DAVID

UNDERSTANDING
THE
HIGH HOLYDAY SERVICES

UNDERSTANDING
THE
HIGH HOLYDAY SERVICES

A popular commentary to the *Machzor*

Dr Jeffrey M. Cohen
BA(Hons), MPhil, AJC, PhD

Foreword by the Chief Rabbi
Sir Immanuel Jakobovits

Routledge & Kegan Paul
London, Boston, Melbourne and Henley

First published in 1983
by Routledge & Kegan Paul plc
39 Store Street, London WC1E 7DD,
9 Park Street, Boston, Mass. 02108, USA,
296 Beaconsfield Parade, Middle Park,
Melbourne, 3206, Australia, and
Broadway House, Newtown Road,
Henley-on-Thames, Oxon RG9 1EN
Set in Baskerville by Input Typesetting Ltd, London SW19 8DR
and printed in Great Britain by
T. J. Press Ltd

ISBN 0-7100-9566-X

To Gloria
with affection and gratitude

CONTENTS

FOREWORD by the Chief Rabbi   ix
   Sir Immanuel Jakobovits
PREFACE   xiii
NOTE ON TRANSLITERATION   xv

Rosh Hashanah   1

The morning service – first day   3
The *Musaph* service   42
Tashlikh   72
The morning service – second day   75
The Jewish doctrine of repentance   88

Yom Kippur   97

The evening service   99
The morning service   128
Memorial of the departed   153
The *Musaph* service   156
The afternoon service   170
The *Ne'iylah* service   176

NOTES   190
BIBLIOGRAPHY   206
PRIMARY RABBINIC SOURCES   209
INDEX   210

FOREWORD

by the Chief Rabbi, Sir Immanuel Jakobovits

Prayer is to the spirit of the High Holydays what Matzah is to *Pesach* and the Sukkah to the Festival of *Sukkoth*. It is the basic essence of *Rosh Hashanah* and *Yom Kippur*, when once a year the Jew regenerates himself to reach his spiritual peak just as nature around him is in its most perfect state at this season. How does prayer achieve this?

Prayer in Jewish thought is primarily not intended to *express* man's emotions and needs. God knows our feelings and wants much better than we do, let alone than we can formulate them. Rather is prayer meant to *impress* us; to stir our conscience, to uplift our spirit, to transport us from our mundane world around us to the inner world of our soul. Prayer is the bridge between Heaven and earth, between man and his Maker, instructing us on the difference between what we are and what we should be. Hence our prayers are fixed. For the truths and ideals they are to teach us do not change from one individual or from one age to another.

This applies to all our prayers throughout the year in their daily routine, but never more so than on *Rosh Hashanah* and *Yom Kippur*. 'Search the Lord when He is to be found, call on Him when He is near' (Isaiah 55:6) – this, our Sages say, refers to the Ten Days of Penitence.

This 'nearness of God' distinguishes the High Holydays from the Three Pilgrimage Festivals. The latter are so called because on these occasions, by biblical law, every Jew was expected *to go up* to the Temple of Jerusalem. The national and religious significance of these festivities could only be fully experienced by *coming to God* 'in the place which he shall choose', in the words of the Torah. On *Rosh Hashanah* and *Yom Kippur* God *comes to us*. Through the intensity of our prayers we are to find his reality close by;

He is 'near', intimately at hand with and within us.

This special feature of the High Holyday season is also illustrated by a striking halachic rule. During the Ten Days of Penitence we insert a number of amendments into every '*Amidah*-prayer. If we miss any of these changes by mistake, the prayer is still valid and we can carry on – with one exception. In the third Benediction 'the Holy God' is changed into 'the Holy King', and if this change was omitted, we have to return to the beginning and repeat the '*Amidah* all over again. Why is this so?

'God' is an abstract Being, remote, transcendent and beyond human comprehension. We worship him as such all the year round, But during the penitential season, we are to relate to him as 'King', a concrete Ruler, almost visible with crown and royal vestments, a Being whose presence is manifest, whom we can address and hear directly. And if at this season we merely perceive him as *God* and not as *King*, a distant abstraction rather than an immediate reality, then we have missed the whole meaning of these festivals and our principal prayer is invalid, requiring repetition in the correct form.

The *Machzor*, with its superb liturgical compositions, is the key to this spiritual transformation. It is a kind of anthology, an imposing literary edifice constructed with building-blocks collected from all layers of our sacred literature: from the biblical foundations of readings from the Torah and the Prophets together with numerous other scriptural passages, especially from the Psalms; from the major prayers composed during the talmudic era, including all benedictions; to the rich poetry of the *Piyyutim* and *Selichot* dating from the earliest to the late Middle Ages; right up to the Prayer for the State of Israel written only some thirty years ago.

In this colourful mosaic every nuance of religious inspiration finds the most diverse expression. Some portray the awe of the Heavenly Judgment in a few bold strokes, deeply moving in their simplicity and grandeur, such as the *Unethaneh Tokeph* prayer. Others are highly intricate compositions, artistically pieced together with biblical and

midrashic allusions which require careful study to be
understood, contrasting Divine omnipotence with human
frailty, or the efficacy of repentance with the doom of the
unrepentant, or describing the ministrations of the High
Priest in the Holy of Holies to secure atonement on *Yom
Kippur*. Yet others are just hymns of glory, or pleas for
compassion, sung to induce spiritual elevation as well as
humility in the presence of God. The liturgy includes long
confessional listings of our failings in alphabetical order,
and serene reflections of the fleeting passage of life.

The impact of all these prayers is further enhanced by
their antiquity and their universality. Whatever the rela-
tively minor local variations between different rites, the
basic texts unite the entire House of Israel both vertically
and horizontally, across the ages and across the continents.
Part of the extraordinary spell exercised by these prayers
– still annually drawing far more Jews together than any
other national Jewish cause or danger, any appeal or demonstration – lies in the very knowledge that these hallowed
texts are recited in essentially identical terms by fellow-
Jews the world over, as they have been by our ancestors
for centuries and millennia. Even the traditional tunes,
likewise matured by age, have an exceptional power to pull
tears and heart-strings otherwise scarcely touched by the
passion of religion or the poetry of the spirit.

Yet much of this ornate splendour is often lost on the
worshipper for sheer lack of comprehension. Unfamiliarity
with the Hebrew language is of course itself a serious impediment. However well this can be overcome by a com-
petent rendering into the vernacular, any translation
remains but a pale reflection of the majesty radiating from
the Hebrew original; and most of the allusions, alliterations
and other literary devices are altogether lost in any foreign
tongue. But even those perfectly conversant with the Hebrew language would find it hard fully to understand the
plain meaning, let alone the deeper interpretation, of these
liturgical compositions without the skilled guidance of a
commentator, in much the same way as a display of
supreme historic art or of some complex scientific exhibits

cannot be appreciated by the uninitiated without the explanations of an informed guide.

This volume seeks to provide such guidance. While it specialises in literary sources and explanations more than in relating the texts to the religious experience they are to evoke, Dr Jeffrey Cohen's painstaking work will convey to the worshipper a much wider understanding of our prayers than can be gained from a mere reading of the plain text, whether in Hebrew or in English. Not every explanation given in this commentary is undisputed or exhaustive. But as an aid to the High Festivals *Machzor* it will be widely welcome for the light it sheds on some of the finest spiritual and literary creations of the Jewish genius.

May this commentary help to make the hours spent at prayer in our Synagogues on the High Festivals ennoble and sanctify our lives throughout the year, thus making us worthy of the blessings for which we plead. For the real effect of our prayers is gauged not by how we feel when reciting them, but by what they have made of us long after the festivals are over – not by their momentary expression but by their lasting impression.

Ellul 5743

PREFACE

The idea of writing this commentary had been germinating in my mind for many years. Already during my student days at Jews' College, where I was given an understanding and love of Hebrew and rabbinic literature, and where I was introduced to the serious study of medieval Hebrew poetry, I had felt the need of such a commentary, both for myself as well as for the vast majority of worshippers on the High Holydays for whom the *Machzor* is a sealed book.

The available commentaries were unsatisfactory for a variety of reasons. The standard work on the subject – *Jewish Liturgy and its Development* by A. Z. Idelsohn – devotes a mere forty pages to the High Holydays and provides no real insights into the individual compositions. The few other available commentaries were equally sketchy and took no account of the fruits of modern scholarship in the field of liturgy.

I waited in vain for such a commentary to appear; and finally, summoning courage from the advice of the Ethics of the Fathers, 'Where there are no men, endeavour to be the man', I decided to undertake this formidable task. I did so in full awareness that the *Chazan*'s admission of unworthiness applies most accurately to me: 'Terror overwhelms me . . . since I am lacking in good judgment and knowledge.'

The ultimate spur to embark upon this labour of love came from friends and congregants in the Kenton Synagogue, London, where I have the privilege of serving as spiritual leader. After I had conducted a lengthy explanatory service one year, which was received enthusiastically, many expressed the desire to receive a copy of my talk in printed form. I immediately launched myself into the preparation of this book.

The major problem confronting a commentator is how

to decide on priorities in the light of the inevitably circumscribed length of his commissioned work. I have had to apply my own blue pencil to many interesting literary features and midrashic ideas in nearly every composition, and I apologise in advance for any injudiciousness in omission, as well as for errors in commission. I have tried to present a blend of traditional interpretations and references together with my own insights and literary appreciation of the poetic creativity. The inspirational appeal of the former will, I feel sure, compensate for any shortcomings in the latter.

I would like to express my sincere appreciation to the Chief Rabbi, Sir Immanuel Jakobovits, for having allocated many hours of his most valuable time to reading the entire typescript and for saving me from a number of pitfalls through his valuable criticisms and suggestions. I also thank him for graciously contributing the Foreword, as well as for his friendship and encouragement over many years. I would also like to thank Mrs Rebecca Pentol, who typed the manuscript and helped with the proof reading.

My greatest thanks must go to my wife, Gloria, and my children, Harvey, Suzanne, Judith and Lewis, without whose encouragement and sacrifice of long hours which, otherwise, would have been devoted to them this work could never have been undertaken.

Jeffrey M. Cohen

NOTE ON TRANSLITERATION

The following system of transliteration from the Hebrew has been employed:

Consonants

א	– '		צ ץ	– tz
בּ	– b		ק	– q
ב	– v		ר	– r
ג	– g		שׁ	– sh
ד	– d		שׂ	– s
ה	– h		תּ	– t
ו	– v		ת	– th
ז	– z			
ח	– ch			
ט	– t		**Vowels**	
י	– y		–	– a
כּ	– k		ָ	– a
כ ך	– kh		short ָ	– o
ל	– l		ֶ	– e
מ ם	– m		ִ	– i
נ ן	– n		ִי	– iy
ס	– s		ֵ	– ey
ע	– '		וּ	– u
פּ	– p		וֹ	– o
פ ף	– ph		ְ	– e

PAGE REFERENCES

The abbreviations, Ro., Bi. and De S., which accompany the page references under the headings of each composition, refer to the Routledge, Birnbaum and De Sola editions of the *Machzor* respectively.

ROSH HASHANAH

THE MORNING SERVICE – FIRST DAY

The morning service on *Rosh Hashanah* commences much earlier than on a normal Sabbath, to ensure that the considerably extended order of service may be terminated at a reasonable hour in the early afternoon, to enable people to enjoy their festive lunch, as well as in order to comply with the law which prescribes that *Musaph* (the Additional Service) should be completed by about 1 p.m.

The Ark curtain, the mantles which enclose the scrolls of the Law and the cover of the Reader's desk, are all in white on this occasion, a colour which symbolises purity.

All who serve as officiants during the services on the High Festivals are also obliged to wear a white linen robe called a *kittel*. It is worn by the Synagogue Reader on three other occasions during the year: on Passover, when intoning a special prayer for the summer dew; on the seventh day of Tabernacles (*Hosha'na' Rabbah*), which has the special character of a day of judgment; and, finally, on the eighth day of Tabernacles when a special prayer is offered for winter rains to fall in the holy land.

The *kittel* calls to mind the white shrouds in which the dead are dressed before burial,[1] an association which should prompt man to reflect upon the brevity of life and the final account he will be called upon to render when he departs this world. Since without rain life cannot exist, the *kittel* was also prescribed for those two occasions on which we pray for rain. It is hoped that the sight of Israel's spiritual representatives, clad in shrouds, will melt the divine heart and wrest his precious blessing from him.

Another explanation of the *kittel*, taking into account its white colour, connects it with the prophetic promise: 'Though your sins are like scarlet, they shall be white as snow' (Is. 1:18). Accordingly, the *kittel* is worn to symbolise the pure state that is attained through repentance.

Some see in the *kittel* a reflection of the angels, who are
said to be clothed in white garments.[2] The repentant souls,
having received absolution, stand like the angels without
sin.

The first part of the morning service follows the almost
identical order of ordinary Sabbaths and holydays. The
only difference lies in the insertion, very early on, of the
'Hymn of Unity'. This is followed by the recitation of the
'Hymn of Glory', the 'Psalm for the (particular) day of the
week' and Psalm 27 (*Le-david ha-shem 'oriy*), all of which are
generally recited towards the end of the *Musaph* service.

It is conceivable that these were removed from the end
to the beginning of the service on *Rosh Hashanah* in order
that the congregation should leave the Synagogue with the
sound of the final notes of the Shofar still ringing in their
ears. This effect would be weakened if those regular concluding hymns had still to be recited. For the sake of
consistency this arrangement was then preserved on *Yom
Kippur*.

The burden of this volume is limited to commenting
upon the compositions which are unique to the High Holydays, rather than to duplicate the existing English commentaries to the daily prayer book. For this reason we have
refrained from providing comments to the early part of the
morning service, other than to Psalm 27 and the 'Hymn of
Unity'.

לְדִוִד ה׳ אוֹרִי וְיִשְׁעִי

The Lord is my light and my salvation (Psalm 27)
(Ro. 39, Bi. 417, De S. 45a)

Neither the significance nor the origins of many of our
early liturgical compositions can be comprehended without
recourse to rabbinic literature. Most of those compositions
gained their place in the liturgy solely on account of a
special interpretation given to them in rabbinic tradition.
Without a knowledge of that interpretation, the presence
and purpose of many a psalm, prayer or formula may
frequently appear enigmatic.

Psalm 27 exemplifies this principle; for the text betrays not so much as a hint of why it was selected as the 'Psalm for the New Year'. Granted, it breathes a supreme confidence that God will protect the psalmist from his enemies. But this is a theme common to a large number of the psalms; and its particular relevance to the High Holydays is tenuous!

Its adoration of the 'house of the Lord', where the psalmist longs to spend his life, would also be more appropriate as a theme for *Pesach*, *Shavu'oth* and *Sukkoth*, when the Jews made a pilgrimage to the Temple! So why was the psalm chosen for this festival?

For the answer we must turn to the opening words of the Midrash on this psalm.

The Rabbis expound this psalm with reference to Rosh Hashanah and Yom Kippur: *The Lord is my light* – on Rosh Hashanah, the day of judgment, as it is written 'He will make your righteousness shine clear *like a light*, and the justice of your cause like the noonday sun' (Ps. 37:6). *And my salvation* – on Yom Kippur, when he grants us *salvation* and pardons all our sins.

The Midrash proceeds to transform totally the import of the psalmist's references to his enemies, particularly 'the evildoers who came upon me to devour my flesh'. In the mystical imagination of the Rabbis, these are viewed as the guardian angels of the heathen nations of the world who assume the role of the accuser, attempting to have Israel condemned at judgment. *They stumble and fall* – because God does not allow them to open their mouths against Israel.

The Midrash develops this theme by pointing out that the Hebrew word for 'the accuser' is *ha-Satan*, whose numerical value (*gematria*) is three hundred and sixty-four. This indicates that there is just *one* special day in the (solar) year – the day of judgment – when the satanic spirit is absent and his demonic power neutralised. On that day, says the Midrash, God takes Satan on a tour of Jewry, making him witness their total preoccupation with fasting, prayers and atonement. At the height of Satan's confusion, God invites him to disclose what faults he has found in God's children. The accuser is forced to say, 'They are, indeed, like the ministering angels; I cannot oppose them.'

The recitation of Psalm 27, at the end of the daily morning and evening services, extends until after the seventh day of the festival of Tabernacles, *Hosha'na' Rabbah*, which also partakes of the nature of a 'Day of Judgment'. The reference to God hiding the psalmist 'in his Sukkah' also made its recitation appropriate for the duration of the Tabernacles festival.

שִׁיר הַיִּחוּד

Hymn of unity
(Ro. 40–60, Bi. 101–26, De S. 46–74)

The 'Hymn of Unity' is so called because its predominant theme is a declaration of the absolute Unity of God, even though this particular concept, as well as the key-word *yichud* ('Unity'), does not appear until the end of the section prescribed for the second day of the week: *Vehinnenu 'al yichudekha* – 'Behold, we are the witnesses ... to your Unity.'

The section for the first day of the week serves as a general introduction, describing the extent of our reliance upon God, as well as puny man's total inability to enter into any meaningful praise of, or dialogue with, the great and glorious Creator. Lines 5 to 17 of this section bear a strong association with ideas contained in the *Nishmath* prayer,[3] and, more particularly, in the *'Aqdamuth* composition recited on *Shavu'oth*. A few lines from the latter poem will illustrate its influence:

If all the heavens were parchment, and all their forests reeds,
If all the swirling waters of the seas were ink,
And all the earth's inhabitants were ready and skilful scribes,

Who could yet declare in words the glory of the
   Universe?

The 'Hymn of Unity' is attributed to Rabbi Samuel He-
Chasid, one of the founders of the famous pietistic movement in twelfth-century Germany, whose members were
known as the *Chasidey Ashkenaz*. His son, author of the
popular *Shir Ha-Kavod* ('Hymn of Glory'), was the most
distinguished leader of the sect, and this composition bears
all the hallmarks of the philosophical and mystical propensities of that movement.[4]

The present writer is of the opinion, however, that the
poem, in the form in which we have it, has gone through
a considerable editorial revision. It has the definite characteristics of a composite work, put together from a number
of poetic compositions, some of which were alphabetical
acrostics. This is obvious from a closer look at the section
for the fourth day of the week, which is a complete alphabetical acrostic, though with no consistency in the frequency with which each letter is employed. Extracts of
alphabetical acrostic material also appear in the sections
of other days of the week; thus, in the concluding section
of the second day, eight of the lines commence with the
letter *'aleph*, a device which is carried over into the first
three lines of the section for the third day of the week.
Furthermore, in the latter section we find six lines commencing with the word *Kiy* and seven lines commencing
with *Kol*. These are scattered throughout that particular
section, but clearly originally belonged together as alternating couplets. Again, in the middle section for the fifth
day, we find a cluster of lines commencing with the word
'eyn, which must originally have been part of a separate
poetic composition.

The *Shir Ha-Yichud* was originally recited in its entirety
only at the *Kol Nidrey* night service, when the contempla-
tive mood of the congregation was suited to its rather
philosophical and mystical descriptions of the deity. Its
introduction into the liturgy met with considerable opposition, however, particularly on the part of the distin-

guished sixteenth-century Polish authority, R. Solomon Luria (*Maharshal*). He prohibited it in the communities under his jurisdiction on account of its rather daring anthropomorphisms whose import could easily be misconstrued by those uninitiated into mystical speculation. These fears were not shared by his famous contemporary, R. Mordechai Jaffe, who allowed its recitation on Sabbaths and festivals also. Although some communities wished to recite it daily, this was objected to by Jaffe and R. Jacob Emden on the grounds that such a practice would undermine the value of the composition, as people would have to rush its recitation in order to get to work. Perhaps by way of compromise, the lengthy poem was then divided up into seven sections, so that at least a part of it could be recited, with the requisite intention, on each day of the week.

Few Ashkenazi communities have retained its regular recitation, even on Sabbaths. On the High Holydays, however, it is still customary to recite it at the beginning of the morning service.

הַמֶּלֶךְ

The king
(Ro. 80, Bi. 169, De S. 98)

The Reader commences here the main part of the *Shachrith* service. Whereas, on ordinary Sabbaths, he commences with the following sentence (*Shokheyn 'Ad*), on the High Holydays, because the central theme of the liturgy is that of God sitting on the throne of justice, it was felt more appropriate to commence the service with the previous sentence (*Ha-melekh*) which encapsulates that key theme.

In some festival prayer books the reading is *Ha-melekh ha-yosheyv* ('The King *who* sits'), a version found in many early manuscripts. This reading, while contextually appropriate when it is linked to the previous verses (as it is on Sabbaths throughout the year), impairs the stylistic smoothness when it stands as part of an independent sentence, as on the High Holydays. Its translation would then be, 'The King who sits upon a high and exalted throne', without any related predicate. The reading found in most printed editions – *Ha-melekh yosheyv* – converts it into an independent statement: 'The King sits upon a high and exalted throne.'

שִׁיר הַמַּעֲלוֹת מִמַּעֲמַקִּים

A pilgrim song. Out of the Depths
(Bi. 171)

The fact that only the Birnbaum *Machzor* has retained the custom of reciting Psalm 130 is indicative of its optional character. In Chasidic Synagogues it still enjoys a respected status, and is recited aloud with great feeling by *Chazan* and congregation.

Its recitation at this juncture is on account of its opening reference: 'Out of the depths, I call to you, O Lord.' The Midrash on this verse observes: 'A man should never pray on an elevated place, but rather on one that is on a low level, as it is written, "Out of the depths I call . . .", since none are elevated in the presence of God.'[5]

As this is the point at which the *Chazan* of the congregation commences the main section of the service, this psalm, with its reference to the most appropriate position from which to utter prayer, was regarded as a fitting prelude.

In talmudic times it was the practice for the Reader to recite the *'Amidah* from a position slightly lower than that occupied by the surrounding worshippers. This gave rise to the term *yoreyd liphney ha-teyvah*, '*descending* to the Reader's desk'. It has been suggested that the practice was abandoned as an anti-Samaritan gesture, since the latter made 'prayer from the depths' a central feature of their worship.

The several references in the psalm to forgiveness of sin, making it most appropriate to *Rosh Hashanah* and *Yom Kippur*, resulted in the custom of many communities to include it only on these two festivals, though some prayer rites recite it on all festivals.

יוֹצֵר אוֹר

Blessed are you . . . who forms light
(Ro. 81, Bi. 171, De S. 99)

This is the opening of the first of the *Shema'* blessings whose theme is praise of the Creator for the gifts of light and darkness, day and night, the former in which to pursue ennobling work, the latter in which to enjoy bodily rest and refreshment. It is a quotation from Isaiah 45:7, with the one notable exception that the final phrase in Isaiah is not *uvorey 'eth ha-kol* ('and creates *all things*'), but *uvorey ra'* ('and creates *evil*').

The reason for the change was probably because retention of the authentic biblical version might have provided fuel for the adherents of the dualist Persian (Zoroastrian) religion. They believed that the world was created and preserved by two opposing forces, light and darkness, which manifest their will through good and evil respectively. The reference to God as the creator of evil was accordingly altered.

אוֹר עוֹלָם – *Yea, eternal light*

This rather abstruse line can only be understood in the light of talmudic folklore, according to which the primordial light enjoyed by Adam was possessed of supernatural properties which enabled him to take in the whole panorama of creation with one glance. The Midrash states that God refused to bestow that gift upon the wicked generations of the flood and the builders of the Tower of Babel, so he stored it away for the exclusive enjoyment of the righteous in the hereafter.

This explains the first part of the line: 'The light (*'or*), by means of which the whole world (*'olam*) could be surveyed, is stored away in the treasury of eternal life (*be'otzar chayyim*).'

Thus, according to this mystical idea, the light of the sun and moon (*'oroth*) which we enjoy is of a far inferior quality to that original unique source of illumination. Our light only merits its name when it is contrasted with darkness (*'Oroth mey'ophel*). And it was our circumscribed light that God commanded (*'amar*) and which came into being (*vayehi*).

PIYYUTIM.

Not surprisingly, since the *'Amidah* was, at first, the only prayer to be led by a *Chazan*, the earliest *Piyyutim* – poetic compositions – were designed for insertion into the *'Amidah*. Because of their position in the '*Chazan*'s Prayer' they were even called *Qerovoth*,[6] after the name given to the *Chazan* himself at that early period. He was known as the *Qarovah*, the one who 'brings near' the prayers of Israel to the heavenly throne.

Until the introduction of *Piyyut*[7] the prayers tended to be rather stiff and prosaic, with the exception, of course, of the book of Psalms which was freely drawn upon as the main font of liturgical inspiration. But the Psalms were rather general in their themes; and, as the liturgy developed with an *'Amidah* of eighteen (later nineteen) blessings, expressing a variety of different needs, theological concepts, national aspirations and historical reminiscences, the need was felt for poetic compositions of an emotional and inspirational nature which amplified specifically each individual blessing of the *'Amidah*. Hence the poetic expansion of the festival liturgy in this way, and its later extension into other parts of the services, particularly into the blessings preceding and following the *Shema'* both in the evening and morning services.

The *Piyyutim* also came to fulfil a need for poetic and emotional compositions which were more relevant to the outlook of the age, more in the spirit of its needs and challenges and more reflective of its particular social, political and spiritual tensions. Where a Jewish community was the victim of persecution or discrimination, for example, or when it was granted a miraculous deliverance, it felt the need to express its feelings of anxiety, relief and

thanksgiving with an appropriate *Piyyut*. As Hebrew literature developed, especially from the third to the seventh
centuries CE, with the rise of the Midrash which gave the
impetus to Hebrew poetry, men of spirit felt the spontaneous urge to be creative and artistic, and to compose
beautiful poems in tribute to the Sabbath and the festivals.

The classical period of the *Payetanim*[8] extended to the
twelfth century. Those compositions that caught the imagination of the communities gained wider currency and
became part-and-parcel of the Synagogue prayer rites for
those occasions. Some composers even succeeded in weav-
ing a poetic web around the mundane ritual laws and
customs of the sacred days.

To win the acclaim of the masses a *Piyyut* had to have
all the hallmarks of artistry. It had to observe the basic
laws of rhythm and metre, it had to employ the choicest
and most appropriate biblical phraseology and it had to
demonstrate the author's ability to mould the biblical
vocabulary into new forms and expressions to suit the
imagery being employed.

It was the *Chazan* alone who recited the *Piyyutim*. The
congregation were unable to join in as handwritten *Machzorim* were a rarity. Frequently a Synagogue only possessed
one *Machzor* for the use of the *Chazan*. It was only with the
introduction of printing in the sixteenth century that this
situation changed.

One of our earliest and most prolific liturgical poets
(early seventh century) was Eleazar Kallir, a pupil of Yannai, the great pioneer of Hebrew poetry.[9] Unfortunately,
very little is known of his life and activity, resulting in a
web of legend being woven around him in the medieval
period. According to one tradition he was killed by his
teacher Yannai in a fit of jealousy at Kallir's growing fame
and influence.

Kallir devoted special attention to *Yotzeroth*, poetic insertions into the blessings before (and after) the *Shema'*.[10] Some
scholars are of the opinion that these were originally written as substitutes for the *Shema'* at a time when the Persians,
who occupied Palestine between 614 and 628 CE, banned

its public recitation. Such a central daily affirmation of the unity of God would have offended against the dualistic beliefs of the Persians. Hidden amid a profusion of poetry, however, it would be difficult to detect or anticipate its recitation.

Kallir – and his teacher Yannai – made significant contributions towards Hebrew philology and the development of the Hebrew language. Where a Hebrew word was not available in the classical literature to express a particular idea, they coined new words or word-formations. Their approach, which frequently involved sacrificing the rules of grammar and syntax, was severely criticised by the later medieval grammarians, particularly the great bible commentator Abraham Ibn Ezra[11] and the illustrious philosopher, Moses Maimonides.[12]

The output of these early poets adorns our Ashkenazi festival and High Holyday liturgies. The Sephardi communities, on the other hand, preferred to adopt the *Piyyut* of their own Spanish poets, such as Ibn Gabirol, Judah Halevi, Abraham and Moses Ibn Ezra.

מֶלֶךְ אָזוּר גְּבוּרָה

King with might begirded
(Ro. 81–3, Bi. 173, De S. 100)

This *Yotzer*-poem is attributed to Eleazar Kallir. It contains twenty-five stanzas, each stanza comprising three short lines with no more than four words to a line. The first word of each stanza is *melekh* ('King'), and the succeeding initial letters of the second word in each stanza create an alphabetical acrostic.

The poem is a paean of praise, alluding to the midrashic idea that God donned a special robe of majesty on each of ten occasions when he went forth to achieve some great cosmic or historic purpose. The ten divine garments referred to here are *might* (see Ps. 65:7), *vengeance* (Is. 59:17), *majestic splendour* (Ps. 3:1), *radiance* (Dan. 2:22), *strength* (Ps. 93:1), *triumph* (Is. 59:17), *grandeur* (Is. 63:1), *crimson robes*

(Is. 63:1), *a snow-white Tallith* (Dan. 8:9) and *zeal* (Is. 59:17).

These different *robes* represent the varied attributes of the divine being and his presence as it is manifested in history. They may appear rather gross to the philosophical or sophisticated modern, whose concept of God is that of a pure spirituality; though religious soldiers, who sensed the active participation of God in the various struggles which led up to the establishment of the State of Israel and to the reunification of Jerusalem, frequently admitted to thinking militaristically in terms of a God of 'might', 'vengeance' and 'triumph'. Again, at times when we are filled with awe at the sight of a wonder of nature, do we not associate God with 'grandeur'? And when we detect his presence among us as we stand in prayer on *Rosh Hashanah* and *Yom Kippur*, does he not also become, in a sense, enwrapped in 'a snow-white *tallith*'?

Judaism in the medieval period struggled hard to defend these anthropomorphic references against their many detractors; and Maimonides, for example, vehemently denied any literal significance for such concrete references to the deity. He did recognise, however, the problem that it is well-nigh impossible for any ordinary intellect to know God, or for any ordinary emotion to be stimulated by contemplation of him, except by means of such anthropomorphic similes.[13]

Devotional prayer itself would be well-nigh impossible without mentally sensing or invoking the proximity of a being who is, in fact, more than just 'pure spirituality'. The vocabulary of our prayers even promotes this through its many references to God's 'name', 'reign', 'throne', 'greatness', 'holiness'. Although these are one stage removed from any of the objected-to biblical references to parts of God's 'body', they nevertheless still direct our emotions towards a conception of God which gives him the trappings of monarchy, with the references to his 'name' completing the image of personalised authority.

כְּבוֹדוֹ אָהֵל

Tent-like he stretched out the sky
(Ro. 86, Bi. 189, De S. 105)

Another *Yotzer* composition from the pen of Eleazar Kallir. Poems of this genre, written for recitation before the section *Veha'ophanim ve-chayyoth ha-qodesh*, are accordingly called by the name *'Ophan*. It follows the alphabetical acrostic form, and opens with the word *Kevodo* in order to provide a contextually smooth link with the last word of the prayer into which it has been inserted (even though this tends to obscure the fact that it is the following word, *'iheyl*, which opens the acrostic with its initial letter, *'aleph*).

The reference to God stretching out the sky 'this day' is in conformity with the opinion of R. Eliezer in the Talmud[14] that the world was created on *Rosh Hashanah*. The word *berachamim* ('in mercy') emphasises the rabbinic view that God's original intention was to create a universe ruled by the inflexible canons of strict justice. Man would have been regimented in the code of moral discipline and ethical behaviour to which he would have had to conform. The noble challenge of free will would have had little place in such a system; but, on the other hand, sin would have been reduced to a minimum.

That God commenced creation with this approach is inferred by our Rabbis from the exclusive use of the divine name *'Elokim* (denoting 'God of strict justice') in the first chapter of Genesis. God revised his scheme, however, and made the quality of mercy (*rachamim*) an equal partner, a fact which underlies the employment of the conjoint names *'Adonai* (God of mercy) and *'Elokim* in the second chapter of the creation story. *Rosh Hashanah* is, consequently, also the anniversary of the genesis of the quality of divine mercy, a fact which gives the author confidence that this will be extended to Israel on this day.

The phrase *mey'ethmol kiddamnukha* ('From yesterday began our petition to beseech you') refers to the ancient practice of fasting on the eve of *Rosh Hashanah*,[15] during the

Selichoth period, and, generally, on as many days as possible during the month of Ellul.[16]

The poet invokes the merit of the patriarchs in order to secure mercy for Israel. This is in line with the popular concept of *Zechuth 'Avoth*, the origin of which is to be found in the Torah itself, where Moses invoked the merit of Abraham, Isaac and Jacob in order to persuade God to have mercy on their sinful descendants after they worshipped the golden calf.[17] In this context, Kallir refers to Isaac, obliquely, as 'the one for whom the King's valiant angels shed bitter tears' (*Lemar bakhu 'erelley melekh*). This is an allusion to the midrashic tradition[18] that, as Isaac lay bound on the altar, the heavenly angels shed tears at his impending doom. His impaired sight[19] is explained as having been caused by some of those heavenly tears which dropped onto Isaac's eyes.[20]*

וְהַחַיּוֹת יְשׁוֹרֵרוּ

The Chayyoth sing

(Ro. 87, Bi. 191, De S.106)

This mystical passage names the five main sections of the heavenly angelic choir, depicted as lustily singing the praise of God. It was recited only in the Polish rite, and is a slightly expanded version of the formula recited on weekdays and Sabbaths which refers to only three angelic categories. These various categories are derived from Ezekiel's famous vision of the heavenly throne and divine chariot, supported by four bizarre beasts (*Chayyoth*) in human form, each with four faces and four wings.[21] The prophet also describes another weird creature which served as the wheels (*'Ophanim*) of the vehicular throne. As a counterpart to the Cherubim (*Keruvim*) which protected the Ark in the desert sanctuary and in Solomon's Temple, there are also heavenly Cherubim which play such an active role that God is frequently referred to in the Bible as 'He who sits enthroned upon the Cherubim.'[22]

---

* For further commentary on this composition, see Second Day, pp. 77–8.

Referred to also here are *Seraphim*, which figure in Isaiah's mystic vision of the heavenly court.[23] Rather than constituting the essence of the divine chariot, the *Seraphim* are probably its guardians.

The nature of the last category, the *'Arelim*, is even more obscure. The name occurs only once in the Bible, in Isaiah 33:7, where they are described as 'angels of peace'. From a talmudic passage[24] it would seem that they were regarded as the angels sent to seize the soul of man and transport it back to its source when the moment of death arrives. This idea might well have been inspired by Isaiah's reference to them, which was re-interpreted in the sense of 'angels conferring *everlasting* peace'.

Again, the modern mind might recoil at the inclusion of such fantastic elements of folklore into our sacred liturgy. It is apposite to point out, therefore, that such ideas do not owe their origin to mainstream rabbinism. Indeed, Judah Ha-Nasi, author of the Mishna, ruthlessly excluded nearly all mystical material of this kind from his pioneering Code of Jewish law and religion.

Mystical speculation regarding the Creation (*Ma'aseh Bereyshith*) and the heavenly Chariot (*Ma'aseh Merkavah*) was indulged in, especially in the Essene circles whose literature was discovered at Qumran, as well as among early Pharisaic circles in the last few centuries before the Common Era. While normative Judaism fought hard to ensure that angelology was never allowed to form the basis of a cult, it must be admitted that the existence of angels was widely believed in, by scholars and laymen alike, in talmudic times (first–sixth centuries CE). Their existence, it was considered, only served to enhance the sense of *mysterium tremendum*, the awful mystery, that surrounds God's majesty;[25] and it was with that objective in mind that mystical references and hymns were introduced into the liturgy. Rudolph Otto terms such hymns 'numinous', by which he means irrational glorifications of God, whose sole purpose is to attempt to reproduce in words a formula that is calculated to induce emotionally an ecstatic state from which must automatically flow a keen sense of great *mys-terium*[26] (see pp. 160–61).

Such references – whether to God's robes or to this strange living Chariot – are not, therefore, to be read literally. They are but stimuli to a religious experience, without which prayer is a meaningless exercise.

THE REPETITION OF THE *'AMIDAH* BY THE *CHAZAN*
(Ro. 95, Bi. 209, De S. 118)

The original, and main, role of the *Chazan* was to lead the congregation in a verse by verse recitation of the *Shema'*, as well as to repeat the *'Amidah* aloud for the benefit of those members of the congregation who were illiterate or who could not memorise it. They would recite it, word for word, together with him, with the addition of the *Qedushah*. It seems that the rest of the service – apart from the Reading of the Torah – used to be chanted, word-for-word in unison, from a seated position, by the congregation, with no one acting as a leader. (The Sephardim today chant the whole service in unison.) Apart from the leaders, elders and sages of the community, who sat on benches or in special seats of honour, the rest of the congregation sat in rows, on rugs, on the floor behind the *Bimah*. The *Bimah* was used exclusively for the Reading of the Torah, and the *Chazan* recited the Repetition of the *'Amidah* from a stand behind the *Bimah*.[27]

At a later period both the *Chazan* and the congregation moved forward towards the front of the Synagogue; and it was from there, before the Ark, that the *Chazan* stood to repeat the *'Amidah*. As Synagogues grew larger, and it became impossible for those at the back to hear the *Chazan*, it became the practice for him to pray from the *Bimah*, and, with the development of liturgical compositions, to take a dominant role as leader of the whole service, not merely the repetition of the *'Amidah*.

פְּתִיחָה – OPENING OF THE ARK

In the practice of opening the Ark for particular compositions we again enter an area where considerable licence
was exercised throughout the centuries. Originally the Ark
was opened during the course of a service only in order to
take out the Torah scroll. This has remained the practice
in all other rites except that of the Ashkenazim who, at a
very early period, employed the practice of opening the
Ark for particularly favoured compositions, in order to
stress their importance and to stimulate a greater degree
of concentration during their recitation.

In Franco-Germany, in the thirteenth century, some
communities adopted the custom of opening the Ark for
the whole of the repetition of the *Shachrith* and *Musaph
'Amidahs*, closing it only for *Qedushah* and the Priestly Benediction. This did not win universal acceptance since many
authorities preferred to open the Ark at intervals in order
to highlight specific compositions. This had the added advantage of enabling the sacred honours to be distributed
more widely around the members of the congregation. It
was probably that consideration which accounted for the
many compositions for which we, quite unaccountably,
stand and honour with a *petiychah*.

מְסוֹד חֲכָמִים וּנְבוֹנִים

From the counsel of the wise and understanding
(Ro. 95, Bi. 211, De S. 118)

One of the problems confronting the composers of *Piyyut*
was the fact that, from the halachic point of view, some
authorities were uneasy about introducing interruptions
into the standard *'Amidah*.[28] Because of this it became customary for the *Chazan* to commence the repetition by seeking the permission of the congregation for such a poetic
interruption. This is the purpose of this particular recurring
composition, which is categorised as a *Reshuth* ('permission').

Its author is unknown. It is basically an assertion that

whatever is being added by way of *Piyyut* is strictly traditional, having been derived from 'the company of wise
men and sages' (*missod chakhamiym unevoniym*), that is, from
the authentic rabbinic tradition, not the author's independent ideas or interpretations. In an age when people were
also most sensitive to the inroads of sectarianism, such as
the Karaite heresy, it was probably also felt necessary to
allay the fears of the community – especially where texts
were unavailable for examination and control – and to
assure them that any poetic innovations were strictly in
line with Orthodox ideology.

יֵרֵאתִי בִּפְצוֹתִי

Trembling, I now pour forth my prayer
(*ibid.*)

Just as Aaron had first to seek atonement 'for himself '
before he could act as intercessor for 'the whole assembly
of Israel' (Ex. 16:17), so the Reader tremblingly (*yarey'thiy*)
asks for divine mercy and indulgence as he presumes to
embark upon this sacred responsibility, though keenly
aware of his own spiritual shortcomings. This type of Reader's personal meditation is an essential part of the *Reshuth*.

The poet, Yekutiel bar Mosheh of Speyer (eleventh century), skilfully conveys the *Chazan*'s prevailing sense of awe
by ending each phrase with the syllable *chil*, the common
Hebrew word for 'trembling'. This was doubly appropriate,
as this *Reshuth* was written to serve as an introduction to
the following composition by Kallir, which opens with the
phrase *'ath chil*.

Yarey'thiy is constructed as a name-acrostic: *Yekutiel bar
Mosheh*, followed by the plea, *chazak ve'ematz yechiy* ('May
he be strong and of good courage; may he live').

אָת חִיל

The terrible day of visitation is come
(Ro. 96, Bi. 211, De S. 119)

In this alphabetical acrostic, Kallir alludes to a midrashic
idea that it was Abraham, through his plea for mercy on

behalf of the Sodomites ('Shall not the judge of the whole earth deal justly?'),[29] who convinced God that strict justice, untempered by mercy, could not possibly serve as a principle upon which to base the world – 'If you want a world, then, Lord, there can be no absolute law; and if you insist upon absolute law, then there can be no world.'[30]

The poet asserts that 'this will be remembered at judgment', to Israel's credit, in recognition of that great patriarch. Kallir alludes to the midrashic idea that God wished to create Abraham even before Adam, on account of the former's unique spiritual attainment. His decision to send Abraham only after twenty generations was in order that he might repair the widespread moral damage inflicted upon the world by the wicked generations before him. Had they followed Abraham, no one could have achieved that.[31]

The birth of a child to Abraham and Sarah, which took place on *Rosh Hashanah*,[32] is regarded as a good omen for their offspring, so that this 'day of visitation' will ever be propitious for divine mercy.

The final reference to the 'ashes' of Isaac is based upon a very obscure Midrashic tradition that Isaac was actually killed on the altar, and his ashes strewn across Mount Moriah. God then brought dew, commingled it with the ashes and brought Isaac back to life.

זָכְרֵנוּ לְחַיִּים

Remember us unto life
(Ro. 97, Bi. 213, De S. 120)

Remember us unto life, O King who delights in life, and inscribe us in the book of life, for your own sake. O God of life.

This line is interpolated into the first blessing of every *'Amidah* recited throughout the Ten Days of Penitence. The opening word, *Zokhreynu* ('Remember us'), was consciously employed in order to serve as a link with the similar phrase, found in the basic formula of the first blessing of the *'Amidah*: *Vezokheyr chasdey 'avoth* ('And *remember* the piety of the patriarchs'). The plea, therefore, is that, when 'remembering' the merit of the fathers, God will, in appreciation, grant the blessing of life to their children.

The image of the 'book of life' is found in the Talmud,[33] which depicts God as opening three records. One contains the names of the wholly righteous, the second those who are indubitably wicked, and the third book contains the names of the average person. The righteous are immediately inscribed for blessing and life; the wicked for punishment and death. The fate of Mr Average, however, is held over from *Rosh Hashanah* until *Yom Kippur*, to give him a chance to tip the scale in his favour.

מִי כָמוֹךָ

Who is like you
(Ro. 98, Bi. 215, De S. 121)

Who is like you, O merciful father, who in mercy remembers your creatures for life.

As in the case of the previous interpolation into the first blessing of the *'Amidah*, so we have a similar sentiment prescribed for insertion into the second blessing of the *'Amidah* throughout the Ten Days of Penitence.

Prayer has been described as 'the expression of a primitive impulse to a higher, richer, intenser life ... a great longing for life, for a more potent, a purer, a more blessed life'.[34] If, indeed, this is the prime motivation of prayer, then the High Holyday liturgy is prayer in its most realistic and instinctive form. Not only the content but the whole spirit of the liturgy focuses the attention and concentration of the worshipper upon an evaluation of life in general and his own existential situation in particular.

These insertions into the first two (and, similarly, those of the last two) blessings of the *'Amidah* express, most directly, our passionate longing for life, by which we mean not mere existence, but a life 'for your own sake, O God of Life'. Franz Kafka,[35] animated by a keen sensitivity

towards the spirit of Judaism, made an apposite and pene-
trating observation, that 'we are not sinful merely because
we have eaten of the Tree of Knowledge, but primarily
because we have *not* yet eaten of the Tree of Life'. This
is one of the fundamental teachings of the Jewish High
Holyday liturgy.

Again, the opening phrase, *miy khamokha*, is consciously
employed in order to link it to the same phrase as contained
in the basic formulation of the blessing: *miy khamokha ba'al
gevuroth*.

תֹּאֲלַת זוּ

Desiring to ease the tribulations of the people
(Ro. 97, Bi. 215, De S. 120)

This composition by Kallir follows a reverse-acrostic structure, commencing with the last letter of the alphabet, *tav*,
and ending with *'aleph*.

The poet departs from the general view regarding the
origin of prayer, that it began as a spontaneous *crie de cœur*
as mortal man sensed his desperate need of God's help in
time of crisis. It is suggested in the opening line of this
poem that the ability to pray, and the recognition of its
power as well as its psychological benefit, was a definite
gift conferred by God upon man.[36]

Reference is made to the nine blessings which constitute
the *Musaph 'Amidah* on *Rosh Hashanah* and the idea[37] that
this number corresponds to the nine invocations of the
divine name in the prayer of Hannah (I Sam. ch. 2). This
concept contains within it a veritable psychology of prayer.
As we stand before God at this time we need to appreciate
how desperately alone and vulnerable we are without God's
guidance and blessings, and how nothing is irrevocable –
not even Hannah's barrenness – if we pray sincerely
enough. The urgency of Hannah's prayer, and the faith
infusing her thanksgiving, are models to which we should
aspire.

אַתָּה הוּא אֱלֹהֵינוּ
You are our God
(Ro. 98, Bi. 217, De S. 122)

An alphabetical acrostic devoted entirely to listing various divine attributes culled from the Bible, predominantly from the books of Isaiah and Psalms. Only two of the attributes are post-biblical: the description of God as *Chay 'Olamim* ('One who lives forever') is talmudic,[38] and the expression *Sithro yosher*, whose meaning is unclear, is not found elsewhere. Birnbaum avoids the problem by translating it merely as 'He is invisible'. Routledge has the rather enigmatic rendering, 'His secret is rectitude', while De Sola has 'His veil is rectitude'. A more probable rendering is 'His secrecy is justifiable', though D. Goldschmidt[39] believes that a textual error has occurred here, and that we should read *Sithro Choshekh*, 'His secret place is in obscurity', a phrase found in Psalm 18:12.

אַדֶּרֶת מַמְלָכָה
Your glorious kingdom
(Ro. 99, Bi. 219, De S. 123)

Another *Piyyut* from the pen of Kallir, constructed out of the name-acrostic *Eleazar biribi Kilir*. The Birnbaum *Machzor* is the only one which sets out the composition in a way that its poetic structure and acrostic pattern are apparent. It comprises five stanzas, each stanza containing three lines, with each line divided up into three phrases, each of two (sometimes three) words. Each stanza concludes with the word *melukhah*, 'kingdom'.

The poem is introduced by, and signs off with, the refrain *ta'iyr vethariy'a*, the first half of which is based upon Isaiah's spiritual war-cry: 'The Lord goes forth like a warrior, he will rouse the frenzy of battle (*ya'iyr*); he will shout (*yariy'a*) . . . and triumph over his foes.'[40] This refrain encapsulates the theme of the whole composition in which the poet complains bitterly at the havoc wrought by the Roman conquerors in the holy land, and the fact that their haughty rule has extended for so long a period. He ends on a note of confidence that the one whose rule is exalted above that of any earthly monarch will presently restore independence to Israel.

אֵם אֲשֶׁר בְּצֶדֶק

Mother who has grown old in the practice of goodness
(Bi. 221, De S. 125)

This composition has been omitted in the Routledge edition. It is a poetic retelling of the story of the birth of Isaac, with special emphasis upon the biological miracle of a woman of ninety years being enabled to suckle her child.

The opening phrase, describing Sarah as 'a mother who grew old in righteousness', is based upon the midrashic tradition that at the age of one hundred Sarah was as free of sin as she was at twenty.[41]

Sarah is supposed to have conceived on *Rosh Hashanah*, as did Rachel and Hannah.[42] Hence the reference in the final stanza to 'the three barren women who were visited (with child) on this day'. The poet, in his reference to Sarah's conception, emphasises that it was 'her Creator (*gochakh*) who visited her'. This emphasis, based upon the actual biblical phrase, 'And *the Lord* visited Sarah as he had said',[43] seems, according to the Midrash, to be playing down the role of her husband in this happy enterprise! This inspired the comment of R. Judah b. Simon that 'although Rav Huna has asserted that there is an angel specifically responsible for (generating) sexual passion, Sarah had no need of such things; for God in his glory visited Sarah!'[44]

אֲאַפִּיד נֵזֶר אָיוֹם

To him who is feared, a crown will I bring
(Ro. 102, Bi. 223, De S. 127)

This poem by Kallir follows a double alphabetical acrostic pattern, in that both the first and third words of each line commence with the same letter. It was composed as an

introduction to the *Qedushah*, with which theme it is inter-
connected, and reference to which is made in both the
opening and closing lines. There are also several references
to categories of angels – *Chayyoth, Seraphim, Peli'im* ('nameless
angels')[45] – which provides a further link with the *Qedushah*
which describes the praise of God uttered by the angelic
choir. The structure of each phrase, with precisely *three*
words, is similarly no coincidence, but is intended to highlight the three-fold formula of sanctification: 'Holy, Holy,
Holy . . .'

אֶתֵּן לְפוֹעֲלִי צֶדֶק

The justice of my creator I will praise
(Ro. 104, Bi. 223, De S. 127)

This poem was composed by Simeon bar Isaac (see pp.
75–6). The alphabetical acrostic pattern is followed by the
name acrostic: *Shim'on bar Yitzchaq chazak*.

The poem is introduced by two lines (*yishpot teyveyl . . .
vehu' ve'echad . . .*) which were intended to be employed,
alternatively, as refrains to each line. Because of the monotony of such unnecessary repetition, which in this instance
does not further either the thematic or the metric quality,
the refrains were omitted, with the first refrain (only) being
repeated at the end of the poem to serve as a conclusion.

The poem opens with a phrase from Job 36:3. The biblical author of this title-verse is actually Elihu, one of Job's
three friends, who attempts to justify the suffering God has
brought upon Job ('The justice of my creator I will praise')
by suggesting to him that suffering is a warning against
sin, and that when the warning is taken to heart, the
victims are always restored to well-being.

Most of the lines of this poem are direct borrowings of
biblical verses, though the word order is frequently re-
arranged, with some words varied or omitted, in order to
conform to the metric and acrostic structure.

The poet points out the unique synthesis of majesty and
modesty which characterises the divine attributes:

Supreme in strength, enthroned upon his height;
Yet mild is He, according to his might.

Though the Almighty controls the workings and destiny
of the great cosmos, he attends, with equal concern, to the
plight of the widow and orphan.

The poet refers to the talmudic idea that while God
judges the whole world on this day yet he calls Israel before
him first. The reason for this is in order that he might be
well disposed to them while he is still in good humour,
before his review of the wickedness of the nations provokes
him to anger.[46] Another reason is that the merit of Israel
may also secure mercy for all mankind, in fulfilment of the
universalistic promise to Abraham: 'And in thee shall all
the families of the earth be blessed.'[47]

יְיָ מֶלֶךְ יְיָ מָלָךְ

The Lord is King, the Lord was King . . .
(Ro. 105, Bi. 225, De S. 128)

This composition was also written by Kallir in order to
provide a poetic and mystic setting for the *Qedushah*. The
Qedushah opens with the statement that 'We (Israel) will
sanctify God's name on earth just as they (the angels)
sanctify it in the highest heavens.' Kallir is inspired by this
vision of Israel as an angelic counterpart; and in this composition he fuses together the attributes of both, making it
difficult, at times, to ascertain whether he is referring to
the angels or to Israel.

The poetic and metric links with the *Qedushah* are subtly
contrived. The core of the *Qedushah* is the triple-evocation
qadosh qadosh qadosh. Kallir keeps this three-fold emphasis
in the forefront. Hence his major refrain, *'Adonay melekh,
'Adonay malakh, 'Adonay yimlokh le-'olam va'ed*, is also a triple
evocation, which Kallir has culled from three independent
biblical phrases, and combined into one verse. (Kallir's
composite verse is also employed in the *Yehiy khevod* prayer,
recited each morning.)

The triple-formulation, inspired by the *Qedushah*, also

infiltrates the metre of this composition, providing three-lined stanzas with each line contributing (before the word *vekol*) a three-word phrase bearing three equal stresses. In addition, each line boasts a rhythmic alliteration established by a three-fold alphabetical acrostic (*Gibborey govahh yagbiyru* . . .).

The different verbs employed in each line are ingeniously wrought synonyms, all conveying a particular nuance of the idea of 'praising', 'exalting'. The word *vekol* ('with a loud voice'), which climaxes each phrase, is a further link with the *Qedushah* which contains the phrase *'az bekol*; and the opening word *'Addiyrey* also links up with another *Qedushah* phrase, *'Addir vechazak*. It will be noticed that Kallir was not concerned about replacing the letter *samech* with the like-sounding letter *sin*.

וּבְכֵן לְךָ הַכֹּל יַכְתִּירוּ

And now let all acclaim your sovereignty
(Ro. 106, Bi. 261, De S. 130)

This composition is recited in the *Shachrith 'Amidah* on the first day, though its recitation is moved to *Musaph* on the second day. This practice might have arisen in order to do justice to both opinions in a talmudic dispute[48] as to the exact time of the day when God judges the world: whether early at *Shachrith* time, or a little later, at *Musaph*. By varying the time of its recitation we ensure that our minds are solemnly directed to the awesome process of judgment, and that we are in the appropriate mood, at the precise moment at which it is being enacted.

The introductory heading of the composition is omitted in a number of early manuscripts. Others have an alternative heading: *Uvekheyn dayan 'emeth 'attah* ('Indeed, you are a true judge').

The composition describes, in alphabetical acrostic form, the judicial qualities of God which prompt him to allow his mercy to vanquish his wrath when sitting in judgment (*baddin*) on the Day of Judgment (*Beyom din*).

וּבְכֵן תֵּן פַּחְדְּךָ

And now impose your awe
(Ro. 107, Bi. 263, De S. 134)

This composition preaches a universalistic message of the messianic era when fear of God will penetrate the hearts of all men and weld them into 'a single band'. This universal recognition of God will bring with it the acceptance, on the part of the other nations, of the primacy and uniqueness of Israel's spiritual heritage. The concomitant of this will be a heightened respect for Israel, as alluded to in the next paragraph: 'And therefore, O Lord, give glory to your people.'

The origin of this prayer is disputed, as well as its specific purpose in the context of the third (*Qedushath Hashem*) blessing of the *'Amidah*. Its universalistic theme has suggested to some scholars that it was originally composed as an introduction to the *Malkhuyoth* section of the *Musaph 'Amidah* which treats of this specific theme.

Although our *Malkhuyoth* section is introduced into the fourth blessing of the *'Amidah*, and the introduction we employ is the famous composition of Rav (later prescribed to be recited three times daily as the second paragraph of the *'Aleynu*), the Mishna[49] refers to the view of R. Jochanan ben Nuri that the *Malkhuyoth* should be recited in the *third* blessing. The *Uvekheyn teyn pachdekha* might well have been R. Jochanan's original introductory prayer which was retained in this blessing even though the verses of the *Malkhuyoth*, which originally accompanied it, were later assigned to the following blessing.

It will be observed that this and the following two paragraphs are all introduced by the word *Uvekheyn*. A popular explanation relates this to the occurrence of this word in the book of Esther – *Uvekheyn 'avo' 'el ha-melekh* – 'and *then* (i.e. after my fasting and praying) I shall go to the king'.[50] The analogy is clear: the way to win proximity to the divine King is to undertake the sincere approach, and the spiritual preparations of prayer and fasting, adopted by Queen Esther.

Notwithstanding this liturgical homily, a no less author-
itative version, current throughout Franco-German communities, began the third paragraph not with the words
uvekheyn tzaddikim but with *ve'az tzaddikim*. This suggests
that our consistent version was, in fact, a later attempt at
literary uniformity.

קָדוֹשׁ אַתָּה

You are holy

(Ro. 108, Bi. 265, De S. 136)

This paragraph, which leads into the closing benediction
of the third blessing of the *'Amidah*, was the original formula
of this blessing (though probably without the accompanying biblical quotation, introduced by the phrase *Kakkathuv*)
according to the ancient Palestinian rite. In Babylon this
was varied, with the opening words being transposed to
read *'attah qadosh . . .*

Throughout the Ten Days of Penitence the concluding
formula of this blessing – *ha'eyl ha-qadosh* – is replaced by
ha-melekh ha-qadosh, in order to emphasise the kingship of
God.

אַתָּה בְחַרְתָּנוּ

You have chosen us

(Ro. 108, Bi. 265, De S. 136)

With the words *'attah vechartanu* we commence the middle
blessing of the seven blessings of the *'Amidah* recited on all
festivals. This is referred to in the Talmud as *Qedushath
Ha-yom* ('Sanctification of the day'), as it contains references to the special quality of holiness with which the
festival days are invested. The form of this blessing as it
appears in the *Musaph 'Amidah* for *Yom Kippur*[51] is the most
expansive because of the fact that the account of the ancient
Temple service (*'Avodah*) and the *Selichoth* were inserted
into it.

The actual mention of the holiness of the particular
(named) festival only comes in the following paragraph,

vatiteyn lanu ('And you gave to us'). The purpose of *'attah vechartanu* is to serve as an introduction, by establishing from the outset why Israel merited to be the recipients of those precious holydays. It was a loving privilege conferred upon Israel because of her willingness to aspire towards spiritual 'exaltedness above all tongues', in order to become a receptacle of holiness through the fulfilment of God's *mitzvoth*.

The *'attah vechartanu* blessing is couched in the second person. The same blessing, though framed in the third person – *'asher bachar banu mikol 'am* (. . . 'who has chosen us . . .') – is employed as the evening *Kiddush* blessing for all festivals. A contracted version of it is also used as the blessing recited before the reading of the Law (*'asher bachar banu mikol ha'ammiym*).

This composition is reproduced almost *verbatim* in the *'Attah yatzarta* prayer, recited on *Shabbat Rosh Chodesh* in the repetition of the *Musaph 'Amidah*.

אֱלֹהֵינוּ ·· מְלוֹךְ עַל כָּל הָעוֹלָם

Our God . . . reign over the whole universe
(Ro. 109, Bi. 265, De S. 138)

We have just referred to the infiltration into our High Holyday liturgy of elements from the ancient Palestinian prayer book. Their presence is undoubtedly due to the fact that that source was the matrix from which so much of our festival *Piyyut* is culled. These compositions were borrowed, therefore, together with their contextual material from the statutory Palestinian *'Amidah*.

This factor explains the presence of the composition *melokh 'al kol ha-'olam*; for this prayer for the kingdom of God to be established was actually used in ancient Palestine not only on the High Holydays but on all festivals.[52]

בָּרוּךְ ···עוֹשֵׂה הַשָּׁלוֹם

Blessed . . . author of peace
(Ro. 111, Bi. 269, De S. 193)

The adoption of elements from the Palestinian liturgy into
our festival prayer books also explains this special concluding formula of the final benediction of the *'Amidah*, in place
of the usual *ha-mevarekh 'eth 'ammo yisra'el ba-shalom*. The
version *'oseh ha-shalom* was, in fact, the common daily formula used in Palestine.

אָבִינוּ מַלְכֵּנוּ

Our Father, our King
(Ro. 111, Bi. 271, De. S. 143)

On *Rosh Hashanah* we define God's relationship to us as
'Our Father, our King', as well as our own relationship to
him (*'im kevanim 'im ka'avadim*) 'as children, as servants'.[53]

A child and a servant both have an obligation to obey
implicitly whatever instruction is given to them by parent
or master respectively. There is, however, a significant
difference. The child is in a special relationship to the
parent which allows for him to question the reasons behind
the parental instruction and to indicate whether he is un-
dertaking it with enthusiasm or with reluctance. The servant, on the other hand, has to suppress his own feelings,
and get on with the task.

In our dialogue with God both of these relationships
coalesce. He is 'our father'. He must allow us the privilege
of analysing his will and examining his instructions. Indeed, this is the unique and most prominent characteristic
of Judaism: the in-depth analysis of God's will, which constitutes our Oral Law which every Jew has the privilege
and obligation to study. Our God is no tyrant; his instructions can all stand up to human inquiry, after which they
will be shown, individually and collectively, to be an integrated mosaic of spiritual and moral refinement of the
highest order. As 'our father' we also believe that he is
indulgent to us when our response to his call is less than

enthusiastic. Without this belief the plea for atonement at this time would be a futile exercise.

Nevertheless, God is also 'Our King'; and even instructions which to our superficial glance may appear irrelevant must also be observed out of humility, love and faith, and in the hope that the day will come when God will 'open our eyes' to true enlightenment.

This coalescent relationship of 'son' and 'servant' is given clear expression by the prophet Malachi (3:17):

> They shall be mine, says the Lord of Hosts, My own possession . . . and I will spare them as a man spares *the son* (*beno*) who *serves* (*ha'oved*) him.

The *'Aviynu Malkeynu* prayer constitutes a lengthy catalogue of concise, direct petitions to God. There are, however, two dominant and recurring pleas: first, for the counsels of Israel's accusers to be destroyed and their malevolent intentions frustrated, and, second, for the sick of our people – whether it be a physical or spiritual malady – to be healed, and for the whole nation to be inscribed for life and blessing. It concludes with a special appeal that God should grant this primarily through the merit of the saints and martyrs of our people in every generation.

The kernel of the *'Aviynu Malkeynu* goes back to talmudic times when the formula was first employed by Rabbi Akivah while officiating as *Chazan* at a special service to intercede for rain during a period of drought.[54] The immediate heavenly response convinced the people that it was this particular mode of appeal that was the key to unlocking the gates of mercy. The inevitable result was that, while R. Akivah's *'Aviynu Malkeynu* contained but five lines, subsequent authorities and *Chazanim* expanded the prayer to suit their particular needs and emotions. Hence, while the Sephardi version has twenty-nine lines, the Ashkenazi rite has thirty-eight and the Polish rite has forty-four lines. The great nineteenth-century liturgist, Seligman Isaac Baer, in his famous commentary on the Siddur, *Yak-*

hin Lashon,[55] testifies to having seen as many as fifty-three variants in the Siddurim and manuscripts he consulted!

The *'Aviynu Malkeynu* prayer, because of its popularity and the efficacy attributed to it, was prescribed for recitation immediately following the *'Amidah* on *Rosh Hashanah*, *Yom Kippur* and at morning and afternoon services throughout the Ten Days of Penitence and on fast days. It is not recited on *Shabbat*, however, because it is patterned on the weekday *'Amidah*, with a direct correspondence of phraseology between the two. A few examples will suffice. The final line contains the phrase *chonnenu va'anenu* ('favour us') which corresponds, in the *'Amidah*, to the blessing *'attah choneyn* ('you favour man'). The second line – *'eyn lanu melekh 'ellah 'attah* ('we have no *King* but you') – corresponds to the phrase in the first blessing of the *'Amidah*, *melekh 'ozer* ('A *King* who helps . . .'). The fourth line – *chaddesh 'alenu shanah tovah* ('renew unto us a good year') – corresponds to the phrase in the ninth blessing of the *'Amidah*, *Barekh 'alenu . . . 'et ha-shanah ha-zo'th . . . letovah* ('Bless *this year unto us* . . . for *good*'). The eleventh line – *Shelach rephu'ah sheleymah* ('send perfect healing') – corresponds exactly to the phrase in the eighth blessing of the *'Amidah*, *veha'aleh rephu'ah sheleymah*.

This direct correspondence to the phraseology of the weekday *'Amidah* explains why it is omitted on Sabbath,[56] and also why it is prescribed for recitation following on immediately after the *'Amidah*.

READING OF THE LAW FOR THE FIRST DAY
(Ro. 117–23, Bi. 287–99, De S. 151–61)

On *Rosh Hashanah*, as on other festivals, we call five people to the Reading of the Law. The Reading (*layening*) is chanted to a special melody, reserved especially for the High Holydays. It is not as lively or wide-ranging a melody as for *Shabbat*, but is rather slower in tempo and more reserved and restricted in vocal range. This conforms to the mood of calm reflection and tranquil introspection which is the order of the day.

The *Miy Shebeyrach* prayers, recited for those called up, are also chanted to that same melody; and, if they are able to do so, the latter may even chant their blessings over the Torah employing the same High Holyday melody.

Genesis ch. 21 is read on the first day of *Rosh Hashanah*. This tells of the birth of Isaac, the problems posed by Ishmael's evil influence upon him, culminating in Ishmael's banishment from Abraham's home. It records the divine promise to Hagar of protection and prosperity for her offspring, and the peace treaty signed between Abraham and Avimelech.

For the *Haphtarah*, the story of Hannah[57] was selected. This describes her mental anguish at her unfulfilled desire for a child, her visit to the sanctuary at Shilo 'to pour out her heart', and the response to her prayer, culminating, happily, in the birth of Samuel.

The relevance of these readings to the message of the festival is not difficult to discover. *Rosh Hashanah* is the time for expressing our firm conviction that 'God is near to all who call upon him in truth'. It is the occasion when we affirm our belief and faith that if our cherished wishes are not fulfilled, it is no reflection on the justice of God. It might well be his inscrutable will that we must suffer years of frustrating waiting, as did both Sarah and Hannah before they were blessed with a child. Faith, prayer, righteous living and patience ultimately wrest blessing from the divine grip. Despair and loss of faith put it even further from our reach.

Another message of the Torah reading is that of God's universal concern for all his creatures. Man may cast out his fellow – the same way that Ishmael was banished from his home – but God will never abandon his creatures. He may have selected Isaac as the repository of his spiritual message to mankind, but Ishmael is still an object of his loving concern. This message is reinforced in the story of Jonah, read on *Yom Kippur*, where God demonstrates to Jonah that *all* men are worthy of salvation, and that God hears the cries of *all* men when they issue forth from a truly contrite heart.

A rabbinic tradition[58] forges another link between the festival and the choice of Torah and *Haphtarah* readings by asserting that both the conception of Isaac (described in the reading for the first day) and his binding (recounted on the second day) actually took place on *Rosh Hashanah*. Similarly, the birth of Samuel was chosen to be read on this day because he was also conceived on *Rosh Hashanah*. This coincidence is emphasised by the choice of the same Hebrew verb, *paqad*, 'to visit (with child)' used in connection with both Sarah[59] and Hannah.[60] This verb has a particular association with *Rosh Hashanah* in that it also means 'to remember', which is one of the major themes (*Zikhronoth* – God remembering the merit of the Patriarchs) of our festival liturgy.

It is, however, amid the exalted prayer of Hannah, with which the *Haphtarah* concludes, that we come closest to discovering the core message of *Rosh Hashanah*: that man's fate is totally in the hands of God and that we are all dependent upon his grace for every breath we take.

> The Lord ends life and preserves it;
> He brings down to the grave, and resurrects.
> He makes poor and invests with wealth.
> He brings low and elevates.
> He raises the poor out of the dust and the needy from
> the dunghill,
> To make them sit with princes and inherit a majestic
> throne.

THE SOUNDING OF THE SHOFAR

(i)   The historic role of the Shofar

Although we sound the Shofar only on *Rosh Hashanah*, and once on *Yom Kippur* to mark the end of the fast, in biblical times its alarming call was heard very frequently.

Every morning in the Jerusalem Temple twenty-one blasts were sounded on the Shofar. As the gates opened three notes rang out summoning the faithful to worship, and perhaps acting at the same time as an alarm-clock for the slumbering priests. Accompanying the morning public sacrifices another nine notes were blown and a further nine accompanied the afternoon offering.

Each Friday eve the Shofar announced the approach of the Sabbath. Six notes were blown. At the first sounding the labourers in the fields stopped work and made for home. At the second Shofar blast the shops closed and city-life came to a halt. The third blast was a signal to light the Sabbath lights. Then, after a brief pause, three further notes were sounded and the Sabbath began.

When Israel went into battle the Shofar proclaimed the moment of attack. It was at the sound of the Shofar that all the Israelites under the command of Joshua shouted aloud to bring down the walls of Jericho (Josh. 6:4). Gideon and a small band of three hundred men put to flight a vast army of Midianites by blowing on Shofars and creating a mighty uproar, thus giving a mistaken impression of Israel's numerical superiority.[61]

The Shofar was also employed at the inauguration of each Jubilee (fiftieth) year to announce the year of release, when all slaves were granted their freedom and all land was restored to its original tribal owners. The Shofar figured so prominently at that inaugural ceremony that the name of the year of release was even called *yovel* (translit. 'Jubilee'), which is the old Hebrew word for the Ram's horn!

In medieval times the Shofar was also used in the ceremony of excommunication which imposed total isolation on any Jew who rebelled against the rulings of the court or who undermined the authority of the Torah. The threatening alarm of the Shofar brought home to the one under ban the full reality of his estrangement from any social, religious or commercial contact with any member of the Jewish community, while at the same time offering a public clarion warning of the penalty for associating with such a miscreant.

The Shofar was also heard on fast days, attempting to rouse the people to repentance. It was heard each month to announce the appearance of the new moon, and at funerals its plaintive notes set the mood of the occasion.

One could add still further to this impressive list which demonstrates the role of the Shofar as herald at almost every major event and occasion in ancient times. Since Numbers 29:1 designates *Rosh Hashanah* as 'a day of blowing', the Shofar must have been particularly conspicuous on that day, and it has even been suggested that it was blown at regular intervals throughout the day.

(ii)   The notes of the Shofar

There are three types of sounds or notes made by the Shofar in the course of the New Year liturgy. The most common one is the *Teqiy'ah*. This is a plain, unwavering note which is held for about five seconds before ending abruptly. The *Teqiy'ah* is always sounded at the beginning and end of each bar; and sandwiched between the two *Teqiy'ah*s is either the *Shevarim* or the *Teru'ah*.

The *Shevarim* must be identical in length to the *Teqiy'ah* that proceeds and follows it. It consists of three short blasts, each ending abruptly. The name *Shevarim* means 'broken', indicative of its structure as a *Teqiy'ah* 'broken up' into three parts.

The *Teru'ah* is likewise of equal length to the accompanying *Teqiy'ah*s. It comprises nine very brief notes, formed by the rapid insertion and withdrawal of the tongue into the mouthpiece of the Shofar.

During the morning one hundred of these notes are sounded at key points in the service. Altogether sixty *Teqiy'ah*s are blown, twenty *Shevarim* and twenty *Teru'ah*s. In order that the officiant who is blowing the Shofar should not become confused he has an aide standing opposite him (the Synagogue Reader being in the centre) at the reading desk, who proclaims aloud the note about to be blown. Both are dressed in a white gown or *kittel*.

The Rabbi is given the honour of blowing the Shofar, as

he is presumed to be the most fitting person to sound the call to repentance. If he is unable to blow the Shofar – which can happen – he will act as 'proclaimer of the notes' or, to give it its Hebrew title, the *Maqriy'*. The one who blows the Shofar is designated *Ba'al Toqea'* ('the master of the blowing'); and if his performance has been particularly faultless he can be sure that at the end of the service, when the last note has faded away, he will receive a loud token of appreciation from the congregation, which will shout the traditional formula of acclaim, *yishar kochakha* ('May your strength be increased').

(iii)   The significance of the Shofar

The most popular explanation of the origin of the ritual of blowing the Shofar on *Rosh Hashanah* relates it to the episode of the *'Aqedah* ('binding of Isaac') in Genesis ch. 22. The life of Isaac was saved, vicariously, by the offering of the ram 'caught in the thickets *by its horns*'. The Shofar thus recalls Abraham's unquestioning and total obedience to the divine will which has represented, ever since, a model and ideal to which his offspring might aspire.

Other explanations have also been suggested, such as that the New Year, as the beginning of creation, marked the moment when God became King of the Universe. Just as trumpets are sounded at the coronation of earthly monarchs, so is the Shofar sounded to mark the enthronement of God.

Another explanation draws attention to the fact that at the revelation at Sinai 'the sound of the Shofar went stronger and stronger'.[62] On *Rosh Hashanah* it is sounded, then, to summon us to renew that pledge made by our ancestors at Sinai.

Further explanations understand the Shofar blowing as foreshadowing its role in the time to come, as herald to the day of judgment,[63] the ingathering of the exiles[64] and the resurrection.

לַמְנַצֵּחַ לִבְנֵי־קֹרַח

To the chief musician: a psalm of the sons of Korach
(Ro. 126, Bi. 315, De S. 164)

Quite apart from the thematic relevance of this psalm to the sounding of the Shofar, there is a poignant and telling message underlying the selection at this time of a psalm composed by the sons of Korach.

Korach was the arch rebel against God and his anointed leaders.[65] He was swallowed up alive into the earth for his sin; yet his sons were untainted, having dissociated themselves from their father's wicked ways. It is most appropriate, therefore, that one of their psalms should have been honourably selected to serve as an introduction to the sounding of the Shofar with its call to repentance.

The psalm is recited seven times, which some have explained on the basis of the fact that the divine name *'Elokim* is repeated seven times. A more mystical explanation regards each recitation of the psalm as efficaciously bringing the divine presence down from the seventh and highest heaven to the throne of mercy at the closest proximity to man.

Psalm 47 is followed by a selection of verses, recited responsively, all but one of which (*Koliy shama'ta*, Lam. 3:56) are from the psalms. Aside from the introductory verse (*min ha-meytzar*), which was included by some authorities in order to make up the significant number of *seven* verses, the initial letters of the last six verses form the acrostic *Kra' Satan*, 'tear in pieces the accuser'. This imprecation was regarded as particularly significant by the sixteenth-century mystics of Safed who prescribed the recitation of these verses, and who, for the same reason, introduced into the liturgy the recitation of the *'ana' bek-hoach* prayer.[66] The second line of that prayer – *kabbeyl rinnath 'amkha; sagveynu taghareynu nora'* – provides the same acrostic. For the sounding of the Shofar the acrostic's sentiment is especially appropriate, as the Talmud[67] explains that the purpose of sounding the Shofar was 'in order to confuse Satan'. According to *Tosaphoth*[68] his confusion arises from fear that this Shofar might well be the messianic alarm which will herald Satan's own demise.

THE *MUSAPH* SERVICE

הִנְנִי

THE READER'S MEDITATION
(Ro. omitted, Bi. 325, De S.1)

The *Chazan* stands in fervent prayer reciting silently a most beautiful and strikingly personal plea to God to accept him as representative of his congregation, however unworthy he might be to assume such a sacred and exalted spiritual role. He asks God to overlook his particular shortcomings when receiving, through him, the prayers and supplications of the congregation.[1]

Here am I, poor in deeds, quaking in dread of the One who sits as recipient of the praises of Israel. I have come to stand and make supplication before you on behalf of your people, Israel, who have appointed me even though I am not worthy or deserving of that privilege.

Therefore I do entreat you, O God of Abraham, God of Isaac and God of Jacob, Lord, Lord, merciful and gracious God, bountiful One, awesome and revered One, make to succeed the task upon which I am setting out: to secure mercy for myself and for them that have appointed me.

Please, let them not be held responsible for my particular sins, nor condemn them for my shortcomings; for I am, indeed, a transgressor. Let them not suffer for my faults. Let them not be embarrassed on my account, nor ashamed. Neither make me ashamed because of them.

Accept my prayer as you would the prayer of a worthy sage, acclaimed for absolute integrity from his earliest youth.[2] Accept it as you would the prayer of one endowed

with maturity and a sweet voice, the prayer of one en-
joying the religious confidence of his fellows. Deprive
Satan of his ability to accuse, and let our love become
your ensign, just as your love banishes all traces of our
transgression.

Convert all Israel's fasts and periods of abstention into
days of gladness and rejoicing, for life and peace. O how
they crave after true peace![3] Let there be no impediment
in my prayer. May it be your will, Lord, God of Abraham, God of Isaac and God of Jacob, the great, mighty
and feared God, the Most High, called 'I shall be what
I shall be', that all the intermediaries that transmit the
sound of prayers should carry my prayer before your
glorious throne, and present it effectively before you, on
behalf of all the righteous people, the pious, the blame-
less and the upright, and to the glory of your great,
mighty and revered name. For you do, indeed, hear
mercifully the prayer of your people Israel. We bless you
for hearing our prayer.

When we consider that in the medieval period the *Chazan*
was also the religious leader, this humble prayer, laying
bare his spiritual inadequacies, is in marked contrast to
the posture of spiritual perfection adopted by the ecclesiastical officials of other faiths.

HALF-*KADDISH*
(Ro. 131, Bi. 327, De S. 3)

The half-*Kaddish* is a kind of liturgical punctuation mark
which serves to separate off certain parts of the service
from other more important sections. Here it sets into
sharper relief the *'Amidah*, the most important prayer. Its
call, that God's name should be 'magnified and sanctified',
suggests that its purpose is also to serve as an exhortation
to the congregation to recite the next section with particular
devotion and concentration.

Ashkenazi tradition doubles the word *l'eyla'* in every

Kaddish recited during *Rosh Hashanah* and throughout the Ten Days of Penitence. The repetition of the word *l'eyla'* ('exalted') is to convey the idea that God is never more exalted than at this time of the year when the thoughts and prayers of all Israel are directed towards him.

The number of words in a particular prayer was regarded as mystically significant and not to be altered. Thus, because an additional *l'eyla'* was being inserted at this time, authorities suggested that we should compensate by taking out one word. The most convenient way was to contract the two words *min kol* (*birkhatha'*) to *mikkol* – a regular contraction which does not affect the meaning.

This practice of doubling the word *l'eyla'* is a comparatively late innovation, there being no reference to it in any source before the fifteenth century, where it is referred to for the first time in the notes to the *Sepher Maharil* of R. Yaakov ben Mosheh of Moellin.[4] There was, in fact, considerable variety of practice in this matter in Ashkenazi communities. In Posen they only doubled the word in the first *Kaddish* which preceded the *Selichoth* services. In Frankfort the extra *l'eyla'* was only inserted on *Rosh Hashanah* and *Yom Kippur* – not during the rest of the Ten Days of Penitence – and only in the *Kaddish* recited by the *Chazan*. Mourners did not include it.

REPETITION OF THE *'AMIDAH*

מְסוֹד חֲכָמִים וּנְבוֹנִים

From the counsel of the wise and understanding
(Ro. 142, Bi. 349, De S. 184 – see pp. 19–20)

אֹפֶד מֵאָז

From of old this is the appointed day

A poem by Eleazar Kallir, it is constructed as an alphabetical acrostic in rhyming, four-lined stanzas. The requirement of providing a concluding response for Reader and congregation gives the mistaken impression that the acros-

tic ends after the letter *reish* (*Rachum zekhor* . . .), support
for which might be adduced from the fact that the next
verse, recited by the congregation, commences with the
letter *nun* (of the word *na'aleh*).

It is probable, however, that Kallir's penultimate line
originally did begin with the (letter *shin* of the) word Shofar,
but that subsequently the first two words of that line were
transposed. The transposition was made in order to take
account of five biblical quotations which were inserted
immediately before that penultimate line, but which we
have not retained in our *Machzorim*. The final word of the
last biblical quotation (Ps. 47:10) was *na'alah*, and it was
therefore felt preferable to juxtapose these two almost
identical words,[5] even though it meant sacrificing the acrostic uniformity. When the biblical quotations were omitted, the original word order was not restored.

The poet alludes to the fact that it was on the first day
of creation – the anniversary of which *Rosh Hashanah* cele-
brates – that Adam sinned and was judged. Because God
spared him the full measure of retribution, 'that day was
established from then on (*'uppad me'az*) as a day of judgment' and divine indulgence.

תֶּכֶן בְּמָכוֹן

When you are seated on your judgment-throne
(Ro. 143, Bi. 351, De S. 186)

A beautiful and direct plea to God to leave his throne of
judgment and occupy the throne of mercy.[6] It calls upon
him to take note of our sincere efforts to extricate ourselves
from the constriction of our own passions. This seems to
be the import of the phrase *mul 'even negeph mithlachamim*,
derived from Is. 8:14. 'The attacking missile' (lit. 'stone of
attack') is one of the designations of the Evil Inclination
according to the Talmud,[7] though some explain it as referring to the Accuser or Satan. The poet asks God to remember us compassionately, and particularly as the
descendants of that Patriarch, Isaac, who was so willing to
surrender his life in the service of God.

The poem is constructed as a reverse alphabetical acrostic, perhaps symbolising the retreat of God from his remotest throne of judgment (represented by the letter *taf*, the last letter of the alphabet) to the throne of mercy at the closest proximity to man (represented by the first letter, *'aleph*). There are four words to a line and four rhyming lines to each stanza.

The biblical and rabbinic allusions blend so naturally into their context in the poetry of Kallir, notwithstanding his masterly economy of words – the veritable hallmark of poetic expression. The second stanza is a prime example of this, wherein, in a mere eight words – *tzarath 'omer lo' yadon, pa'amayim lo' thaqum la'avaddon* – he expresses a lengthy and complex sentiment.

Lo' yadon is an allusion to the curse *lo' yadon ruchiy ba'adam* (Gen. 6:3) – 'My spirit shall not abide in man' – uttered by God prior to bringing the flood. *Tzarath 'omer* here means 'the threat of the utterance'; and the second line of the stanza says 'it shall not occur a second time for destruction'. Thus, in a mere eight words the poet has called upon God not to repeat that terrible curse which he directed against the generation of the flood, but to ensure that his spirit remains eternally with us.

This device, of employing just two or three key-words from a quotation, Kallir utilises with great effect, leaving to his reader the task of mentally filling in the rest of the quotation in order to appreciate the full impact of the association. This is especially effective in the final line of the poem where the three words *eylleh divrey ha-brith* (Deut. 28:69), which climax the *tokhechah*, the fearful retribution which is threatened if Israel rejects her Torah, are employed as a pregnant allusion to that lengthy catalogue of punishments. Again, the final three words, *bezikhron shillush brith* ('remembering the three-fold covenant'), employ the same device, as an allusion to the verse 'And I will remember (*zakharti*) my covenant (*brithiy*) with Jacob, and I will remember my covenant (*brithiy*) with Isaac, and also my covenant (*brithiy*) with Abraham' (Lev. 26:42). Thus, again, in a mere eight words, Kallir succeeds in expressing the complex plea that, in recognition of God's promise to each of the patriarchs to grant rewards to their offspring, the fearful punishments detailed in the Torah must, of necessity, be neutralised.

Another important allusion is contained in the line, *'olam 'asher be'arba'ah nadon* ('World which is judged at four times in the year'), based upon the mishnaic statement[8] that there are, in fact, four 'New Years' when God's verdict on the world is given practical expression in terms of the richness or meagreness of the harvest bestowed. Passover is the 'New Year' for grain, Pentecost for fruits, *Rosh Hashanah* for mankind and Tabernacles for water.

The concluding plea of the Reader, asking for 'a year of plenty, of dew, rains and warmth', is based upon the prayer of the High Priest[9] which he uttered on leaving the Holy of Holies. It is quoted in full in the *Musaph 'Amidah* of *Yom Kippur*.[10]

אַף אוֹרַח מִשְׁפָּטֶיךָ

Though your path is judgment
(Ro. 144, Bi. 363, De S. 187)

This composition by Kallir employs the very complicated construction of a double alphabetical acrostic with *At-bash* formation, according to which the first line of each couplet follows the usual alphabetical order while the second line of the couplet creates a reverse alphabetical acrostic pattern.

The theme of the poem will be seen to be well suited to the alphabetical acrostic pattern, as it sketches in the history of repentance, demonstrating it to have been an active agent from the creation, through the patriarchal age, and throughout history, even until the longed-for Messianic era. The alphabetical progression furthers the idea of this long history of repentance from the beginning to the end of time; and the reverse acrostic was perhaps intended to convey the vicissitudes of fortune – from periods of appeal and influence to others of *reversal* and rejection – suffered

by the spirit of repentance as it strove for a permanent
place in the hearts of men.

The third line makes reference to Israel having 'sought
thee *since yesterday*' – a statement which seems hardly appropriate for the *first* day of *Rosh Hashanah*! It appears again
(*mey'ethmol qiddamnukha*) in the *Shachrit* composition, *kevodo 'iheyl*, and is to be understood in the context of an
ancient pietistic practice, of certain groups since the talmudic period, to fast on the day preceding *Rosh Hashanah*[11].
This was probably in compensation for an earlier custom
of fasting on *Rosh Hashanah* itself, and during all the Ten
Days of Penitence, including Sabbath. It was subsequently
felt to be improper to impair the joy of holy days by fasting.
Consequently, the four days on which fasting was suspended (two days *Yom Tov*, the intermediate Sabbath and
the day before *Yom Kippur*) were compensated for by hold-
ing them on the four days immediately preceding *Rosh
Hashanah*. This explains why, if there are not four clear
days for *Selichoth* in the week of *Rosh Hashanah*, we commence *Selichoth* from the preceding week.

Kallir, having referred in the previous composition to
the missiles of the Evil Inclination, or human passion, is
moved to include here a reference to Joseph, who valiantly
resisted the charms of the wife of Potiphar. He is referred
to allusively as *hasarath shekhem missevel*, 'the one whose
shoulder was relieved of the fetters' (Ps. 81:7), in accordance with the talmudic opinion that Joseph was released
from prison on *Rosh Hashanah*.[12] The poet pleads that the
vindication, on this day, of Joseph's innocence from the sin
of lust, should, vicariously, be credited to the merit of his
children if ever they should fall prey to its temptation.

מֶלֶךְ עֶלְיוֹן

Highest divinity[13]
(Ro. 145, Bi. 355, De S. 190)

A cursory glance at the alphabetical acrostic pattern of this
composition immediately discloses the fact that it has been
abridged from a longer composition in which all the letters

of the alphabet were represented. The full version appears, in fact, in the Avignon *Machzor* and in some fragments of the Cairo Genizah collection.

An editor has removed each alternate stanza, which commenced with the phrase *melekh 'evyon* ('The inconsequential king') and ended with the refrain *'ad mathay yimlokh* ('How long can he reign?'), and whose purpose in the composition was to serve as a foil by which to contrast 'The Supreme King, who reigns forever and ever' (*la'adey 'ad yimlokh melekh 'elyon*) with the mortal, earthly monarch in whom people naively put their trust. It is conceivable that before each of the *melekh 'evyon* verses the Ark curtain was originally drawn, and that it was in order to avoid performing this distracting activity that those alternate verses were subsequently taken out. It might also have been removed as an act of internal censorship so as not to offend the monarchy of the host country, since the original version contains some rather strong expressions which, although motivated only by a pious attempt to enhance the total superiority of God, yet inevitably appear as an attempt to demean the earthly monarch.

The first (*balah*) and last (*tenumah*) stanzas of the *melekh 'evyon* verses were subsequently re-admitted before the final line (*toqpo la'ad*), though with the precondition that they were recited in an undertone, so as not to give offence.

וּנְתַנֶּה תֹקֶף

We will celebrate the mighty holiness
(Ro. 146, Bi. 361, De S. 191)

This is probably one of the most moving compositions in the whole of Jewish liturgy, despite the fact that it is unrhymed, not artistically constructed to include any poetic or acrostic devices, and the phraseology employed is not the rich biblical language which most of the *Piyyutim* draw on. Simplicity and directness are the hall-marks of this composition, with its message couched in short, clipped phrases of three or four words, suggestive of the brevity of man's life-span and the sudden twists of fate. It opens with a glimpse into the heavenly Hall of Justice where the Almighty judge is engaged in reviewing the deeds of man. Unlike our administration of law, wherein a witness cannot act as a judge for fear of subjective impression or bias, God alone may act not only as 'witness' to the crimes committed, but also as 'judge, arbiter and discerner'.

וְתִפְתַּח סֵפֶר הַזִכְרוֹנוֹת – *And you open the book of records*

The phrase *Sepher Ha-zikhronoth* is found in the book of Esther (6:1). It refers there to the royal chronicle of every significant event that occurred in the realm. It was while reading that record that Ahazuerus discovered the hitherto concealed fact that Mordechai had not been rewarded for his loyalty. God, similarly, has his royal 'Book of Records', symbolic of the fact that nothing remains concealed from him – 'for you remember all that has been forgotten'. Like Mordechai, if we have deserved reward it will be forthcoming, sooner or later; and if, God forbid, we deserve punishment – that fact is also indelibly recorded.

וְחוֹתָם יַד כָּל אָדָם בּוֹ – *The seal of every man's hand is set thereto*

This idea is derived from a Midrash which states that, at the time when we depart this world, God presents the sinners with a full record and reminder of their wrongdoing, and they sign it as a true record. The author of *Une-thaneh Toqef* has taken this idea and transferred it to the events of each *Rosh Hashanah*.

וּמַלְאָכִים יֵחָפֵזוּן – *The angels are dismayed*

The reference to the heavenly angels 'quaking with fear' is inspired by Job 4:18 – 'Behold, he puts no trust in his servants, and his angels he charges with folly.' It is a philosophically perplexing notion. In the context of the book of Job it might be explained as referring specifically to the Satan – a free agent whose task is to exploit human weakness. The heavenly accusers also have cause for fear on the judgment day, 'for they will not be vindicated in

thy sight in law'. God will, as it were, spring to the defence
of his wayward children as they stand in the dock facing
the onslaught of the accusing angels' condemnation.

כִּבְנֵי מָרוֹן – *As a flock of sheep*

This expression, used by the author to describe the manner
in which all creatures pass before God's throne, is borrowed
from the Mishna.[14] Even the later talmudic authorities
were not too sure, however, of the precise meaning of the
phrase. The universally accepted interpretation, adopted
by all translations, is 'like sheep', on the basis of the Aramaic noun *immra'*, 'a lamb'. *Bney maron* would therefore
mean 'young (lit. the offspring of) sheep'.

The suggestion of the nineteenth-century scholar, N.
Brüll,[15] that a textual error has occurred here, whereby a
single word *ki-venumeron* has been erroneously split up into
two words, has now received corroboration from the research of Professor N. Wieder into a number of medieval
liturgical manuscripts.

The word *numeron* was a Greek word, the equivalent of
the Latin *numerus*, meaning 'a troop (lit. "numbered formation") of soldiers'. Thus, the Mishna's intention was to
depict Israel 'as in (*Ki-ve*) military formation', filing by the
heavenly reviewing-stand.

בְּרֹאשׁ הַשָּׁנָה יִכָּתֵבוּן – *On the first day of the year it is inscribed*

'. . . And on the Day of Atonement it is sealed.' This
extended period, before man's fate is finally sealed, applies,
according to the Talmud,[16] only in the case of one particular category of offenders. The truly righteous do not require
a deferment of final judgment – they are inscribed, and
their fate sealed, immediately on *Rosh Hashanah*. The truly
wicked likewise have their doom sealed on that day. It is
for those who occupy a mid-way position, whose spiritual
pendulum frequently vacillates between virtue and sinfulness, that a period of grace – the Ten Days of Penitence
– is granted, for the exalted influence of *Rosh Hashanah* to
inspire them to remorse and pious resolution.

Ironically, the authorship of this most popular and awe-some composition is shrouded in mystery. Perhaps that is as it should be, for its sentiments are universal. Praise of God can be framed by numerous poets, each with his own individual style and emphases; but *Unethaneh Toqef* indentifies the singular mood, the deep-seated apprehension, that grips all alike at this period. Will we, and our dear ones, escape 'the net which is spread for all creatures'? Will sickness, accident, violence, anxiety and financial ruination stalk our lives this coming year? Will the angel of death knock on our door? We are *all* the authors of the *Unethaneh Toqef* sentiments if the High Holyday spirit has at all penetrated our hearts.

Its popularity is generally attributed to the efforts of Rabbi Kalonymos ben Meshullam, the celebrated eleventh-century liturgical poet of Mainz, Germany, though its attribution to the legendary Rabbi Amnon, who is supposed to have composed it as he lay dying in the agony of martyrdom, has become an inspirational axiom of Jewish folklore. Amnon is credited with having appeared to Rabbi Kalonymos in a dream, three days after his death, to teach him the prayer in order to popularise it in Israel.[17]

וְכֹל מַאֲמִינִים

And all believe
(Ro. 149, Bi. 367, De S. 197)

Another alphabetic acrostic. The authorship is not known for certain but it is now generally attributed to the earliest Palestinian Hebrew poet, Yannai (sixth–seventh centuries CE), who also composed the *Piyyut 'Az Rov Nissim* in the Passover Haggadah.

Yannai's pioneering contribution to Hebrew poetry, his personality and his numerous poetic compositions were only brought to light this century with the discovery of the Cairo Genizah. He was known hitherto only through some scattered references to him in early medieval sources. Through modern research many anonymous fragments of poetry have been discovered and attributed to Yannai's authorship, and this important literary figure has been rescued from the oblivion of antiquity.

The poem proceeds in a stair-like progression of ideas. An idea of God is presented in the first stich (introduced by the definite article, *ha*), and the key word is then taken over to form the subject of the succeeding affirmation, introduced by the words *Vekhol ma'amiyniym*. Thus:

> *HABOCHEYN uvodeyk ginzey nistaroth . . . Vekhol ma'a-miyniym shehu' BOCHEYN kelayoth.*

The popularity of this hymn ensured for it a place among the select group that are recited on both *Rosh Hashanah* and *Yom Kippur*.

The opening line of this two-fold alphabetical acrostic poem describes God as 'the one who takes firm hold of the scales of justice', a phrase derived from Deuteronomy 32:41. The Midrash[18] on that verse states that 'in the same way that God does not influence the judicial process when reviewing the deeds of the other nations, so Israel must expect to be subjected to a comprehensive inquiry into her own actions'. That the concept of the 'Chosen People' does not confer upon Israel special immunity in the face of divine judgment, is the import of this poem.

The poem lays special emphasis on the divine quality of mercy which is extended to those who exhibit even a trace of remorse – 'He opens the door to those who knock in repentance' (line 17). God is so long-suffering and indulgent that 'he closes an eye to the rebellious' (line 15).

The phrase *vekholelam yachad* (line 11) has been misunderstood by all translations. The general rendering is 'He is all-perfect' (Routledge), 'all-embracing' (Birnbaum), 'able to accomplish all things' (De Sola). None of these take account of the objective suffix (*am*) 'them', attached to the verb. This relates back to the previous subject, namely, God's creatures whom he had 'formed in the womb'. M. Zulay has shown that the verb *Kalal* means 'to complete an act of creation'.[19] The whole stanza may, therefore, be loosely rendered, 'And all believe that he fashioned them in the womb. He that is all-powerful *sees them safely born.*'

The following line – *ha-lan beseyther betzeyl shadday* ('He dwells in the secret place in the shadow of the Almighty') – is most perplexing. The subject – as in all the corresponding lines – can only be God. How, then, can we speak of *God* dwelling in the shadow of the Almighty?

This line is borrowed directly from Ps. 91:1 – *yosheyv beseyther 'elyon betzeyl shadday yithlonan.* The classical commentators – Rashi, Ibn Ezra, etc. – all assume that the subject of the phrase is a righteous human being. They render accordingly, 'He who dwells in the shelter of the Most High, who abides in the shadow of the Almighty . . .', a rendering followed by most modern translations. From our poem, however, it is clear that early Jewish tradition took the subject of this phrase to be God himself, a fact supported by the rendering of the official Aramaic translation of the Targum![20] The doctrine is to be seen against the backcloth of the various manifestations – or extra concentrations[21] – of God's presence which are hypostatised in rabbinic literature, such as *Shekhiynah* ('In-dwelling'), *Ruach Ha-Qodesh* ('Holy Spirit'), *Memra'* ('created word'), *Kavod* ('glory').

וְיֶאֱתָיוּ

All the world shall come
(Ro. 151, Bi. 373, De S. 201)

In the preceding three paragraphs a vision of the future is presented when righteousness will be vindicated, the national restoration under the royal Davidic line effected, and all nations will be united in submission to the will of God.

The present composition, in blank verse, echoes this messianic hope, though emphasising exclusively the universalistic theme and omitting any reference to the restoration of Israel's national fortunes.

The alphabetical acrostic pattern is not so easily discernible here. It makes its appearance as the initial root-letter of the verbs employed as the opening word of each phrase (viye*v*archu, veya*gg*idu, veyi*d*reshu, viye*h*alelu, etc.). It will be noticed, however, that the letter *zayin* is represented twice, by the verbs *veyizbechu* and *veyiznechu*. What has occurred here is that these were originally separate, variant versions, one of which was probably inserted in the margin. A later copyist mistakenly embodied it into the main text, where it has remained!

The final word *melukhah* ('kingdom') enables the poem to blend into the context, as a link with the opening word of the next passage *vethimlokh* ('And you shall be *King*'). It forms, therefore, an appropriate poetic climax to the third blessing of the *'Amidah* which concludes by blessing God as *ha-melekh ha-qadosh* ('The holy King').

וּמִפְּנֵי חֲטָאֵינוּ

But because of our sins
(Ro. 153, Bi. 805, De S. 45)

This composition appears in the *Musaph 'Amidah* recited on all festivals. On *Pesach*, *Shavu'oth* and *Sukkoth* a phrase, *la'aloth veleyra'oth ulehishtachavoth lephanekha* – ('And we are unable to go up to appear and worship before you') is included in the opening lines, since those are festivals when the pilgrimages to Jerusalem were made. This composition also inspired the *'Attah yatzarta* prayer, recited on *Shabbat Rosh Chodesh* in the repetition of the *Musaph 'Amidah*.

This poignant plea to God, to restore the national independence of his people in the holy land and to reintroduce the Temple service, is accompanied by an admission, in the opening sentence, that it was 'on account of our sins that we were exiled from our country and banished far from our land'. This may appear to some as a simplistic philosophy of Jewish history, one which would appear to be contradicted by the fact of our national restoration in the twentieth century, the very period of unprecedented assimilation! A popular response is to suggest that the gift of the land of Israel in our day is, indeed, totally undeserved, and is to be justified only as a token of divine love and mercy towards his reprobate children.[22]

The great thirteenth-century Bible commentator and halakhist, Moses ben Nachman (*Ramban*) expands upon the basic principle enunciated in the opening line of this composition – that sin and exile are linked by cause and effect – and he even suggests that the early stories in Genesis were included solely to promote this fundamental principle:

> God placed Adam in the Garden of Eden, which was the choicest place on earth and the residence of the divine spirit, until Adam's sin caused his banishment from there. The generation of the flood was removed from God's earth because of their sin, and only the righteous man (Noah) and his family escaped. Again, the sin of their descendants (who built the tower of Babel) caused them to be banished and scattered over the face of the earth. . . . God drove the wicked Canaanites from his holy land and settled there the people who performed his will. The history contained in Genesis would have served to teach Israel the lesson that by serving God they merited to inherit the land, and if they sinned against him, the land 'would vomit them out as it did the nation that came before them' (Lev. 18:28).[23]

The plea for the rebuilding of the Temple and the restoration of the sacrificial system, contained in this composition as well as in the *retzey* blessing recited in every *'Amidah*, has taken on a new significance in our day with the reunification of Jerusalem and Jewish possession of the Temple Mount.

The rebuilding of the Temple is universally accepted as an event linked to the advent of the messianic age. Rashi and Maimonides differ only in the method, not the period, of its restoration. Rashi,[24] inspired by the verse 'The sanctuary which *your hands* have established, O Lord' (Ex. 15:17),[25] maintains that the third Temple will appear miraculously as a fully built edifice provided by God. This view is clearly expressed in the *Nacheym* prayer, recited in the *'Amidah* of the afternoon service on the Fast of Av:

'. . . For with fire you did consume it, O Lord, and with fire you will, in future, restore it.'[26] Maimonides, on the other hand, believed that the Temple would be built in the normal way, but by the Messiah, and that his ability to achieve its construction would serve to substantiate his messianic claims.[27]

The Talmud states that the future restoration will follow a particular sequence: First Jerusalem will be restored, then the monarchy of the house of David will be re-established, after which the Temple will be rebuilt to become a place of prayer for all nations. Finally, the sacrificial system will be re-instituted.[28] Our prayers for the restoration of these several spiritual institutions, none of which will function until the messianic era,[29] are, therefore, rather vague evocations of our desire to experience something akin to a national and spiritual state of vindication and fulfilment at the dénouement of God's cosmic plan.

עָלֵינוּ

It is our duty
(Ro. 154, Bi. 377, De S. 205)

Although in the second half of the Middle Ages this prayer became invested with such importance that it was introduced as the main conclusion to each of the three daily services throughout the year, it was originally reserved exclusively for the High Holyday recitation, as an introduction to the *malkhuyoth* verses (which acclaim the 'Kingship' of God) of the *Musaph* Service on *Rosh Hashanah*.[30]

The popularity of the prayer grew because of its association with martyrdom. It was used, for example, as the dying prayer of the martyrs of Blois in Southern France who were massacred in 1171. Its choice was probably determined by a particularly fierce reference which they applied to their merciless murderers: 'For they worship vanity and slabber (*lehevel variq*) and pray to a God who cannot save.' This phrase was subsequently expunged by the censor, but it is still widely recited, as, for example, in the popular *Rinath Yisra'el* edition. In order to foster a spirit of

tolerance, *The Authorised Daily Prayer Book* (Singer's edn) of
Anglo-Jewry has consistently omitted the reference.

Such bitter condemnation of their persecutors' faith by
the victims of crusades and *autos da fé* is wholly pardonable.
They must have been totally mystified as to how a religion
of love could initiate, foster and carry out such atrocities.
(One is reminded of a comment by Elli Wiesel that the
holocaust is as much a problem for Christians as it is for
Jews!)

Christian authorities in subsequent centuries were particularly incensed by the insulting reference to the founder
of their religion, and were unimpressed by some Jewish
efforts to demonstrate that the author never had Christianity or its founder in mind when he created his composition. To buttress this latter polemical assertion a variety
of theories were offered as to its period of authorship –
ranging from Joshua (who had in mind the idolatrous
Canaanite religion) to the Men of the Great Assembly (fifth
century BCE) who were attacking the Persian dualists.[31]
What all these theories had in common was the crucial
point that it was a pre-Christian prayer with no offence
intended to the dominant religion.

It was through the testimony of converted Jews that
medieval Christianity got wind of an unauthoritative and
mischievous re-interpretation of the meaning of the prayer
which was suggested by some through highlighting the fact
that the numerical value (*gematria*) of the word *variq* ('slabber') added up to 316, equivalent to that of *Yeshu* (Jesus)!

Through the researches of Professor N. Wieder,[32] we now
see that others even managed to include an additional
oblique defamatory reference to the Muslim religion. This
was achieved by insisting on a variant reading, (*lehevel*)
veLariq. With the additional letter, *lammed*, inserted into the
second noun *variq*, the two words now added up to a numerical value of 413, the equivalent of *Yeshu Muchamet* (Je-
sus/Mohammet)!

Some congregations have a custom of reciting '*Aleynu*
aloud, word for word. This goes back to a decree of the
Russian government in 1703, accompanied by the appoint-

ment of inspectors to visit Synagogues in order to listen to its recitation so as to ensure that the offending phrase was omitted.

Because of the wide attention focused upon this prayer, Jewish internal censorship became particularly sensitive to any other expression which could be misinterpreted. This resulted in the practice of reciting in an undertone the verse *Shelo' sam chelqeynu kahem vegoraleynu kechol hamonam* ('He has not made our portion like theirs, nor our fate like their multitude'), which explains why we close the Ark while reciting that sentiment silently.

While all these medieval vicissitudes suffered by the *'Aleynu* are of great interest, its reputed author, the great talmudist, Abba Arikha[33] (third century CE), had only one purpose in mind: to highlight the sole kingship of God and to deride all idolators and the objects of their veneration. It breathes such an adoration of God that one medieval commentator, R. Eleazar of Worms (twelfth–thirteenth centuries), actually called the prayer 'the Song of Songs of our liturgy'.[34]

'Aleynu is written in a style similar to that of the early *Piyyut*, with short lines, of about four words to a line, and with a simplicity and clarity of expression. The reference to Israel 'bowing and prostrating' is especially appropriate to the Temple practice of full prostration on the ground,[35] especially on *Yom Kippur* when these prostrations were increased in response to the extra invocations of the divine name. In recollection of this, it is still our common practice to make a full prostration on the ground during the *Musaph* recitation of *'Aleynu* on the High Holydays – this being the only time when Jews are permitted to perform prostrations on account of the significance it assumed in non-Jewish worship.[36]

הֱיֵה עִם פִּיפִיּוֹת

Inspire the lips

אוֹחִילָה לָאֵל

I will hope in God
(Ro. 155, Bi. 379, De S. 206–7)

We have referred above to the diffidence with which the
composers of liturgical hymns introduced them into the
statutory services, and the need felt by them to preface
their new compositions with a *Reshuth*,[37] which assured the
congregation that their hymns were fully in line with Orthodox sentiment, and which, at the same time, expressed
the sense of humility and inadequacy which burdened them
as they assumed the role of representative of the
congregation.

These two compositions were inserted here precisely to
serve this purpose: as an introductory *Reshuth* to the major
divisions of the *Musaph 'Amidah*: the *Malkhuyoth*, *Zikhronoth*
and *Shopharoth*. These same two *Reshuth*-compositions are
utilised in the identical position (following *'Aleynu*) in the
Musaph service on *Yom Kippur*. Their purpose there is,
likewise, to serve as an introduction to another major di-
vision of the *'Amidah*, the *'Avodah*, describing the order of
the service of the High Priest in Temple times.[38]

It is clear then, that these *Reshuth*-compositions were not
originally written for the particular prayers to which they
now serve as introductions. The *'Ochilah la'eyl*, for example,
is employed in Sephardi rites as the opening *Reshuth* for the
repetition of the *'Amidah*. That, indeed, seems to have been
its original purpose, a fact which explains the presence of
the verse *'Adonay sephathay tiphtach*, the prefatorial verse of
the *'Amidah*.

The composition *heyey 'im piyphiyyoth* has clearly been
adapted and expanded in order to make it contextually
suited, particularly to the composition *'Al keyn neqavveh*
which follows. This is apparent from the fact that the
version in the Sephardi rite is considerably shorter, com-

prising merely the opening requests for divine inspiration ('Our God . . . Teach them . . . and make known to them how they may glorify you'), followed by the plea that no impediment should be found in their speech ('Suffer them not to falter with their tongue . . . and guard their lips from uttering any word that is not according to your will'). This, then, was the kernel of this *Reshuth*. It was expanded to include references to the sacred role of the *Chazan* and the reliance of the congregation upon his ministrations, as well as to include an allusion to the following composition. This is achieved by means of the phrase *berekh lekha yikhre'un* ('They bend the knee unto you') which corresponds to the verse *kiy lekha tikhra' kol berekh* in the *'Al keyn neqavveh* composition.

The second *Reshuth*, *'Ochilah la'eyl*, is, similarly, an expanded version. Its kernel comprises one four-lined stanza, with four words to each line, and the opening word of each line commencing with an *'Aleph* to emphasise the personal nature of the plea. The added section contains three biblical verses (Ps. 16:1, Ps. 51:17 and Ps. 19:15), though the usual introductory formulae (*ka-kathuv*, *vene'emar*, etc.) have been omitted before each verse.

Attention is drawn by the Birnbaum footnote (p. 380) to one phrase in the text – *bam she'onam* – which, it is claimed, 'does not seem to make sense unless it is read as one word'. There is no basis for this conjecture, especially in the light of the universal acceptance of the existing reading according to all rites and manuscripts. Had the text been suspect, alternate readings would have certainly presented themselves. Birnbaum, rather inconsistently, offers a textual emendation to solve the problem, while at the same time omitting the phrase entirely from his translation! The sense of the phrase which Birnbaum finds difficult, is, simply, 'Let not their great communities[39] be let down *by them* (*bam*),' namely, by any unworthy spiritual leaders.

MALKHUYOTH

עַל כֵּן נְקַוֶּה

Therefore we hope
(Ro. 156, Bi. 381, De S. 357)

This composition was certainly created in order to serve as
an introduction to the *Malkhuyoth* verses which give expression to the 'Kingship' of God. It emphasises the scope of
this concept which is not merely a graphic anthropomorph-
ism but a real messianic expectation that, in the hereafter,
wickedness will cease and all mankind will clearly and
potently sense the nearness of God and be moved to give
him their total spiritual allegiance as monarch of the
Universe.

The universalism of this composition is marvelled at by
one commentator in his comment on the phrase 'when *the
world* shall be subject to the Kingdom of the Almighty, and
all humanity shall call upon your name, and you will cause
all the wicked of the earth to turn back to you'. The *'Iyyun
Tephilah*[40] observes:

> How uniquely long-suffering Israel is may be inferred
> from these sentiments. For the Jew, who, throughout his
> history, has suffered anguish and oppression at the hands
> of the evil-doers, is, nevertheless, as concerned for the
> fate of his tormentors as he is for his own. So he stands,
> in solemn prayer, petitioning the Almighty to grant en-
> lightenment to his enemies so that they may recognise
> God's sovereignty and share in the reward that is
> treasured up for the faithful.

כַּכָּתוּב בְּתוֹרָתֶךָ – *As it is written in your law*

This verse, which throughout the year we regard as an
intrinsic part of the second paragraph of *'Aleynu*, will be
seen in the present context to display its true purpose,
namely to serve as the first of the ten biblical verses employed here, in the *Malkhuyoth*, as proof-texts to depict the

Kingship of God. In our daily version of '*Aleynu* we conclude by adducing merely the first and the penultimate of the ten verses.

Modern scholarship has proved that the *Malkhuyoth* section was not introduced into the High Holyday liturgy until the period of Rabbi Akivah and the Bar Kochba revolt against the Roman occupation of Palestine. Its introduction may have had a nationalistic motive to strengthen determination in order to prepare the nation for the forthcoming struggle to overthrow the foreign kingship and replace it with *the Kingdom of God*.[41]

That the *Malkhuyoth* section was a later innovation may be inferred from the fact that, whereas the *Zikhronoth* and *Shopharoth* each have their own special concluding blessing, which makes a direct reference to the theme of the section, the *Malkhuyoth* section does not. The latter had to be artificially provided with a blessing that was already an intrinsic element of the '*Amidah* (*Barukh . . . meqaddesh yisra'el veyom ha-zikkaron*).

SOUNDING OF THE SHOFAR

The list of notes sounded at this point to herald the *Malkhuyoth*, as given in the Routledge and De Sola editions, is misleading. *Ten* notes are, in fact, sounded for each of the three sections (as correctly given in Birnbaum ed.), according to the following pattern:

Teqiy'ah	Shevarim-Teru'ah	Teqiy'ah	(4 notes)
Teqiy'ah	Shevarim	Teqiy'ah	(3 notes)
Teqiy'ah	Teru'ah	Teqiy'ah	(3 notes)

At the end of the third (*Shopharoth*) section a *Teqiy'ah Gedolah* is sounded. Again this has been omitted from those two editions.

הַיּוֹם הֲרַת עוֹלָם

This day the world was called into being
(Ro. 157, Bi. 383, De S. 210)

These verses reflect a fatalistic attitude towards human destiny. Just as man has no control over whether he is born 'a son (of a household)' or 'a servant', but, in either situation, can merely hope to be the recipient of as much favour as is consonantal with his particular position, so man has no control over the determination of his own status in the eyes of God. God assigns a position to man in accordance with the nature of the relationship with him which God desires. We must hope and pray for a filial relationship; but we must also accept that, inevitably, there will be epochs when we are undeserving, and are relegated to the subordinate status of servants.[42]

Within the context of the sounding of the Shofar, which, in biblical times, heralded the manumission of all slaves in the Jubilee year, these particular verses may be regarded as a challenge to Israel to improve her relationship with God; and, if her status has hitherto been that of 'servant', to regard the sounding of the Shofar on *Rosh Hashanah* as heralding the end of that status and the opportunity for initiation into a new relationship with God as children of a loving father.

ZIKHRONOTH

אַתָּה זוֹכֵר מַעֲשֵׂה עוֹלָם

You remember what was wrought from eternity
(Ro. 158, Bi. 385, De S. 211)

This composition, also attributed to *Rav*, serves as an introduction to the *Zikhronoth*, the second major section of the *'Amidah*, which emphasises the infallibility of the divine memory, and the absolute comprehensiveness of God's surveillance of human actions: 'There is no forgetting before the throne of your glory; there is not a thing hidden from your eyes.'

Judaism's essential doctrine of reward and punishment is predicated upon this concept of the existence of a permanent record of all man's deeds, a record indelibly imprinted upon the divine memory. Herein may be the key to an explanation of the vagaries of divine proximity or distance from mankind – the latter situation enabling the spread of evil, oppression and holocaust in a world supposedly filled with the spirit of God. For, just as in human relationships the degree of our emotional responsiveness towards our fellow is conditioned by the 'memory', the cumulative stimuli and recollection of past dealings – and just as proximity flows from trust, loyalty and shared experience, and distance is the corollary of distrust, neglect and indifference – so the divine emotion is motivated by the stimulus of its 'memory' of human dealings. Our evil drives God from an immanent relationship to a more distant, transcendent relationship with his world, wherein the intensity of his spirit is weakened and opposing forces are enabled to surface.

Just as God 'remembers all the events of the Universe', and responds to good and evil accordingly, so Israel is, similarly, commanded never to forget both the kindnesses extended to her by her allies and friends, on the one hand, as well as the evil perpetrated against her by Amalek (Deut. 25:17), on the other. *Imitatio dei* thus extends to the cultivation of a collective historical memory.

Whereas the usual procedure in quoting biblical proof-texts is to follow the order of *Torah*, *Neviy'iym* (prophetic literature) and, finally, *Kethuvim* (sacred writings), it will be noticed that in the *Malkhuyoth*, *Zikhronoth* and *Shopharoth* sections the three *Kethuvim* verses (from the Psalms) always precede the three verses quoted from the *Neviy'iym*, with the tenth, and final, proof-text being chosen, once again, from the *Torah*.

Already in talmudic times it was a received tradition to give precedence here to the Psalm verses from the *Kethuvim*,[43] though the reason for this change of the usual order did not seem to be known. *Tosaphoth*[44] offers the unconvincing reason that, chronologically, the verses from the

Kethuvim were *composed* before the verses from the prophetic literature, since King David, traditional author of the Psalm verses, lived before the period of the prophets. The objection to this explanation is obvious; for if this historical consideration was, indeed, a valid criterion, then the Rabbis should have consistently followed this order in all their expositions!

In the view of the present writer, the order we have before us in these sections dates back to an early (pre-first century CE) period, before the traditional order of precedence – *Torah*, *Neviy'iym* and, lastly, *Kethuvim* – was established as the official norm for exegesis. It is possible that it was only in the wake of the introduction of prophetic *Haphtaroth* into the Synagogue order of service – which did not become statutory until the first century CE[45] – that the prophetic literature established its claim to precedence over the *Kethuvim*. Indeed, the very reason for establishing that order of precedence, giving second place to the *Neviy'iym*, might well have been in order to bolster the authority of the innovation of reciting *Haphtaroth*. As the *Zikhronoth* and *Shopharoth* predated that period, they were obviously not bound by any rule of precedence, other than that the verses from the Torah must come first. Obviously, when the *Malkhuyoth* were later appended,[46] consistency had to be maintained.

SHOFAROTH

אַתָּה נִגְלֵיתָ

You revealed yourself
(Ro. 160, Bi. 389, De S. 214)

This final section of the special triad of *Musaph 'Amidah* compositions draws attention to the important role of the Shofar in the majestic revelation of God on Mount Sinai to bestow the Torah upon Israel.

In a sense then, as we stand, listening in awe to the urgent appeal of the Shofar on this holy day, we – like our biblical ancestors – ought also to be able to feel that we likewise have been witnesses to a 'revelation' of the divine spirit.

The ten verses of the *Shopharoth* include the whole of the Psalm 150 (*Halelu 'el beqodsho*), even though only one of its phrases refers to the sounding of the Shofar. R. David Avudarham suggests that the purpose of this was on account of the fact that ten times the expression *haleluyah* occurs in this Psalm, corresponding to the ten verses in each of the *Malkhuyoth*, *Zikhronoth* and *Shopharoth* sections; and just as this Psalm serves as the climax to the biblical book of Psalms, so it is intended here to serve as a climactic paean of praise to Almighty God as we conclude the last main section of the *Rosh Hashanah 'Amidah*.

The final quotations, from the prophetic literature, move from historical recollections of the Sinaitic revelation to our future messianic expectations when the Shofar will herald the ingathering of our exiles and the re-establishment of Jerusalem as the supreme spiritual capital and sanctuary of the Jewish nation.

וְתֶעֱרַב לְפָנֶיךָ

May our prayer be acceptable
(Ro. 163, Bi. 395, De S. 218)

This prayer is inserted into the *retzey* blessing on all our festivals, and the formula of its concluding blessing replaces, on these occasions, the usual formula: *ha-machaziyr shekhinatho letziyyon*.

The reason for this substitution is, simply, that the version we use on *Yom Tov* was the original daily version of ancient Palestine which was subsequently displaced by Babylonian traditions. Because, on *Yom Tov*, we make use of the old Palestinian *Piyyutim*, it was regarded as most appropriate to resuscitate the original version of the prayers for which those poetic compositions were created.[47] In this way the poems are left, partially, amid their original setting, and, at the same time, nationalistic sentiment was kept

alive with the nostalgic preservation of the ancient liturgical traditions of the homeland.

The priests ascend the steps of the Ark immediately the
Reader commences the *retzey* blessing. This is in order to
preserve the biblical precedent of Aaron the High Priest
who blessed the people *before* leaving the altar, on comple-
tion of the *'Avodah* (sacrificial ritual) in the sanctuary.[48] By
taking up their positions during the *retzey* blessing – which
makes a particular plea for the restoration of the sacrificial
ritual – the priests symbolically associate their blessing
with the *'Avodah* ritual.

בִּרְכַּת כֹּהֲנִים

The priestly blessing
(Ro. 164, Bi. 399, De S. 220)

Dukhaning is a popular term applied to the priestly blessing
of the congregation. The name derives from the word for
the platform (*dukhan*) on which they stood for that purpose.

The Torah (Nu. 6:23–7) provided the priests with the
exact wording (*Yevarekhekha . . .*) of the formula they had
to use when blessing. Because the priests in the Temple
had to perform ritual washing of their hands before commencing their sacred duties, our priests do likewise before
ascending the Ark. Their hands are washed by Levites –
members of their own ancestral tribe. A basis for this
washing was found in the verse, 'Lift up your hands in
holiness (i.e. in cleanliness) and bless the Lord' (Ps. 134:2).

The priests are not permitted to wear shoes while blessing, and these are generally removed before washing. The
hands of the priests are outstretched and their fingers
parted in a specially prescribed manner, making a total of
five 'spaces' between the fingers of both hands. This is
achieved by having the thumb of the right hand hovering
above that of the left hand and spacing out the middle of
the four fingers of each hand. The mystics believed that
these spaces were a kind of lattice window through which
the divine spirit 'peeps' to see whether Israel deserves the
blessing.

Because the priests have to concentrate intently upon their sacred duty, in order to ensure that they make no mistakes in the recitation of the exact formula, the *Chazan* recites the blessing, word by word, before the priests. It is the duty of every priest over the age of thirteen years (*Bar Mitzvah*) to 'dukhan'. It should be realised that the priest is only the mouthpiece of God. He is not conferring his own private blessing; so the question of religious competence or degree of observance must not be considered – either by the congregation or the individual priest.

In order to induce extra concentration on the part of the priests, as well as to ensure that the attention of the recipients of the blessing does not become distracted by the priestly actions, the priests cover their faces and hands with their large *tallith*. The congregation should face the priests, but not fix their gaze upon them.

Before commencing their task the priests petition God to grant them fluency in their blessing, after which they recite in unison the benediction on the mitzvah: 'Blessed are you . . . who has sanctified us with the sanctity of Aaron, and has commanded us to bless your people Israel in love.' At the conclusion of the priestly blessing the priests recite a private prayer, affirming that they have performed all that was prescribed for them, and that it now only rests with God to fulfil his side of the agreement, and to accord his blessing to Israel and to her land.

הַיּוֹם תְּאַמְּצֵנוּ

This day you will strengthen us
(Ro. 166, Bi. 405, De S. 225)

No more fitting poem could have been chosen than this, with which we close the *Musaph* service. It is not a prayer, but rather a stirring evocation of optimistic faith – almost certainty – that God will, indeed, bless and forgive us because of our whole-hearted prayers and confession. The Birnbaum translation has totally missed this sense of the Hebrew by rendering the verbs as imperatives ('strengthen us') rather than as imperfects ('You will, indeed, strengthen us').

Ha-yom Te'amtzeynu is an alphabetical poem, each verb (*'Amz, Barech, Gadel*) commencing with a succeeding letter. The version we have is only a fragment of the complete alphabetical poem which appears in full in the *Machzor* of the Italian rite.

Interestingly, if we compare the Birnbaum, Routledge and De Sola editions, we find that, after the fourth line, they differ from each other in one or more respects: the Routledge has one extra line, making a nine-line poem; the last line in Routledge and De Sola is omitted in Birnbaum, and the line commencing *Ha-yom Tishma'* precedes *Hay-yom Tekabbeyl* in both Routledge and De Sola, whereas in Birnbaum it follows it (in conformity with the correct alphabetical order!).

A detailed study of the *Piyyutim* will demonstrate that a great deal of licence was applied to them, and no reservation was felt by later religious authorities when it came to abbreviating, omitting, selecting, combining and even altering compositions.

אֵין כֵּאלֹהֵינוּ

There is none like our God
(Ro. 168, Bi. 409, De S. 226)

This joyous hymn seems to have been based upon the verse in the *Qedushah*, beginning *Echad hu' 'eloheynu* ('Our God is One'). The recurring emphasis upon '*Our* God', '*Our* Lord', '*Our* King' and '*Our* Deliverer' is clearly intended to contrast our true God with the erroneous conception of him espoused by the theologies of some other faiths.

A more logical order would have been to interchange the first two verses, in order to provide a question – 'Who is like our God?' – followed by the answer: 'There is none like our God.' The reason for not doing so was clearly in order to maintain the acrostic *'Amen ba'* ('Amen has arrived'), a mystical kind of doxology with a messianic overtone.[49] Another, homiletical, explanation is that philosophical speculation on the subject of God ('Who is like our God?') can only yield constructive insights when it is undertaken from the starting-point of faith, by a mind already convinced that 'There is none like our God.'

TASHLIKH

תַּשְׁלִיךְ

Ceremony of casting away sins
(Ro. 175, Bi. 460, De S. 234)

The ceremony of *Tashlikh* is beloved among observant Jews, though more for the enjoyment of its performance than for its inspirational appeal! How pleasant it is, on the first afternoon of *Rosh Hashanah* (or, if that day is a Sabbath, on the second afternoon), to take a stroll to a nearby park, there to meet one's friends and acquaintances and, together, to perform this brief, quaint ceremony of symbolically throwing away one's sins into a running stream. Some preserve an old custom of throwing pieces of bread into the water after reciting the prayers.

Although we find no clear reference to the *Tashlikh* ritual in rabbinic writings until the *Sepher Maharil*[1] of Jacob Moellin (fourteenth century), it is clear that by that time it had already undergone a long and chequered history dating back possibly over a thousand years to early talmudic times.

The origin of *Tashlikh* is obscure. According to Professor Jacob Z. Lauterbach[2] its genesis was as a superstitious act of intercession with the satanic demons of the sea. The throwing of crumbs was, accordingly, to serve as a propitiatory gift, to win the favour of those harmful forces, so that their accusations would be silenced and that they might even intercede on behalf of their benefactors on the judgment day. It has been suggested that the practice of throwing crumbs was curtailed in order to avoid fuelling the malicious gentile charge that the Jews were throwing poison into the wells! Lauterbach draws a parallel between *Tashlikh* and the *Yom Kippur* ceremony of sending away one of the goats into the desert – another place where demons were believed to lurk.

Many popular interpretations of the ceremony have been suggested, beginning with Jacob Moellin who connected it with the midrashic idea that Satan transformed himself into a river to block the path of Abraham in order to frustrate his progress to the 'Aqedah. Another view associates the ceremony with the crowning of monarchs which, in biblical times, always took place near a perennial stream[3] to symbolise the blessing of a long reign.[4] Rosh Hashanah, likewise, focuses upon God as King, and according to this interpretation the Tashlikh becomes a symbolic crowning of the heavenly monarch.

The mystic school of Isaac Luria insisted that for Tashlikh one must go to a river in which there are fish. According to their interpretation of the symbolism, water was a merciful element (Moses, as a baby, had been saved by water), and the fish, which have no eyelids, are symbolic of God's ever open-eyed, sympathetic supervision of his people. The Lurianic practice was also to shake out the edges of their garments into the water. A writer of that school[5] states unashamedly that the purpose of this is to banish the evil spirits, created by our sins, which adhere to the hems of clothes.

The term Tashlikh is derived from Micah 7:19, 'And you will cast (vethashlikh) all their sins into the depths of the sea', which verse forms the core of the formula to be recited at this ceremony. Other verses and psalms – notably Psalms 33 and 130[6] – were added in the course of time.

Psalm 33 refers to the creation of the seas. Its introduction here might have been in order to refine the gross idea of the river as a residence of the demons – as suggested by this ceremony – and focus attention rather upon the role of the deep in the first act of creation ('He gathers the waters of the sea as a heap; he lays up the deep in storehouses') which, according to our tradition, took place on Rosh Hashanah.

Psalm 130 commences with the phrase 'Out of the depths', which again links up with the verse from Micah

'And you will cast ... *into the depths* of the sea', as if to suggest that, were it not for God's mercy, the sinner – rather than his sins – would have been deserving of a watery grave.

מֶלֶךְ אָמוֹן מַאֲמָרֶךְ

O King, your word has stood steadfast
(Ro. 177, Bi. 177, De S. 237)

For the second day of *Rosh Hashanah* we cannot draw upon the inspirational poetry of Eleazar Kallir, as, at that early period in which Kallir lived, Palestinian Jewry still observed the original practice of keeping only one day of *Rosh Hashanah*. The Ashkenazi communities found here an opportunity to give honour to one of their own distinguished sons, Rabbi Simeon bar Isaac, Cantor of Mainz (b. 950) and one of the earliest composers of *Piyyut* in Germany.

Besides being an inspired poet in his own right, Simeon bar Isaac was also an authority on the works of the famous poets of earlier generations. His own style is clearly influenced by them, and particularly by the poetry of Kallir. But it also possesses a tragic quality of its own, born out of the domestic tragedy into which he, personally, was plunged, combined with the bitter experiences of the Jewish communities of the Rhineland which are reflected in many of his compositions.

Legend has it that Simeon's brilliant young son, Elchanan, was kidnapped by a Christian maid and forcibly baptised. He was trained for the Ministry, distinguished himself as a theologian and pastor, and ultimately rose to become Pope. The only heritage that remained with him of his early upbringing was the recollection of his initiation into the game of chess by his father, and, in particular, one unique opening gambit that he had been taught by him and which he had never seen any other player employ.

The legend relates how Rabbi Simeon once came to Rome to beg the Pope to rescind some anti-Jewish measures he had introduced. During his audience the Pope challenged the Rabbi to a game of chess; and when the latter employed that particular gambit, the identity of his Jewish petitioner – and his own – was immediately discovered. At this point the legend divides into two versions. One claims that the son, Elchanan, abandoned his high position and his adopted faith to return secretly to the practice of Judaism in his home town. The second, more plausible, version has it that, after confessing his allegiance to Judaism before his father, he committed suicide. Support for the martyrdom version of the legend is forthcoming from this opening *Piyyut* for the second day of *Rosh Hashanah*, which contains the acrostic 'Elchanan my son, may he be granted eternal life, Amen.'

The acrostic pattern is not as easily recognisable as, for example, in the poems of Kallir. The author signs his name – *Shim'on bar Yitzchak* – by means of an acrostic pattern running through the initial letters of the *second* phrases of each three-phrase stanza. He repeats this in the fourth stanza – *S̄homrey m̄itzvōth . . . n̄attleym* – the initial letters of the first five words of which make up the name *Shim'on*. The usual continuation, giving the patronymic (*bar Yitzchaq*), nestles amid the words of the eighth stanza (ending with the key word, *qadosh*): *b̄erachamim ȳaqqer l̄ze'iyrey ha-tzo'n c̄huq̄q̄am. . . .*

The reference to his son's name occurs in the twelfth stanza, in the opening two words *'el chanan*. The first two letters of the fourth word (*b̄eño'am*) of that line, and the initial letter of the sixth word (*ȳidd'am*), make up the word *beniy*, 'my son'.

The prayer that he should be granted eternal life begins with the sixteenth stanza (*ȳēra'eh . . . c̄haȳoth*), making up the word *yechiy* ('may he live'), and continues in the twentieth line which actually commences with the words *lechayyey 'olam* ('for eternal life'). The twenty-fourth stanza – *ī̄mrey n̄ichumekha* – adds the formula *'Amen*.

The poem is closely related to the three central themes of the *Musaph 'Amidah*, the *malkhuyoth*, *zikhronoth* and *shopharoth*.[1] Hence the words *melekh*, *zekhor* and *shophar*, successively employed three times as the initial word of each stanza.

The opening reference, to God's 'word' (*ma'amar*) being steadfast, is probably intended here as *synecdoche*, representing the ten occasions (*'asarah ma'amaroth*)[2] in the Genesis account of Creation when the term *vayyo'mer Ha-Shem* ('And God said') is employed. On this anniversary of the creation of the world the poet marvels at the fact that God has allowed his precious handiwork to remain the possession of sinful mankind. That privilege, he avers, is not by reason of the merit of Adam's descendants, but merely because God has determined to judge man mercifully.

כְּבוֹדוֹ אָהֶל

Tent-like he stretched out the sky
(Ro. 181, Bi. 189, De S. 241)

This composition, constructed according to the alphabetical acrostic pattern, is attributed to Eleazar Kallir, though, as we have observed above, he would have written it for the first day of *Rosh Hashanah* at a period when only one day was observed in Palestine.

The idea that God stretched out the heaven 'like a tent' is derived from Isaiah 40:22:

> God sits throned above the circle of the earth,[3] whose inhabitants are like grasshoppers. He spreads out the skies like a fine curtain, he stretches them out *like a tent* to live in.

It is a moot point whether or not this verse may be interpreted as a directive to man to contain his explorations and restrict his activities to the planet earth.[4] What is clear, however, is that the prophet conceives of the earth and heavens, in a mystical sense, as supporting the divine spirit like a throne. Isaiah expresses this concept with even greater clarity in the last of his utterances, 'These are the words of the Lord: The heaven is my throne and the earth my footstool' (Is. 66:1).

Each line ends with the word *melekh* ('King'); and the poem is a plea to the divine King to shower upon Israel the full measure of his mercy when reviewing all our actions. In the fourth stanza the poet describes his people as 'Sons of the King' (*beney melekh*), an idea expressed in Deut. 14:1 and amplified in *Avoth* 3:17. The Talmud[5] draws attention to the fact that Israel retains the title of 'sons' even in the context of denunciation: 'foolish *sons*' (Jer. 4:22), 'faithless *sons*' (Deut. 32:20), 'corrupt *sons*' (Is. 1:4).

In the fifth stanza the poet asks for God to show 'kindness' (*chesed*) to Abraham,[6] who is referred to as 'the one to whom the three mighty messengers of the King were sent', an allusion to the visit of the three angels as described in Genesis, ch. 18. The 'kindness' is that the prayers and petitions of his offspring should be accepted. He then proceeds to invoke the merit of Isaac, 'for whom the angels shed bitter tears',[7] and Jacob, who spent the night on the place where the angels ascended and descended.

אֱתִיתִי לְחַנְּנָךְ

I come to supplicate you
(Ro. 190, Bi. 229, De S. 254)

This poem was written by the illustrious German poet, Simeon bar Isaac.[8] As he himself acted as a cantor in Mainz, it is probable that he would have composed this as a purely personal meditation, or *Reshuth*,[9] prior to leading the congregation in the recitation of the *'Amidah*.

It follows an alphabetical acrostic pattern, ending with the author's name *Shim'on* interwoven into an acrostic formed by the initial letters of each word of the concluding lines: *Shelach me'ittekha 'eyzer ūtheruphah ña'amkha*.

It expresses the usual sentiments of the *Reshuth*: the abject lowliness and unworthiness of the cantor to represent his congregation, his profound dread and awe at the task imposed upon him, his lack of both knowledge and merit, and his confidence that God will, notwithstanding, send mercy and deliverance to his people.

The poet likens the cantor, standing before God begging for mercy, to 'a poor man begging at the door'. The reference is borrowed from the midrashic statement that 'when a poor man stands at your door, God stands at his right hand (– as it says, "For he stands at the right of the needy" (Ps. 109:31)). If you give to him, remember that he who stands by him will reward you; but if you refuse, he will punish you. . . .'[10] The poet gives this idea an ironic twist by employing it as a lever with which to wrest mercy from God. We stand at God's door begging for mercy. God, as it were, has a religious obligation to accede to our petition!

The poet has no qualms about referring to himself as of absolutely no consequence: 'What am I and what is my life? I am a worm and a maggot.'

Such sentiments flow as a natural concomitant of true fear of God, as defined by Maimonides.

When a man contemplates the divine achievements analytically, he is immediately overwhelmed and over-awed by the knowledge of how puny and lowly a creature he, himself, is, and how restricted is his own knowledge by comparison with the Omniscient One. As King David said: 'When I see your heavens, the work of your fingers – What is man that thou art mindful of him or the son of man that thou takest account of him?'[11]

'Fear of God' – as defined by Maimonides – has been responsible for generating a genre of prayer characterised by an almost Kierkegaardian intensity of self-conscious restlessness and despairing self-deprecation.[12] One such gem is recited every morning:

Sovereign of all the worlds. . . . What are we? What is our life? What is our piety? What is our righteousness? What our success? What our strength? What our might?

What shall we say before thee, O Lord our God and
God of our fathers?

Are not all the mighty men as nought before thee, the
men of fame as though they had never existed, the wise
as if without knowledge, and men of understanding as
if devoid of discernment? For most of their achievement
is inconsequential before thee, and the pre-eminence of
man over the beast is an illusion, for all is vanity.[13]

The cantor's *Reshuth* was composed in this same spirit,
though the despair is never quite so profound as to deflect
him from his purpose or make him believe that divine
mercy is unattainable. As an individual he is acutely aware
of his particular unworthiness, though he never imputes
this to the holy congregation which he represents. A congregation may be comprised entirely of sinful individuals,
but collectively the spirit of God descends upon them all.
As *Kneseth Yisrael* – the congregation of Israel – they become
transformed and elevated into a spiritual entity with the
mystic power to storm the very gates of heaven.

אִמְרָתְךָ צְרוּפָה

Your word is pure

(Ro. 191, Bi. 232, De S. 255)

Another poem from the pen of Simeon bar Isaac, following
the alphabetical acrostic pattern. The concluding lines
form a name acrostic followed by the appeal, *yechiy*, 'may
he live', thus: *Bo šhu'annu me'olam vayya'aneynu nora'oth,*
beriytzuy chinnuneynu qabbel . . . yechaltzeynu . . .
mittachalu'ey.

This composition was created to follow on from the fore-
going poem, and it opens with the concluding phrase of the
latter, 'All your words, O God, are pure and tested' (Prov.
30:5).

In the second line the author calls upon God not to
probe too deeply (*'al tedaqddeq*) when reviewing Israel. The
verb *ledaqddeq* occurs in the oft-repeated rabbinic axiom
that 'God probes the righteous (*medaqddeq 'im ha-tzaddikim*)

as finely as a hair's breadth'. God is reminded that he, himself, employed the quality of mercy when creating the world,[14] and that his biblical attribute of being *rav chesed* ('abundant in mercy')[15] means that when judging the average person – whose sins and good deeds are in counterpoise – God is believed to nudge the scale of merit so that it comes down in favour of acquittal.[16]

At the beginning of the fifth stanza Abraham is alluded to as *'Ezrachiy*, 'the one who came from the east'. This is based upon the rabbinical identification of *'Eythan ha-'ezrachiy* (mentioned in the heading to Psalm 89 as its author) with Abraham.[17] The poet asks that Abraham's merit, as the prince of mercy who entreated God to spare the wicked inhabitants of Sodom and Gomorrah, should stand to the everlasting credit of his offspring, so that 'the accuser would be silenced'.

Abraham, in our tradition, is the paramount exemplar of the quality of *chesed* ('mercy'). The third verse of this Psalm 89 – as ascribed to Abraham – states 'the world must be established by *chesed*', and the prophet Micah ends his prophecies with the words 'ascribe truth to Jacob, *chesed* to Abraham' (Micah 7:20).

תָּמִים פָּעֳלֶךָ

Your work is perfect
(Ro. 192, Bi. 233, De S. 257)

Writing under the influence of the works of Kallir and his imitators, Simeon bar Isaac introduces here a variety of the ordinary alphabetical acrostic. This poem employs the reverse alphabetical acrostic (*Tashraq*), whereby the first line commences with *tav*, the final letter of the alphabet, and subsequent lines continue working backwards to the letter *'aleph*.

As with the composition *'Athithi lechanenakh*,[18] the poet, on reaching the letter *'aleph*, signs off with a line (in this case, two lines), the initial letters of each word of which make up his own name. While this is easily discernible in the final stanza (*Šephathenu medovevoth 'ōz uvetzidqatho nichyeh*), it is not so easy to discover in the penultimate stanza. It is, in fact, compressed into the three words, *Shemeynu ʿal . . . veñiyv*.

In the second stanza the poet petitions God to accept the prayers offered on this holy day as substitutes for the sin-offerings that would have been brought in Temple times. This is in accordance with the prophecy of Hosea who already foresaw the time when 'our lips will make payment for bulls' (Hosea 14:3).

The next stanza contains an interesting midrashic allusion. The poet states that if Israel has indeed strayed from the true paths, 'let there be remembered the ordered altar (of Abraham) together with the *ritual slaughter-knife* (*ma'akheleth ha-ma'akhiylah*) which was provided from then onwards.'

The term *ma'akheleth ha-ma'akhiylah* means, literally, 'the knife which enables us to eat', and the Midrash explains this to mean that 'any meat which Israel enjoys in this world is only through the merit of Abraham when he took the slaughter-knife with him to the *'Aqedah.*'[19] This concept underlies the familiar rabbinic idea of the table as an altar and one's food as representing an act of sacrifice. Abraham's readiness to perform the supreme sacrifice was rewarded by God by transforming his knife into a ritual slaughtering-knife for the future satisfaction of his offspring. In the context of the vegetarian ideal – which represented God's original plan for man – this Midrash suggests that the slaughter and consumption of meat is merely a concession to Israel, won through the merit of the *'Aqedah*.

שְׁלַחְתִּי בְּמַלְאֲכוּת

I am sent on the mission
(Ro. 193, Bi. 235, De S. 258)

Another poem from the pen of Simeon bar Isaac who strongly favours this four-lined stanza construction, technically referred to as *meruba'* ('quatrain'). Each line contains four words, the rhyme being provided by the last syllable of each line. The four lines of each stanza all commence with the same letter, and as the stanzas form an acrostic of the author's name, this becomes converted, in fact, into a four-fold name-acrostic!

The charge of conceit is frequently levelled at those *Payetanim* who employed this device of the name-acrostic. In fairness to them, however, one must appreciate that they were offering the public the fruits of their talent in an age when there were no regulations to restrict plagiarism. They were also writing before the age of printing, at a period when the name of the author was too easily separated from his work. The name-acrostic was, therefore, one of the only methods of ensuring the author's recognition.

The first stanza is detached from the rest of the poem, and assigned for recitation by the Reader. In the Birnbaum edition the Ark is opened especially for this stanza, while in the De Sola edition the rubric, incorrectly, has the Ark opened before the end of the previous blessing, *mechayyeh ha-meythim*. The special attention given to the first stanza is clearly on account of its purpose, which is to serve as a brief *Reshuth*, the Reader's personal petition for God to accept his prayers on behalf of the 'select community' which he represents.

The third stanza (*'eyrekh teqiy'athenu*) asks God to enable the objective of our particular system of Shofar blowing – which is 'to confuse the accuser' (*'arbeyv qatteygor*)[20] – to be realised. It is the Talmud which suggests that the system of Shofar blowing we employ is 'to confuse the accuser', or, more accurately, 'to confuse Satan'.[21] The specific aspect of the system which aroused the talmudic curiosity was the splitting up of the blowing into two separate groups of notes: one group blown before the *Musaph 'Amidah*[22] and the rest blown during its repetition.[23]

The way in which this particular system of blowing helps to confuse Satan, and to deflect him from his intention to condemn, is not too clear. *Tosaphoth*[24] explains that Satan is aware that the great Shofar will herald the final day of judgment when 'God will make death to vanish forever'.[25] Thus, when he hears the first group of notes 'Satan becomes quite agitated', believing that the final moment might well be at hand when his own powers are to be curtailed. Just as he is recovering from that shock, realising that he must have been mistaken, Israel embarks upon her main crescendo of blowing. This totally overwhelms Satan, who is put to flight long enough for Israel to conclude all her prayers and for her to receive divine mercy.

This must be regarded, however, as a quaint homiletical justification of a custom whose origin was uncertain to the talmudists. A tradition, elaborated in the Palestinian Talmud, attributes the bipartite blowing to a period of religious persecution when the Romans prohibited the sounding of the Shofar out of fear that it might be used as a signal for an insurrection. They used to send inspectors to the Synagogues to ensure that the Jews complied with the edict. As the original custom was to blow during *Shachrith* the inspectors left satisfied at the end of that service. Because of these extenuating circumstances, the rabbinic authorities permitted the communities to delay the blowing until *Musaph*. When the persecution was over a compromise was effected between those who wanted to retain the *status quo* and the purists who wished to return to the original practice. Thus the Shofar is blown both in the *Musaph 'Amidah* as well as – not *in*, but immediately after – the *Shachrith* service.

שְׁמוֹ מְפָאֲרִים

They glorify his name
(Ro. 195, Bi. 239, De S. 261)

The poem *Shemo mepho'arim*, by Simeon bar Isaac, was chosen for recitation on the second day of *Rosh Hashanah*. For the first day we recite Kallir's *ta'iyr vethari'a*.[26] Because the latter contains a reference to 'the Shofar's blast', it was regarded as inappropriate for the Sabbath day when such blowing is suspended. For this reason, if the first day falls on a Sabbath we interchange the two compositions, reciting *Shemo mepho'arim* on the Sabbath and *ta'iyr vethari'a* on the Sunday. The former composition is especially appropriate for the Sabbath as it makes specific reference to that day and to the fact that we have to content ourselves then with *Zikhron teru'ah* – 'a (mere) mention of the command of blowing'.[27]

This composition extends for four or five pages in most editions. It commences with seven stanzas all of which are subsequently used, successively, as the refrains for the rest of the poem. Each stanza is comprised of three rhyming lines.

Each of the first *six* stanzas of the introductory section employs the name acrostic, *Shim'on*, in a form which, as we have seen in some of his other poems,[28] is not so readily apparent. The letter *nun*, with which the second lines of each stanza commence, forms the ending of his name. Another point to notice is that the themes of these introductory stanzas follow successively the order of *malkhuyoth*, *zikhronoth* and *shopharoth*, ending, at the seventh stanza, with another *malkhuyoth* line.

In the remainder of the poem – commencing with the line *'eder vahod* – the opening lines of each stanza follow the ordinary alphabetical acrostic pattern, the middle lines of each stanza form the acrostic *Shim'on bar Yitzchaq chazaq ve'ematz* ('Simeon bar Isaac, be strong and of good courage'), and the third lines of each stanza are all biblical quotations. As with the introductory verses, the latter follow through the themes of *malkhuyoth*, *zikhronoth* and *shopharoth*, with three successive stanzas being devoted to each theme.

The poet describes God's greatness as too intense to be contained within the world. He challenges all God's creatures to deepen their awareness and knowledge of God's ways. He recalls the *'Aqedah* sacrifice – which was responsible for the introduction of the ritual of blowing the ram's horn – in order to keep alive the spirit of that unique demonstration of faith. He calls upon God to 'bare his arm to save us from our foes', though, as usual, Simeon bar Isaac does not specify which particular enemies he has in mind.

The poet fervently prays for God to destroy the chains of bondage and to gather his dispersed people to the promised land, there to restore the Temple, its courts, altars and sacred vessels.

READING OF THE LAW – SECOND DAY
(Ro. 216–21, Bi. 299–309, De S. 289–95)

The reading for the second day of *Rosh Hashanah* is the account of the *'Aqedah*, the binding of Isaac,[29] surely one of the most inspiring and challenging monuments to the power of faith and its ability to instil absolute confidence into the hearts of the devoted, even when they, or those most dear to them, are 'walking in the valley of the shadow of death'. No wonder then that the *'Aqedah*, as a unique symbol of martyrdom, became a favourite theme in wider religious thought, art and literature.

The essential character of the *Rosh Hashanah* festival could be said to have been moulded by the *'Aqedah* account; for the blowing of the Shofar is explained[30] as a reminder of the ram sacrificed by Abraham at the *'Aqedah*, a substitution forced upon him as he prepared to make the supreme sacrifice in absolute and loving obedience to the divine command.

Furthermore, in the *zikhronoth* ('Remembrance') prayers of the *Rosh Hashanah Musaph*, the merit of Abraham's faith at the *'Aqedah* is asked to be accounted to the eternal credit of his offspring:

> Consider then the binding with which he bound his son upon the altar, suppressing his compassion in order to perform your will with a perfect heart. So may your compassion conquer your anger against us, and in your great goodness may your great wrath turn aside from your people, your city and your inheritance.

The reading of this episode on *Rosh Hashanah* serves to provide us with a glimpse into the way a unique man of faith responded to the divine call. We cannot be expected to match those standards of self-sacrifice. We are expected, however, to provide some reflection of them in our own lives.

The *Haphtarah*, from the prophecies of Jeremiah, expresses the reciprocal divine response to all that faith, loyalty and sacrifice displayed by Israel. Its message exudes encouragement and love, promising Israel that the dark night of exile and suffering will ultimately give way to a dawn of national restoration.

The link with *Rosh Hashanah* appears in several passages of the *Haphtarah*, most notably in the two images employed to describe God's relationship with Israel: 'I am *a father* to Israel and Ephraim is my first born', and, 'He that scattered Israel will gather him, and watch over him *as a shepherd watches his flock.*' Both of these images figure prominently in our *Rosh Hashanah* liturgy.

A further link with *Rosh Hashanah* is forged by the reference in the *Haphtarah* to the matriarch Rachel, who is depicted as lamenting and weeping for her children in exile. This echoes the references, in the Torah and *Haphtarah* readings for the First Day, to the longings for maternity expressed by Sarah and Hannah. Whereas they both longed for the personal fulfilment which motherhood confers, Rachel longs for the national fulfilment which can only be secured by the rebirth of her children and their restoration to the ancestral homeland.

The *Haphtarah* ends with one of the most poignant pleas for God's mercy, while at the same time expressing the conviction that, because the penitence was sincere, it must be accepted:

Turn to me, and let me return; for you are the Lord my God. For after I repented I was filled with remorse, and after I realised my errors I beat my thigh in agitation. I was ashamed and confounded. . . .

THE JEWISH DOCTRINE OF REPENTANCE

What constitutes repentance? Is it sufficient to feel remorse and to resolve in one's heart not to repeat any unworthy act, or does Judaism demand some practical expression of regret in the form of a *penance*? In biblical times there was a prescribed ritual whereby an individual or community manifested its contrition. This consisted of rending one's garments, praying, fasting, putting on sackcloth and sitting in the ashes. The penance of the people of Nineveh, as described in the book of Jonah,[1] was so demonstrative that even their beasts were made to share in its expression. Like their owners, they also were draped in sackcloth and deprived of food or drink.

In the sacrificial system there was a specific sin-offering – the *Chatta'th* – prescribed for individual sins. It goes without saying that the mechanical act of sacrifice was never intended to effect atonement of its own accord. A code that called upon its adherents to love God with all their 'heart, soul and might'[2] would never have been so inconsistent as to require nothing more than a mere formalistic act in order to heal the strained relationship between God and man caused by the intrusion of sin. The sacrifice was meant to be without any doubt only the climax of a very strenuous act of invocation and petition along the lines enumerated above.

A fundamental part of the sacrificial cult was the laying of the hands on the head of the beast and the public acknowledgment of guilt by specifying the particular sin committed.[3] Human pride being what it is, it is difficult to imagine that anyone emerged from such an ordeal with anything other than a deflated ego and a very real sense of humility. The sacrifice was secondary in importance to the cry of confession; and it may be said to have existed only in order to evoke such an emotional response. When David was severely censured by the Prophet Nathan for his sin with Bathsheba, his first words were 'I have sinned'.[4] There is no mention of any subsequent sacrifice brought by David. His spontaneous confession sufficed to obtain forgiveness.

For the Rabbis of the Talmud repentance was entirely a state of mind. The Temple having been destroyed, prayer and study replaced the sacrificial cult as a means of communication with the deity. It was natural, therefore, that they should have redefined repentance as a psychological state and played down any external forms of penance other than private fasting which was often employed as a means of atonement.[5]

The classical rabbinic definition of true repentance takes account of the overriding passion in man which is ultimately responsible for leading him into sin. R. Judah said 'the truly penitent man is one who is able to resist when the same opportunity for sin recurs a few times with the same woman, at the same season, in the same place.'[6] In other words, true repentance can only be gauged by the strength of resolve that the individual has built up within him and which, if the repentance had been sufficiently sincere, would give him ample resistance even to repeated, alluring and sensuous enticements. The repentant sinner, who has resisted the urge to sin a second and a third time, is, according to some Rabbis, more beloved of God than the purely righteous man who was never exposed to such a temptation and who consequently has had no opportunity to vanquish his baser instincts.[7]

When it came to offences against one's fellow man, an inner remorse was not regarded as sufficient. 'The Day of Atonement', declares the Mishna, 'only effects atonement for transgressions between man and God; but for transgressions against one's fellow man one must first appease one's fellow.'[8]

In their practical concern to protect the rights of every citizen, the Rabbis denied the possibility of pardon to the man who had defrauded his fellow man until he had made full restitution. In the case of tax and customs collectors who, in talmudic times, were notorious for their indiscriminate fraudulence, it was well nigh impossible for them to locate and recompense every individual whom they had robbed. The Rabbis[9] instructed them – and others who had defrauded the public – to reimburse those individuals whom they definitely knew to have been defrauded by them, and to devote the balance to the communal funds. One who had assaulted, insulted or stolen from another was not entitled to assume that, merely on payment of a monetary recompense, he had fulfilled his penance. It was equally necessary for him to offer a humble request that his victim should forgive him his offence. So important was it for a man to obtain a verbal pardon from the one he had wronged that Jewish law specified the steps that might be taken if the victim is cruel enough to withhold forgiveness from a true penitent.

The penitent should bring three of his acquaintances, and, before them, he should again entreat his victim's forgiveness. If he still withholds it, the penitent should repeat the encounter with two further groups of people. If forgiveness is still not granted he need do nothing further, but rather is the sin transferred to the one who will not forgive.[10]

There is a special procedure to be followed if the victim had died before the penitent had had a chance of obtaining his pardon.

He should assemble ten men at the grave of the man he had wronged and he should confess before them his sin and his sincere repentance. If he had extorted money he should return it to the heirs. If he did not know their whereabouts, he should deposit the money with the court of law.[11]

Although the Talmud, as we have seen, considers repentance as an attitude of mind calling for few outward manifestations, there were pietists in the Middle Ages who firmly believed that in order to be cleansed of sin one had to submit oneself to bodily mortification. The chief exponents of this doctrine were the so-called 'Chasidey Ashkenaz', the German pietists who flourished in the Rhineland during the twelfth and thirteenth centuries.[12] They found a scriptural basis for their concept of a mortifying penance in the account of the Prophet Isaiah's 'call':

> And one of the Seraphim flew to me, having in his hand a burning coal which he had taken with tongs from the altar. And he touched my mouth and said: 'Behold, this has touched your lips, your guilt is taken away and your sin forgiven.'[13]

These teachers distinguished four types of penance, all prerequisites for the total eradication of the taint of sin. The first is 'the repentance of opportunity'. This is the mildest form of penitence, corresponding to the established talmudic definition: the opportunity to repeat a sin presents itself but the penitent does not succumb. The second type is 'the preventive form of penitence'. Within this category the penitent must hold aloof from any experience or situation which might present him with the temptation to repeat his sin. Third in order of severity is 'the penance of correspondence', wherein the penitent is expected to endure that intensity of physical pain which corresponded to the amount of pleasure he derived from committing the sin. Finally comes 'the biblically-prescribed repentance', whereby the truly penitent has to inflict upon himself tortures corresponding to the pain that would have accompanied the imposition of the penalties prescribed by the Bible for his particular sin. Where the Pentateuch prescribed flogging the penitent must submit to the forty lashes, and where the biblical penalty was death he was expected to undergo 'tortures as bitter as death'. Penitents were known to lie in the snow for hours in the winter and to expose their bodies to ants and bees in the summer in order to fulfil this last category of repentance.

While the masses of Jews could never have been expected

to aspire to the standards of those pietists, yet the existence of such pockets of extreme piety acted as a vital counterweight to the opposing forces of indifference and assimilation. The sight of such a pietist performing his rigorous penance would not have left the heart of the everyday Jew unmoved. His thoughts must inevitably have turned to the matter of his own sins and the means he might employ to achieve his own spiritual regeneration. A religion enriched by the literary legacy of such movements, and spurred on by the lofty ideals of such saints, acquires an extra spiritual dimension.

What is the divine response to human sin and atonement? Does the God of justice administer judgment according to the strict letter of the law or does the 'quality of *mercy* drop as the gentle rain from heaven'?

The whole basis of the prophetic ministry rested firmly on the assumption that the God of Israel was a forgiving and merciful father. 'Have I any pleasure in the death of the wicked, says the Lord God, and not that he should turn from his evil way and live?' Ezekiel[14] here expresses a conviction shared by all the prophets. It was, in fact, more than a conviction; it was their whole *raison d'être*. The prophet could never accept – nor was he intended to accept – the role of passive 'foreteller' of the nation's fate. He saw himself rather as a 'forthteller'. His message of doom was always conditional upon the nation's refusal to accept his call to repentance. The inevitability of doom was alien to his whole thinking. The announcement of doom is, in reality, merely the pronouncement of the penalty that is compatible with the nation's crimes.

The prophet's duty is to shake them out of their complacency, to prosecute, to condemn, to cry 'guilty' until the nation trembles, and to threaten them with the punishment they truly deserve. But the prophet's moment of supreme fulfilment comes when his threats are negated, and his promises invalidated, by the nation's repentance and the divine decree of forgiveness. The role of the prophet is thus unenviable. His victory as a prophet lies in his defeat as an individual. He can never claim the affection of men; for even in the moment of their salvation his threat of doom must appear to have been misguided. If the prophet is the counsel for the prosecution, God is the counsel for the defence.

This dilemma of the prophet represents the theme of the book of Jonah, the reading of which is prescribed for the afternoon service on the Day of Atonement. Jonah could not rationalise that paradox of prophetic pronouncement and divine indulgence. Summoned by God to go to Nineveh, capital of Assyria, and there to pronounce her imminent downfall, his whole belief in the reliability and infallibility of God's word was shaken to its foundation when the people repented, and God revoked his decree.

Jonah had been more concerned to witness the accurate fulfilment of his prophecy than with the fate of 'the great city in which there are more than a hundred and twenty thousand people who do not know their right hand from their left'. Jonah wished to be a foreteller rather than a forthteller. Compassion had no place in Jonah's conception of divine judgment. If God had proclaimed doom, then surely he had foreseen the ultimate repentance, and rejected it. Otherwise, why compromise his elected prophet by putting into his mouth a false prediction? Jonah's chief concern was to find a solution of this problem.

The lesson Jonah – and mankind – had to learn was that the ways of God and his method of dealing with his world are indeed inscrutable. They do not conform to our own preconceived notions of logic, neither do they show deference to the reputation of a prophet, priest or saint. If any consistency may be found at all, it is in the divine sensitivity to sincere atonement. God will not disclose the fact or time of the repentance of an individual or a nation even to his prophets – and certainly not to a Jonah. The moment of repentance is sacred and intimate. For God to have granted foreknowledge of it to a third party would have been an act of betrayal. The true prophet should rejoice with God that his mercy has been given the opportunity to vanquish his anger.

The talmudic Rabbis further developed the doctrine of the divine eagerness to grant forgiveness. Man is helped by

God along the path of repentance. He has only to exhibit the early flutterings of a remorseful heart for God to implant within him additional strength of purpose. Rabbi Issi said: God says to the Israelites, 'My children, open to me the gate of repentance as minutely as the eye of a needle, and I will open for you gates wide enough for carriages and waggons to enter through them.'[15]

The Rabbis were aware that the existence of such a belief could lead to abuse, whereby people might salve their consciences by deluding themselves into thinking that divine mercy is inexhaustible and extends even where only a token gesture of penitence is offered, unaccompanied by sincere resolve. They therefore took pains to disabuse the naive of such a contention:

He who says: 'I will sin and then make repentance; I will sin again and make repentance,' no opportunity for true repentance will ever be granted to him. He who says, 'I will sin and the Day of Atonement will grant absolution,' the Day of Atonement will not, in such a case, confer absolution.[16]

The motive for repentance does have a bearing upon the divine reaction to it. The Talmud distinguishes three motivations: one who repents out of conviction based upon *love of God*; one who repents out of simple *fear of the consequences of sin*; and, the lowest category of repentance, that which is prompted by *suffering and affliction*.[17] The Rabbis were cautious in their statements about the comparative effect of these three motives for repentance. According to one view,[18] repentance occasioned by love of God has the effect of totally effacing any trace of the individual's sin, whereas repentance out of fear prompts the Almighty merely to disregard the record of that particular sin. Penitents in both of these categories are regarded as 'sons' of God, whereas those whose penitence was only brought about as a result of suffering are relegated to a servant-master relationship with him.[19]

Repentance cannot be confined to the non-repetition of

a particular sin. The consciousness of sin, and the positive desire to remove its taint, impose upon the penitent a duty of striving for a total regeneration, whereby his whole way of life becomes re-consecrated. An oft-repeated phrase in rabbinic literature is 'Repentance and good deeds'.[20] Good deeds are considered as the logical corollary of the act of repentance. The implication is that it is inconceivable for a true penitent to regret and desist from one act of sin while perpetuating another. Repentance must be unconditional and unrestricted to qualify for acceptance.

Is divine forgiveness ever withheld? The rabbinic concept of divine mercy allowed for even the most inveterate sinner to obtain immediate mercy. The Rabbis took their lead from the case of Manasseh, King of Judah (696–641 BC), whose reign stands out as one of the darkest periods in the religious history of Israel. Idolatry, apostasy, murder and immorality are all included in the list of charges made against him. Yet, according to the testimony of II Chronicles 33:12–13,

> When he was in distress, he entreated the favour of the Lord his God and humbled himself greatly before the God of his fathers. He prayed to him, and God received his entreaty and heard his supplication. . . . Then Manasseh knew that the Lord was God.

For one grave sin, however, divine forgiveness is withheld: for leading a multitude into sin. Such a man, declare the Rabbis, is not even given the opportunity to repent. For profanation of God's name there can be no forgiveness during the lifetime of the offender; but the combined efforts of his penitence, the Days of Atonement, his suffering, and, ultimately, his death will succeed in securing for him eventual redemption.[21] Within the definition of profanation of God's name the Rabbis particularise the case of a religious leader who by his conduct brings religion into disrepute.[22]

Allowing for a few notable exceptions, it can be said in general that Judaism believes that salvation is within the easy reach of man. The paths to it are not tortuous or

strewn with pitfalls and trials. Man has but to face in the
right direction, and God will lead him to his destination.

YOM KIPPUR

THE EVENING SERVICE

THE PROHIBITION AGAINST WEARING SHOES

The Rabbis explained the biblical injunction of 'afflicting one's soul'[1] on this day as referring to five specific 'afflictions' or abstentions (*'iynuyyim*): from eating, drinking, perfuming the body, cohabitation and the wearing of shoes.[2] While the first four are normally conducted in the privacy of one's home, it is the abstention from wearing shoes (*ne'iylath ha-Sandal*) which is the one most obvious to the eye of the observer at Synagogue on Yom Kippur.[3]

Today we hardly identify the wearing of shoes as one of life's basic pleasures, though, in biblical and talmudic times, shoes attracted much attention as a status symbol. When the psalmist said, 'Against Edom I cast off my shoe,'[4] he was symbolising the low estate to which that country was about to fall. It was to become a vassal state; and the prophet accordingly performed the same symbolic act – removing the shoes – which served in later talmudic times as a symbolic token of acquisition when transferring possession of a slave to a new owner.[5]

Wearing shoes was the prerogative of the upper classes. In the Song of Songs the King pays this tribute to his beloved: 'How comely are thy steps *in shoes*, O high-born daughter.'[6] Because shoes were regarded as an important adornment they were proscribed on those occasions when a spirit of humility and dejection was appropriate, as in the cases of a mourner, or on the Fast of Av when lamenting the loss of the Temple and on *Yom Kippur* when standing in the dock of the heavenly court.

In the course of time a distinction was made between leather shoes and those made of other materials, such as cloth or wood, with the result that only leather shoes are now regarded as affording 'pleasurable' comfort, and are therefore forbidden to be worn. Slippers or plimsoles are permitted, as are shoes made of synthetic materials, though most of those who observe this abstention would not wear the latter in order to avoid contravening the principle of *mar'iyth ha'ayin*, not giving a mistaken impression (that one is breaking a religious law). White plimsoles – to match the white *kittel* – are the most popular choice.

WEARING A *TALLITH*

Kol Nidrey is the only occasion in the year when the congregation wear a *tallith* for the evening service. This practice is peculiar to the Ashkenazim, and became widespread through the influence of the famous authority, Rabbi Meir of Rothenburg (d. 1293), who officiated as Reader on the High Holydays wearing the *tallith*. His congregation felt compelled to do likewise, and from there the practice spread.

As the duty of wearing *tzitzith* only applies to daytime,[7] the *tallith* has to be donned while it is still daylight, and the *Kol Nidrey* service is commenced, accordingly, in the early evening.

Rabbi Meir's innovation was based upon the circumstances attending the original divine disclosure to Moses of God's thirteen attributes. Rabbinic tradition has it that 'God enwrapped himself in a *tallith*, like a *Chazan*, and disclosed these attributes to Moses.'[8] Since the attributes are recounted in the *Kol Nidrey* service, Rabbi Meir felt that it was appropriate, therefore, for the *Chazan* to be wearing the *tallith*.

בִּישִׁיבָה שֶׁל מַעֲלָה

By authority of the heavenly court
(Ro. 15, Bi. 489, De S. 12)

The footnote in the Birnbaum edition asserts that this formula was introduced by the famous thirteenth-century authority, Rabbi Meir of Rothenburg, in order to encourage Jewish transgressors to return to Synagogue and pray with the community on this holiest night of the year. It had the dual purpose of serving as an invitation to those defectors, as well as as a plea to the regular worshippers to accept them in their midst and to welcome them back. Birnbaum refers to the talmudic statement that 'any fast wherein Jewish transgressors do not participate is no fast' (*Kerithoth* 6ᵇ).

Birnbaum follows here the popular theory of the great nineteenth-century liturgical authority, Leopold Zunz. However, Zunz's attribution of the *Biyeshivah shel ma'lah* formula to Rabbi Meir of Rothenburg has now been shown to have been erroneous, since there is a clear reference to such a declaration in the writings of Rabbi Eliezer bar Yoel HaLevi (*Raviah*) of Bonn, the teacher of Rabbi Meir of Rothenburg. He already refers to it as 'an established practice to enter Synagogue and declare the absolution of the vow, in order to enable the congregation to pray together with any person who has transgressed by disobeying any decree *of the community*.'[9]

It is now clear that this formula was a solemn declaration, lifting any *local* decree of excommunication that had been imposed upon a reprobate member of the community. Among the terms of such a ban were that he could not be given a Jewish burial, his child was not to be circumcised and *the community was not to allow him to attend a service in Synagogue*. On *Kol Nidrey* night this last condition was relaxed; but, since the ban had been solemnly imposed with a formula invoking 'the authority of the heavenly court and the authority of the earthly court; with the consent of the Omnipresent One and with the consent of this congregation', the very same formula had to be employed in order to suspend the ban on this occasion.

Although this formula originated, as we have seen, in Ashkenazi circles, it was soon adopted also by the Sephardi communities. Having established itself, some rationale for its continued recitation had to be offered for those situations – the majority – wherein there were no excommunicants present in Synagogue. The popular rationale was to quote the talmudic tradition that 'any fast in which there

are no transgressors participating is no fast.'[10] The weakness of such a rationale is clearly apparent, in that the
talmudic statement was hardly intended to be taken strictly
literally. Furthermore, it would have been most unchar-
acteristic to create a prayer or formula – postulating the
presence of transgressors and granting authority for them
to be included in the congregation – merely in order to
substantiate a rather abstruse talmudic maxim!

כָּל נִדְרֵי

All vows

The theory that has gained the widest popularity in the
past is that of Joseph S. Bloch who suggested in 1917 that
the origins of *Kol Nidrey* go back to the Visigoth persecution
of the Jews of Spain – and their forced conversion to Christianity – in the seventh century CE.[11] Their conversion vows
were made under the most fearful oaths and adjurations.
They had solemnly to profess their belief in the new faith,
and they had to renounce Jewish practices under penalty
of death. They remained secretly faithful, however, to their
ancestral beliefs; and on the holiest night of the year these
Marranos made an effort to celebrate it with their fellow-
Jews by sneaking into Synagogue.

They were sorely troubled, however, about the fact that,
in so doing, they were breaking solemn oaths and vows,
even though they had been taken under duress. Bloch
asserted that the *Kol Nidrey* was introduced for their benefit,
to enable them first to crave absolution.

This theory is linked to an explanation of the term *'avaryanim*, in the preceding formula, which regards it as a
transliteration of the term 'Iberians' – that is Spanish Jews,
residents of the Iberian peninsula. It also explains the
presence of the succeeding biblical verse, *venislach lechol
'adath* (Nu. 15:26), which occurs in the context of idolatry.

The standard melody for *Kol Nidrey* is also stylistically
most appropriate to either of the above theories. 'The
motifs alternate between solemn syllabic "proclamations",
as in the opening, intensely devotional wave-like phrases,

and virtuoso vocal runs.'[12] The slow, deliberate, almost mournful notations would have the effect of impressing upon the Jewish defectors the seriousness of their actions and their urgent need of divine forgiveness.[13]

This theory of a Spanish origin, however plausible, is, nevertheless, historically unsubstantiated. The first references to this prayer in our literature come from eighth-century Babylonia, the main centre of Jewish life and culture. Spain was not yet on the Jewish map; and, in any case, the Babylonian authorities in a Muslim country would hardly have adopted, on the holiest night of the year, a composition recited for Spanish converts to Christianity and related exclusively to their personal dilemma!

Another theory, suggested by Samuel Krauss, is that the Rabbis of the eighth century introduced the *Kol Nidrey* declaration of absolution of vows for polemical reasons, in order to refute the Karaite denunciation of that practice as being totally without basis in Jewish tradition.

The Bible[14] restricts the privilege of granting absolution to a husband and a father, who may absolve their wives and unmarried daughters, respectively, of any vows they express, providing they are cancelled on the day they are uttered. Oral tradition extended the scope of this privilege, granting a *Beth Din* (Ecclesiastical Court) the right to annul the vows of any Jew, under clearly established conditions. This innovation was hotly contested by the Karaites who accepted no institution without a clear biblical foundation. The Rabbis themselves were forced to concede that 'the absolution of vows hovers in the air and has no basis upon which to lean for support',[15] and Karaite writers, especially Daniel al-Qumisi, their vigorous ninth-century spokesman, poured scorn on the Rabbis 'who break vows even on the eve of the Day of Atonement'.[16]

There were two, diametrically opposite, Jewish reactions. Some Babylonian Geonim[17] wilted under the criticism, and actually abolished this entire judicial procedure. Even the talmudic tractate *Nedarim*, which is devoted to the subject, was withdrawn, by the Geonim Yehudai (eighth-century CE) and Natronai (ninth century), from the curriculum of their academies.

An entirely different, and most courageous, response was emphatically to insist upon the validity of the institution of absolution. This resulted in an exaggerated over-emphasis, culminating in the creation of a special formulation – *Kol Nidrey* – to be recited at the most solemn moment of the year, when the entire community was assembled. It was considered by the protagonists of this approach that the whole integrity and authority of the Oral Law was at stake here, and that such a dramatic gesture of confidence was both required and fully justified at such an impressionable hour.

Even this theory of the origin of *Kol Nidrey* has been subjected to sound criticism on the grounds that it would appear that the composition actually antedates the period of the Karaites, since the Gaon Yehudai (circa 750 CE) refers to it as being an already firmly established custom!

The true circumstances surrounding its origin have still to be demonstrated beyond any shadow of doubt.

The Ashkenazi and Sephardi version of *Kol Nidrey* is written in Aramaic. However, the Italian tradition and the Babylonian liturgical manual, *Seder Rav 'Amram*, have a pure Hebrew version.

Various categories of oaths, vows and promises are enumerated:

(i) *Nidrey*: Religious obligations. The *neder* is a comprehensive term for any kind of religious obligation that a person takes upon himself, such as a vow to bring a sacrifice or to become a Nazarite. It should be stressed that absolution for any of the categories listed in *Kol Nidrey* can be secured only for obligations unpaid to God. No prayer can excuse or absolve a Jew from any firm promise or commitment to his fellow man unless released by the latter.

(ii) *'Esarey*: Obligations. The term *'issar* is found in Nu. 30:3 as a cognate accusative of the verb *Le'ssor*, 'to impose upon oneself a restriction'. The basic meaning of the verb is actually 'to tie', and it is used widely in rabbinic terminology to denote 'that which is forbidden', *'asur*. While the *neder* denotes a recognised and standard religious obligation, the *'issar* suggests a personal obligation to which the donor wished to bind himself.[18]

(iii) *Charamey*: Pledges. The *cherem* is used in the bible to denote an object devoted to God or for a sacred purpose, such as for use in the sanctuary. It is also used to denote 'spoils of war' which escaped destruction (from the verb *charam*, meaning, basically, 'to destroy').

(iv) *Qonamey*: Promises. This is in the same category as the preceding, except that it refers to pledges made by employing the dedicatory formula, *qonam*, 'consecrated!'[19]

(v) *Kiynuyey*: Substitute terms. This is an allusion to the mishnaic principle that 'any terms used by people as substitutes for the official formulae for uttering vows are as binding as the officially accepted terms'.[20]

(vi) *Qinnusey*: Variant terms. This term is also enumerated in the Mishna as a formula which must be regarded as binding. Such terms as *qonam* and *qonas* (sing. of *qinnusey*) were actually gentile mispronunciations of the Hebrew term *qorban* ('I sacrifice, devote'). Maimonides blames the Ethiopians and the French for having popularised such inaccurate variants, which were even adopted later by Jews.[21]

(vii) *Shevu'oth*: Oaths. The terms *shevu'ah* and *neder* are the most common. The term *shevu'ah* also occurs in the biblical passage dealing with a father and husband's right of annulling the vows of their family.[22] The term is used when taking a vow to deny oneself any benefit from a particular object.

מִיּוֹם כִּפּוּרִים זֶה

From this Day of Atonement until the next one

A fundamental difference exists between the Ashkenazi and Sephardi versions of the above formula. The Ashkenazi formula is 'prospective', declaring that any unfulfilled vows uttered during the coming year should be null and void. The Sephardim, on the other hand, have a 'retrospective' formula, annulling any vows made 'from the last Day of Atonement until this Day of Atonement'.

The latter version is undoubtedly the original one, as evidenced by all the Geonic sources from the period of Yehudai Gaon (*circa* 750).

The change to the prospective version was made in the eleventh century by Rabbi Meir ben Samuel, son-in-law of Rashi and father of the great Rabbenu Tam. The latter supported his father's objections to the retrospective formula on the grounds that: (a) annulment of past vows has to be performed by an experienced *dayyan* (judge) or by three laymen acting as a court of law, whereas, according to the prevailing custom, the Reader alone recites the declaration of annulment; (b) according to Jewish law, the actual vow has to be specified; (c) a prerequisite for annulment is the expression of regret (*charatah*) at having made the vow, whereas our congregations merely sing along with the *Kol Nidrey*; (d) there is no one to annul the vows of the Reader!

To overcome these objections, the retrospective formula was changed to the current Ashkenazi prospective version, which is not so much a ritual of annulment as a plea that God should preserve us from making unfulfilled vows, and, in the event of their being made, that he should regard them as non-binding commitments.

However, the discarding of a time-honoured version met with considerable resistance which resulted in many communities rejecting its recitation altogether. The Sephardim opted to retain the original version; the Ashkenazim generally accepted the innovation, and some communities compromised and recited both versions!

Our adjusted version has been left, however, with an

anomaly: for, while the key sentence now refers to the future ('from this Day of Atonement until the Day of Atonement to come'), the verbs have been left in the past tense: 'All vows . . . which we *have vowed* (*dindarna'*) and *have sworn* (*ude'ishteva'na'*)'!

Kol Nidrey is recited slowly three times, with the Reader raising his voice a little at each recitation. Surprisingly, the repetition was not introduced for any mystical or halachic reasons, but merely in order to prolong the service for the sake of latecomers. This was in order to enable them to catch up with the congregation and finish praying *ma'ariv* at the same time as the rest. This was especially important as Synagogues were generally only permitted to be built outside the towns, and it was dangerous for people to make the return journey home on their own in the darkness.

בָּרוּךְ אַתָּה ... שֶׁהֶחֱיָנוּ

Blessed are you . . . who has kept us in life . . .
(Ro. 17, Bi. 491, De S. 13)

This blessing over the festival (*birkath ha-zeman*) is recited on other festivals together with the *kiddush*. Since, on a fast day, obviously no *kiddush* can be made, the blessing was transferred to an honoured position just before *borkhu*. In the *Siddur* of the great Babylonian Gaon, Saadia (882–942), however, it is prescribed for insertion in its usual position after the *'Amidah*.[23]

יַעֲלֶה

O let our prayer ascend from eventime
(Ro. 31, Bi. 521, De S. 32)

The unique appeal of this poem is grounded in its simplicity. The basic structure of the corresponding lines of each three-lined stanza is identical. Only the middle word of each line changes from stanza to stanza, and the added words follow a reverse acrostic design. The three verbs, employed consecutively in each stanza, are culled from the prayer *ya'aleh veyavo' . . . veyeyra'eh*, recited on all festivals

and *Rosh Chodesh*. The poet employs these three verbs consistently in the masculine form of the third person, even
though several of the subject nouns are feminine. Grammar
was clearly secondary in his mind to the maintenance of a
simple and uniform setting.

The poem serves as an introductory petition to all the
prayers recited on *Kol Nidrey* night and throughout the
following Day of Atonement, expressing the fervent hope
that they will all ascend (*ya'aleh*) to the heavenly throne
and be efficacious.

The final word of the first line – *mey'erev* – and the last
phrase of the third line of each stanza – *'ad 'arev* – together
form the biblical phrase, 'from evening unto evening',[24]
which specifies the duration of this great fast day.

All the subject nouns listed in this poem – *tachanuneynu*,
shav'atheynu, etc. – are both appropriate and readily com-
prehensible. The one exception occurs in the first line of
the fourth stanza – 'O let our *menuseynu* ascend at sunset'.
Routledge renders the noun freely as 'hope'; Birnbaum as
'trusting faith'. The meaning of the noun *manos* is, however,
beyond question: 'flight', 'escape', which gives little sense
in this context. Some manuscript versions of the poem
substitute the noun *milluleynu*, 'our words', others *mechilath-
eynu*, 'our pardon'. D. Goldschmidt tortuously justifies the
present reading by explaining that 'if our prayers are
accepted, then that will be the instrument of our "escape"
from the evil decree'.[25]

The identity of the author of this poem is not established
with certainty, though it is thought to have been written
by Yose ben Yose, a very early Palestinian poet (*circa* fifth
century CE). Yose is the author of the composition *'omnam
'ashameynu*, recited later, and of various compositions on the
theme of the Day of Atonement ritual in Temple times
(*'Avodah*). Although the latter were not incorporated into
the Ashkenazi tradition, they have been preserved in the
Siddur of Saadia Gaon who was a particular admirer of
Yose's poetry. Yose's poetry is characterised by a simple
style, an uncomplicated technique and a fervent piety.[26]

שְׁמֵעַ תְּפִלָּה

O you who hear prayer
(Ro. 32, Bi. 523, De S. 33)

This composition comprises a medley of biblical verses, culled mainly from the psalms but including one verse from Deuteronomy, two from Jeremiah, two from Isaiah and one each from Job and I Chronicles. The verses pay tribute to the majestic holiness of God, his mighty acts at creation, his omnipotence and omniscience, and, in consequence, our paramount duty of praising and worshipping him. The climax of the passage is a simple, direct appeal for clemency, arguing that 'the soul is thine, and the body is thy work: have pity on thy labour'. What more effective and guileless argument could be adduced? Which artist would want to destroy the masterpiece into which he had invested all his skill and his unique spirit? Thus, it is 'for thy name's sake' that God must pardon our iniquity, 'however great it is'.

These verses were not randomly chosen merely because they reflect the central themes. A close examination will reveal that a literary device is employed here governing the particular choice of verses. There is a stair-like progression – as used effectively in the parallelism of some of the psalms – whereby either the basic or a subsidiary idea in one line, or a key-word in the line, is carried over as a link with the following line. The ideas thus progress smoothly and impressively towards the climactic plea for mercy.

Many will be surprised by the quotation from Psalm 74:

Thou didst crush the heads of Leviathan,
Leaving him a prey to beasts of the desert . . .
By thy power thou didst divide the sea,
Crushing the dragon's heads upon the waters.

Such mythological references to God having had to struggle with primeval creatures before being enabled to create the world are clearly in blatant conflict with our pure notion of the unity and omnipotence of the Creator!

Professor Yehezkiel Kaufmann[27] suggests that the later biblical writers were actually unaware of the status of these references as pagan concepts, particularly in the light of the fact that paganism is nowhere even hinted at in the biblical account of creation. The author of these psalm-verses would have regarded such references as native to Israel's legendary tradition.

Kaufmann believes that these motifs were actually inherited not from Babylonian mythology – wherein *before creation* God had to struggle for supremacy over *contending gods* – but from pre-Israelite, native, Canaanite tradition (known to us from Ugarit).[28] In our biblical version of these myths God has to deal exclusively with his own rebellious *subject-creatures*. Furthermore, this is always *after creation*, once God's rule was already clearly established.

In our own, recast version of the myths, Leviathan, the serpent,[29] the great sea monsters,[30] Rahab and the fleeing serpent,[31] etc. are all portrayed merely as demonic creatures of God. Their rebelliousness – like man's – becomes a source of real or potential evil and a danger to the stability and survival of the world. In that sense, God is constantly in a relationship of contention with them, as reflected in these rather gross anthropomorphic references.

The literary form of this composition reflects one of the earliest stages of formalised liturgy. Before our great sages of the talmudic period made so bold as to express publicly their own devotional sentiments, which paved the way for the development of sacred poetry, prayer was restricted to the recitation of biblical verses. These were probably chanted antiphonally, by leader and congregation.

דַּרְכְּךָ אֱלֹהֵינוּ ··· לְמַעַנְךָ אֱלֹהֵינוּ

Our God, it is your wont . . . For your sake, O our God

אָמְנָם אֲשַׁמְנוּ עָצְמוּ מִסְּפֵר

Truly our transgressions are more than can be numbered
(Ro. 34, Bi. 527, De S. 35)

The composition 'Omnam 'ashameynu is introduced by the

two verses which serve, alternately, as the refrains to each stanza. Most editions of the *Machzor* fail to appreciate this function of the opening verses, and do not insert, therefore, the usual initial word reference to them in the appropriate places at the end of each stanza.

The author of this composition was the great pioneer of Hebrew liturgical poetry in Palestine, Yose ben Yose.[32] His first refrain-verse reminds God that one of his essential attributes is that of 'being long-suffering towards both the righteous and the wicked'. Yose had in mind here the talmudic explanation of the dual form (*'erekh*) *'appayim*, '(slow to) anger' – instead of (*'erekh*) *'aph* – in the list of divine attributes.[33] The dual form is to indicate that God's tolerance is extended, in equal measure, to both.[34]

The second refrain-verse, 'Act for your own sake, not ours', reflects a similar sentiment to that of the concluding verses of the preceding composition. We are God's handiwork, over which he has laboured. It is for his sake and in his interest, therefore, for his plan to end in success, and for man's destiny to lie in salvation rather than destruction.

The poem *'Omnam 'ashameynu* – considerably abbreviated in our *Machzor* – follows an alphabetical acrostic pattern. A separate, four-lined stanza is devoted to each letter of the alphabet, each line of which commences with that particular letter. This provides a lengthy poem of eighty-eight lines, which, when allowances are made for a refrain after each stanza, makes a total of one hundred and ten lines! It is no wonder that the poem has suffered much abbreviation at the hands of editors. The Routledge and De Sola editions end the poem after the letter *yod*. Birnbaum, following a fairly widespread Ashkenazi practice, omits the poem entirely, while somewhat incongruously maintaining the introductory refrain-verses followed by the very last stanza of the poem, *Ta'aleh 'arukhah*.

Another reason for the abbreviation of Yose's poem is the fact that its despairing and nationally self-deprecatory sentiments, coupled with its chronicle of woes, transform it almost into a dirge, which is not in keeping with the spirit of the *Yom Tov* of *Yom Kippur*.

אֵל מֶלֶךְ יוֹשֵׁב

Almighty King who sits on the throne of mercy
(Bi. 527, De S. 37)

Routledge consistently omits this introductory section to
the thirteen divine attributes, as well as the attributes
themselves. While the other editions repeat these sections
four times, as accompaniments to the various *Selichoth*
('Penitential hymns'), Routledge includes it only once
(p. 40).

God is addressed as 'King who sits upon the throne of
mercy', in accordance with the rabbinic belief that
although God begins by occupying the throne of justice,
yet, at the sound of the Shofar on *Rosh Hashanah*, he aban-
dons it for the throne of mercy.[35]

The phrase *mithnaheg bachasiduth* ('you govern with piety')
is unclear. Some commentators connect it with the biblical
phrase 'with the pious (*chasid*) you show yourself as pious
(*tithchassad*)',[36] which the *Targum* relates to the three patriarchs, each of whom received the full measure of reward
for their piety. This does not explain, however, the particular nuance of the term *chasiduth*, which suggests a reward in excess of what was deserved.

Gersonides[37] comes closest to a satisfactory explanation.
He relates the expression to the experiences of King David
who composed the verse. David was reflecting here on the
fact that, whereas his own heinous sin with Bathsheba was,
nevertheless, instantly pardoned,[38] his predecessor, King
Saul, lost his Kingdom for a comparatively minor offence![39]
David's rationale of this is expressed here. Because he
strove to be a pious man (*chasid*) throughout his life, and
only once was vanquished by the onslaught of his passion
for Bathsheba, God, in return, also displayed *chasiduth*, a
unique degree of loving indulgence. Saul, on the other
hand, who showed indifference to God all his life, was
punished with a commensurate absence of such divine *chasiduth*. In this introduction to the thirteen divine attributes,
the author asserts that the quality of *chasiduth* governs God's
relationship with his people.

מַעֲבִיר רִאשׁוֹן רִאשׁוֹן – *You make them (the sins) pass away one by one*

Rashi explains this rather vague talmudic statement[40] to mean that, rather than placing all the good and evil deeds in the scales together, and risk having to condemn man, God places them in in small clusters. If, in the first cluster, they are equal in number, or if the good deeds outweigh the bad, God then 'removes the sins' from that cluster, and pardons them, leaving only the good deeds in the scale, to augment the good deeds of the subsequent clusters.

אֵל הוֹרֵיתָ לָנוּ לוֹמַר – *God, who did instruct us to recite the thirteen divine attributes*

This is based upon the well-known talmudic statement that,[41] when disclosing to Moses his attributes,[42] 'God enwrapped himself in a *tallith* like a Reader and indicated to Moses that when Israel sins, if they recite these attributes in prayer, God would pardon them.'

וְנַקֵּה – *And acquitting*

According to our *Selichoth* version of the Thirteen Attributes, the single word *venaqqeh* ('And he acquits') represents the final divine attribute. However, if we compare this with the actual biblical source,[43] we find, rather surprisingly, that we have curtailed the full version of this attribute, which, in the original, conveys the very opposite sense! The biblical text has *venaqqeh lo' yenaqqeh* – 'And he does *not* acquit (the guilty)'.

The reason we have abbreviated the attribute is in order to convert it into a positive formulation, to conform with the other attributes. According to our version we must understand the word *venaqqeh* in the sense of 'he acquits *the righteous*'.

Abbreviating a biblical verse in this way does, however, run counter to a talmudical principle that 'we may not stop in the middle of a verse (in order to create a separate verse) at a place where Moses did not stop.'[44] This prohibition was understood, however, to apply only when reading from the Torah. To employ a half-verse in the context of prayer and petition was regarded as outside the scope of the prohibition.[45]

אֱלֹהֵינוּ ··· סְלַח נָא אֲשָׁמוֹת

Our God . . . Forgive the errors
(Ro. 36, Bi. 531, De S. 38)

This *selichah* composition follows on from a miscellany of biblical verses all of which deal with the theme of forgiveness. One of the verses commences with the phrase *selach na' la'avon* ('Forgive, I beseech thee, the iniquity of this people'), and this is employed here by the author to provide the initial words for each line of his rhyming couplets. The succeeding word of each line provides an alphabetical acrostic pattern.

This poem is attributed to the pen of the distinguished thirteenth-century talmudist and leader of German Jewry, Rabbi Meir ben Baruch of Rothenburg. He is best known for his elegy *Sha'aliy seruphah ba'esh*, composed after witnessing the public burning of cart loads of Torah scrolls in Paris in 1242. This is recited by Ashkenazim among the *Qinnoth* for the ninth of Av.

The poet calls upon God to forgive his people notwithstanding their degeneracy and rebelliousness. He offers no defence; he proffers no extenuating circumstances. Although he employs some very strong terms when particularising his people's acts of treachery, yet, for all that, sinful Israel still remains in the closest proximity to God. Hence his description of Israel as 'thy people', 'thy children', 'thy faithful', 'thy chosen', 'thy worshippers', 'thy flock', 'thy loved ones'.

Suspicion has been cast on the authenticity of the opening word of the fifth line *ha-kol modiym* – 'Forgive . . . *all those* who confess their sins.' All the other object-clauses refer to Israel's several misdemeanours, whereas this solitary line would stand as a complimentary designation. It has been suggested that the original version was *hevel modiym*, 'the *insincerity* of those who confess'.

It has also been suggested that a word has dropped out

of the line commencing with the letter *pey*. This line alone
has no direct object: 'Forgive I beseech thee, lest they be
punished from thy heaven.' D. Goldschmidt[46] conjectures
that a word like *piggulam*, 'their detestable behaviour',
might have been originally in the text. He was probably
influenced by the expression *vegam paggel* in the second
stanza of the next composition.

אֱלֹהֵינוּ ⋯ אָמְנָם כֵּן

Our God . . . Yes, it is true
(Ro. 38, Bi. 533, De S. 41)

This *selichah* hymn is believed to have come from the pen
of Rabbi Yom Tov ben Isaac of Joigny, who perished in
the York massacre of 1190. In 1978, when a memorial
tablet to the Jewish victims was unveiled at Clifford's
Tower, this composition was appropriately chosen to be
intoned.

Our editions have omitted the opening stanza wherein
the initial words of a two-lined introductory couplet form
the author's name acrostic 'Yom Tov'. Our version starts
at the beginning of the alphabetical acrostic, *'omnam*.

There might also be an intended allusion to the King,
Richard I, whose absence on a crusade enabled the massacre to take place. His soubriquet was *cœur-de-lion* ('The
Lion-Heart'); and the fourth line employs the verb *sho'eyg*,
'to roar', with the specific nuance of 'a lion's roar'.[47]

The metre of the poem, following the medieval system
which was inspired by Arabic metre, achieves its effect by
having each line conform to a regular pattern of stresses.
Throughout the poem a pattern of 3-3-2 stresses is maintained, as may be observed in this example of the scansion
of the first stanza:

Ómnám kéyn / yétzér sokhéyn / bánú
Bákh lehátzddéyk / ráv tzédék / va'anéynú

The opening words *'omnam keyn* are supercharged with
biblical allusive significance. They were first uttered by

Job: 'Truly, I know, it is so' (*'omnam yada'ti kiy kheyn*),[48] as an admission of the truth of the assertion made by his friend, Eliphaz, that mere man can never be justified or found to be pure in the eyes of his Maker.[49] The implication was clearly that all Job's troubles must have been justified, and attributable directly to his sinfulness.

In employing these words, the poet is making a similar assertion: that Israel must indeed have sinned, but that she was an unwilling party to a sinfulness which was engendered by the *yetzer sokheyn*, the 'evil impulse which holds total sway'.[50]

In the second stanza, Satan, the accuser, is described as *meraggeyl*, 'a spy', the same term used to describe the spies sent by Joshua in order to discover the weaknesses and the most vulnerable areas in the defences of the holy land.[51] Satan, likewise, attempts to penetrate our people's moral and spiritual defences. He is, therefore, also to be regarded by God as 'a fabricator', whose book (of charges against Israel) must be rejected as a forgery. He is a *qatteygor* ('prosecuting counsel') who must be silenced forthwith.

The merit of Abraham, the *'ezrach* ('easterner')[52] is invoked in the fourth stanza to ensure that 'the lily flourishes'. This phrase is an allusion to Hosea 14:6, wherein the prophet summons Israel to repent, promising them that, as a reward for faithfulness, they would blossom and 'flourish like the lily'.

The low estate of pre-expulsion Jewry, who 'by the Crown were regarded as domestic animals to be milked and utilized, and by the common people and the Baronage . . . were regarded as wolves to be extirpated',[53] is forcefully reflected in the final three stanzas, wherein the poet alludes to the plight of his people and asks God to account their insults, tears and humiliation as representing a total retribution for all their sins.

כִּי הִנֵּה כַּחוֹמֶר

As clay in the hand of the potter
(Ro. 39, Bi. 537, De S. 42)

This composition, by an unknown author who lived probably during the eleventh or twelfth centuries, is based upon
Jeremiah's famous parable of the potter:

> These are the words which came to Jeremiah from the
> Lord: Go down at once to the potter's house, and there
> I will tell you what I have to say. So I went down to the
> potter's house and found him working at the wheel. Now
> and then a vessel he was making out of the clay would
> be spoilt in his hands, and then he would start again and
> mould it into another vessel to his liking. Then the word
> of the Lord came to me: Can I not deal with you, Israel,
> says the Lord, *as the potter deals with his clay?*

The Hebrew of the last phrase – *hinney kachomer beyad
ha-yotzeyr* – provided the theme and inspiration for this
composition, wherein the poet expands upon Jeremiah's
imagery to include a variety of craftsmen – stone masons,
blacksmiths, seamen, glaziers, drapers and silversmiths –
all of whom mould, select and reject their raw material at
will. Israel is God's raw material; and the plea is that we
will always be regarded as the choicest material with which
God will choose to carry out his purpose.

The recurring final line of each stanza – *labrith habbeyt
ve'al teyphen layyeytzer* ('consider the covenant and disregard
the evil inclination') – links the composition to the context
of the Thirteen Divine Attributes of mercy. 'The Covenant'
actually stands as a synonym for those attributes, in an
allusion to the talmudic statement that 'a covenant (*brith*)
was signed with the Thirteen Attributes that (whenever
they are invoked in prayer by Israel) they will never be
disregarded'.[54] The attributes are a kind of mystical key to
unlock the treasury of mercy.

God is also asked to 'disregard the *yeytzer*'. This is a plea
for him to overlook his own value-judgment that 'the in-

clination (*yeytzer*) of man's heart is evil from his youth upwards'.[55]

While Modern Hebrew has popularised the word *hegeh* (found here at the beginning of the fourth stanza) in the meaning of 'a steering wheel', the precise sense in which our medieval author understood it is not too clear. It has, consequently, been rendered variously as 'an anchor' (Routledge, based on Heidenheim), 'helm' (Birnbaum), 'rudder' (De Sola) and 'oar'.

The third words of each stanza follow an alternating alphabetical progression (*ʾeven, ḡarzen, hegeh, zekhukhiyth, yeriyʿah, keseph*), which suggests that we have represented here a mere remnant of an originally complete, alphabetical acrostic poem.

זְכֹר רַחֲמֶיךָ

Remember your mercies
(Ro. 40, Bi. 539, De S. 44)

The remainder of the *Selichoth*, from this point onwards, follows, almost identically, the liturgy of the *Selichoth* services for the week preceding *Rosh Hashanah*, the Ten Days of Penitence and for fast days.[56]

The present composition comprises biblical verses from the books of Psalms, Exodus and Deuteronomy, all of which have as their key-word, *zekhor*, 'remember'. God is implored to remember that his relationship with his people has always been grounded in mercy and love. He is called upon to remember that he chose Zion to be the residence of his divine presence, and that God, therefore, has a close interest in securing its immediate restoration. He is also asked to remember the age-old covenant with the patriarchs, and the promise that their offspring would inherit the holy land, not only in those far-off days, but *leʿolam*, 'forever'.

כִּי אָנוּ עַמֶּךְ

For we are your people
(Ro. 45, Bi. 545, De S. 50)

This popular composition is generally sung to a cheerful and optimistic melody, in the spirit of its sentiments which emphasize the inextricable bonds uniting God and Israel. These bonds connote a multi-faceted relationship: we are his people, his children, his servants, his congregation, his inheritance, his flock, his vineyard, his product, his beloved, his treasure. And God is no less possessive of this relationship than is Israel to be its beneficiaries.

The inspiration for this artless outpouring of mutual dependence was derived from the midrashic comment on the verse 'My beloved is for me and I am for my beloved' (Song of Songs 6:3). The whole book of the Song of Songs was viewed by our sages as an allegory on the love between God and Israel; and the above verse led the Rabbis to exemplify the many metaphors used in the bible in order to define this reciprocal love-relationship. Our poet has excerpted these from that midrashic exposition.[57]

In the last few stanzas, prescribed for recitation by the Reader, there is an unexpected change of mood and sentiment. Having highlighted all that which unites God and Israel, attention is suddenly focused upon that which divides: 'We are brazen-faced, but thou art merciful and compassionate; we are full of sin, but thou art full of mercy.'

The objective of this transition is, undoubtedly, to pave the way for the confession of sins which follows. It would have been a presumptuous contradiction to sing of our total and righteous immersion in God and then immediately to have proceeded to a lengthy confession of sin. However, since the transitional, self-condemnatory sentiments are themselves in sharp conflict with the happy and confident tenor of the main composition, they were prescribed for recitation by the Reader alone.

וִדּוּי

Confession of sin
(Ro. 46–51, Bi. 547–55, De S. 51–7)

The *Vidduy*-confessional follows on shortly after the recitation of the 'Thirteen Divine Attributes' because of the tradition, referred to above, that God promised Israel that the recitation of that formula, which emphasises God's qualities of mercy, would never fall on deaf ears, but that forgiveness would immediately be forthcoming.

In Temple times the High Priest invoked the *Tetragrammaton*, the personal name of God, ten times while making confession. Hence the Talmud[58] prescribed that, in our liturgy, we recite the *Vidduy*-confessional a corresponding number of times: in the silent version, and again during the repetition, of the *'Amidah* of the five statutory services of *Yom Kippur*.

In talmudic times there was no uniformity of opinion as to the precise formula of confession to be recited; neither could the talmudists agree on the central issue of whether it was necessary to specify the individual sin or whether a blanket confession would suffice.[59] It was only in the third century that Rav and Shemuel – who had a formative influence on the development of the liturgy – popularised appropriate confessionals. Rav's composition *'Attah yodey'a razey 'olam* ('You know the mysteries of the Universe'),[60] which is quoted in full in the Talmud,[61] won its way into all prayer rites.

The Talmud quotes the opening words of various confessionals composed by a number of sages, though only a few of these have been identified with existing passages in our liturgy. Rabbi Jochanan's prayer, *Ribbon ha-'olamim*, is mentioned, as well as Shemuel's *Mah 'anu meh chayyeynu* ('What are we? What is our life?'). The latter is recited in the *Vidduy* of every service during *Yom Kippur*;[62] and, as a measure of their popularity, these two compositions were combined into one which is recited near the beginning of the daily morning service throughout the year.[63]

Another prayer quoted in full by the Talmud is the

composition of Rav Hamnuna, *'Elohay 'ad shelo' notzartiy* ('My God, before I was formed I was of no worth . . .'). Because this confession of human worthlessness was couched in the first person singular, it was felt to be more appropriate for recitation by the individual worshipper in the silent *'Amidah*.[64] Perhaps its sentiments were also regarded as a little too embarrassing for a Reader to recite publicly. In recognition of its popularity it was prescribed as the closing confessional for every service.

אָשַׁמְנוּ

We have trespassed
(Ro. 46, Bi. 547, De S. 51)

The *Vidduy* section of the *'Amidah*, which commences with the alphabetical confessional *'Ashamnu* ('we have trespassed'), is introduced by a short, humble preamble, *tavo' lephanekha tephillatheynu* ('Let our prayer come before thee'), acknowledging our full awareness of the need for confession. The closing words, *'aval 'anachnu chata'nu* ('Truly we have sinned'), represent, in the view of Shemuel,[65] the basic formula of confession.

Though this confessional is generally attributed to the Geonim of Babylon (ninth–twelfth centuries), it has been demonstrated by A. Marmorstein[66] that during that period the basic confessional consisted of a mere four words: *chata'nu 'ashamnu he'eviynu vehirsha'nu*. This was expanded into our alphabetical version during the thirteenth century, and only won its position as a generally accepted version during the following century.

The *'Ashamnu* confessional was dubbed *Vidduy Zuta'*, 'the short confessional', as opposed to the *'Al Chet*, which is called *Vidduy Rabba'*, 'the long confessional'. The catalogue of sins listed in the *'ashamnu* betrays repetitiveness occasioned by the need to fill up all the letters of the alphabet. Hence we have two identical verbs used twice: *he'eviynu* and *'aviynu*, as well as *hirsha'nu* and *rasha'nu*. It should also be observed that in the confessional of the High Priest he employed only three verbs: *chat'u*, *'avu* and *pash'u* ('They have sinned, committed iniquity and transgressed'),[67] proving that we have in our *'ashamnu* an artificially expanded composition. Its popularity and appeal are in no way impaired, however, by this consideration.

It is significant that our formulae of confession are all couched in the plural, as if to suggest that it is society which fosters the climate and conditions wherein sin is engendered in the heart of the individual. An unfeeling society will nurture despair on the part of the disadvantaged. From despair flows crime and sin. An irresponsible society will, similarly, breed delinquency, violence and sin. The plural formulation indicates that, though the individual commits the act, society at large must bear the responsibility.

It will be noted that, throughout the confessional, there is not one reference to sins of neglect or omission in the performance of specific ritual practices. The catalogue of sins is restricted to the domain of ethics and morals, as if to emphasise that no Jew who strives after piety may ignore his responsibilities to his fellow man.

This was not the case, however, in the prayer book used by pre-expulsion Jewry in England, as preserved in the *'Etz Chayyim* of Jacob ben Yehudah, *Chazan* of London.[68] There, the 'short confessional' – which was recited each day at the beginning of the morning service[69] – was considerably expanded to include enumeration of ritual offences, such as 'I have desecrated the Sabbath' ... 'I have eaten forbidden foods' ... 'I have eaten without reciting the prescribed blessings.' So wide-ranging is that version of 'the short confessional' that it includes confession for sins as serious as 'neglect of Torah study' and 'profaning your holy name', on the one hand, and as inocuous as 'calling a friend by a nickname', on the other!

עַל חֵטְא

'For the sin wherein we have sinned . . .'
(Ro. 49, Bi. 551, De S. 54)

Just as our 'short confessional' is an expanded version, so the '*Al cheyt* – the 'long confessional' – is a considerably expanded version of an original composition containing a mere six lines confessing sins committed (i) *be'ones* (forcibly), (ii) *beratzon* (willingly), (iii) *bishgagah* (in error), (iv) *bezadon* (brazenly), (v) *baseyther* (in secret) and (vi) *bagaluy* (openly).

Maimonides and many other prayer rites present a single alphabetical version of twenty-four lines, whereas the Ashkenazim expanded this into a double acrostic composition of forty-four lines. It is conceivable that the Ashkenazi version is actually a conflation of two totally independent alphabetical confessional compositions. This would explain the several examples of tautology, such as confessions for 'the utterance of the lips', 'the words of the mouth' and 'the expressions of our lips'.

If we examine the list of confessions in '*Al cheyt* we find repeated references to parts of the body: *'immutz ha-leyv* (hardening of the heart), *bittuy sephathayim* (utterance of the lips), *dibbur peh* (words of the mouth), *chozeq yad* (violence of the hand), *lashon ha-ra'* (evil tongue), *'eynayim ramoth* (haughty eyes), *'azzuth metzach* (an obdurate brow), *qalluth ro'sh* (light-headed levity), *qashyuth 'oreph* (being stiff-necked) and *riytzath raglayim lehara'* (allowing one's legs to run to do evil).

As we stand, on *Yom Kippur*, denying ourselves every bodily pleasure to enable our souls to soar upwards, un-fettered, in order to plead our cause, this confessional's emphasis upon crimes committed by the body assumes a special significance.

It offers, in effect, a plea of extenuating circumstances by placing the blame upon the several parts of our bodily frame, and their propensity towards sin. The real 'self', it is inferred, is our indestructible soul, whose purity we acknowledge each morning in the '*Elohai neshamah*: 'My

God, the soul which you have placed within me is pure. You have created it; You have formed it and breathed it into me. You preserve it within me; You will take it from me and restore it to me in the hereafter.'

Thus, we assert that our nucleus is pure, for it is exclusively the physical frame which the soul inhabits that is its source of contamination. And in our confessional we leave God in no doubt as to the many organs of the body at whose door we lay the guilt. We ask, however, that the merit of the soul should secure forgiveness at the same time for its corporeal partner.[70]

וְעַל חֲטָאִים

And for the sins

In this short list forgiveness is petitioned for any act which in Temple times would have necessitated the bringing of any of the specific categories of sacrifice enumerated or which would have attracted one or more of the biblical or rabbinic penalties listed. Though the Temple and sacrificial system has long since vanished, the ancient ritual is referred to here in order 'to impress upon us the nature of the tribute which it would be our duty to offer by way of atonement, and which, today, can be adequately replaced only by means of prayer and sincere repentance.'[71]

Imagine the expense and the effort a penitent was involved in, in making the journey to the Temple at Jerusalem, selecting and purchasing his sacrifice, queuing up to have it ritually slaughtered and offered, as well as the expenses of accommodation and the loss of income during the stay if he came from the provinces. Though this is impossible to quantify, it does give us some idea of the equivalent effort we are expected to put into our self-scrutiny, our expression of remorse and resolution, our prayers and meditations, in order to remove the evil decree.

וְעַל כֻּלָּם אֱלוֹהַ סְלִיחוֹת

And for all these, O God of forgiveness

This line is repeated, as a refrain, at the end of each of the four divisions of the *'Al Cheyt* confessional. The specific designation of God as *'eloah selichoth*, 'God of forgiveness', was inspired by Numbers 14:20 where God announced his decision to reverse his sentence and pardon Israel with the words *salachtiy kidevarekha*, 'I have forgiven, as you petitioned.' This reprieve was granted to the Israelites on the tenth day of Tishri; and henceforth Jews believed that this date, on which *Yom Kippur* occurs, is a blessed day when atonement is annually granted.

SELICHOTH

אֵל רַחוּם שְׁמֶךָ

Your name is merciful God

עֲנֵנוּ יי עֲנֵנוּ

Answer us, O Lord, answer us

מִי שֶׁעָנָה לְאַבְרָהָם

He who answered our father Abraham
(Ro. 53–5, Bi. 559–63, De S. 59–62)

While we have applied the nomenclature *vidduy* (confession) to the *'Ashamnu* and *'Al cheyt* compositions, they actually belong to the genre of *Selichoth*, 'prayers for forgiveness'. Indeed, they and their preceding section, *zekhor lanu berith*,[72] together with these three compositions, appear as one unit which serves as the concluding section of the daily *Selichoth* prayers recited during the week preceding *Rosh Hashanah*, as well as during the Ten Days of Penitence and on fast days.

These *Selichoth* are also somewhat similar to those recited on the festival of *Sukkoth*, which we popularly call

Hosha'noth. Indeed, the alphabetical list in the first of our three compositions – commencing *'Asey lema'an 'amitakh* – is identical with that contained in the *hosha'na'* for the first day of Sukkoth, *Lema'an 'amitakh.* Again in our first composition, following on after the end of the alphabetical acrostic, there is an appeal to God for forgiveness on account of the merit of all our biblical ancestors (this is also the subject of the third composition, *Miy she'anah le-Avraham*), our holy places and our saints and martyrs. This is paralleled very closely by the composition for the second day of Sukkoth, *'Even shethiyyah.*

The common origin of all these compositions lies in a very old Temple ceremony enacted as a special petition for rain. These *Selichoth* originated as a liturgy for the regular fast days introduced in Temple times because of a lack of rain. From that context they were borrowed for recitation on the historical fast days also, as well as during the High Holydays period. Their recitation on the festival of *Sukkoth* is clearly because of the association of that festival with petition for rain.

These very old *Selichoth* and *Hosha'noth* represent one of the earliest forms of post-biblical poetry known to us. Professor Joseph Heinemann, who made a special study of their origin and literary form,[73] has enumerated their main characteristics: (i) they are made up of a large number of short, stereotyped lines; (ii) each line consists of but two or three words; (iii) the alphabetical acrostic is generally employed; (iv) there is a primitive type of rhyme achieved by the employment of a recurring pronominal suffix at the end of each line (*'amitekha. . . . berithekha. . . . tiphartekha . . .*); (v) they have none of the features of style characteristic of the *Piyyut* in general, nor do they possess any internal structure whatsoever.[74]

The first two of our compositions certainly betray these features; and Heinemann tells us that they belong, like the *Hosha'noth*, to the category of *litanies* originally chanted during processions or circuits around the altar. Such processions were a common feature of the service for fast days in

Temple times, and to this day the procession is the central
feature of the *Sukkoth* services.

The third *selichah* composition – *miy she'anah le-Avraham*
('He who answered our father Abraham on Mount Moriah,
he shall answer us') – is based upon the formulae, preserved in the Mishna,[75] of the expanded blessings of the
'Amidah which were recited on special fast days instituted
during periods of drought in Temple times. In seven of the
'Amidah blessings they would insert a plea to God to 'answer' and deliver them from famine, just as he had delivered (i) Abraham (from Nimrod's fiery furnace), (ii) our
ancestors at the Red Sea, (iii) Joshua at Gilgal (Gilgal was
his base at the time of the miracle of the walls of Jericho),
(iv) Samuel at Mitzpah (when he won a decisive battle
against the Philistines), (v) Elijah at Mount Carmel, (vi)
Jonah (from the belly of the fish) and (vii) David[76] and
Solomon[77] in Jerusalem (when they were confronted with
famine).

The Ashkenazi version of this *selichah* is considerably
expanded by the addition of other biblical examples of
righteous people who were miraculously delivered, and the
list is subject to much variation in other prayer rites. The
Ashkenazi version has departed but slightly from the formula of the Mishna which has *miy she'anah . . . hu' ya'aneh
'ethkhem* (instead of *ya'aneynu*).[78] In the French, Italian and
Yemenite rites the formula appears as, *keshe'aniytha . . . keyn
'aneynu*, 'just as you answered . . ., so answer us'. This is
an interesting version, as it provides a link, for this composition also, with the structure of the *Hosha'na'* composition, *kehosha'ta 'eyliym belud . . . keyn hosha'na'*, recited each
day of *Sukkoth*. (For some more general remarks on the
nature of the *Selichoth*, see pp. 166–61).

אָבִינוּ מַלְכֵּנוּ

(Ro. 55, Bi. 565, De S. 62) (see pp. 32–4)

עָלֵינוּ לְשַׁבֵּחַ

(Ro. 58, Bi. 571, De S. 65) (see pp. 57–9)

THE MORNING SERVICE

(For commentary to first part of morning service, see pp. 3–10)

סְלַח לְגוֹי קָדוֹשׁ

Forgive a holy nation
(Ro. 35, Bi. 585, De S. 134)

This self-designation as 'a holy nation' is not to be considered as presumptuous, for God himself so describes Israel: 'For you shall be unto me a kingdom of priests *and a holy nation*' (Ex. 19:6). Psychologically, to regard oneself as holy is, in itself, a great stimulus to holiness. Israel is encouraged, therefore, to think of itself as a holy entity. It is for this reason that Synagogues preface their names with the letters ק״ק , an abbreviation of *qehillah qedoshah*, 'holy congregation'.

To impugn this holy state was regarded almost as an act of blasphemy. Thus, according to the Talmud,[1] the prophet Isaiah died a violent death at the hands of the wicked king Manasseh as a punishment for having impugned the holiness of his people by saying, 'I dwell among a people of unclean lips' (Is. 6:5).

The composition *'Az beyom Kippur*, to which the line *selach legoy qadosh* forms a refrain, as well as the composition *Qadosh 'addiyr ba'aliyyatho*, which follows, are designated *yotzeroth*,[2] as they were composed for insertion into the first of the two blessings preceding the *Shema'*: *yotzeyr ha-me'oroth*.

The latter blessing of the *Shema'* pays tribute to God as 'creator of the luminaries' (sun and moon), and this particular theme is emphasised in the *yotzeroth*. In the present composition it is linked to the theme of repentance, particularly in the last line of the second stanza (line 8): *dophqey bitheshuvah leyotzeyr 'or*, 'knocking repentant at the door of *the Creator of light*'. An examination of the composition will reveal a further twelve references to 'light', as the poet extends the imagery from the literal context of heavenly luminaries to a general metaphor for enlightenment. His licence for this was inferred from the last verse of the actual *Shema'* blessing itself – *'or chadash* ('O cause a new light to shine upon Zion') – which was a later messianic sentiment introduced into a blessing that refers exclusively to the light of the planetary luminaries.[3]

The composition opens with the line, 'On Yom Kippur *you taught* pardon'. This is based upon the rabbinic tradition that it was on the 10th of Tishri – *Yom Kippur* – that Moses descended from Mount Sinai, carrying the second set of tablets of stone. That day of reconciliation between God and Israel was established forever as the most spiritually propitious time when 'you will pardon our iniquity and our sins, and you will take us as your own possession' (Ex. 34:9).

The poem is full of allusions to rabbinic interpretations, which would necessitate a far longer and more detailed commentary than the present one in order to elucidate fully. We may draw attention to just two, as an example of the poet's approach. The opening line of the second stanza (line 5) – *gavru chata'im ba'aniy yesheyna* ('Sins swell mightily when I am asleep') – gives little sense when read literally, for it is hardly possible to sin while asleep! The poet is clearly writing in the spirit of the midrashic interpretation of this verse:

> *I am asleep but my heart is awake* (Cant. 5:2) – The assembly of Israel says this to the Holy One, blessed be He: *I am asleep* [i.e. I may well be indolent] when it comes to fulfilling all the commandments, *but my heart is awake* [i.e. sensitive] to the fulfilment of acts of kindness.[4]

Our poet was thus employing the verse *'aniy yesheyna* ('I am asleep') in the midrashic sense of 'indolence', which gives good sense to his assertion that indolence is the cause of 'sins swelling mightily'.

There is another midrashic allusion in the opening line of the tenth stanza (line 37) – *qarveynu leyesh'akha be'or sheney 'ophariym* ('Draw us near to your salvation by the grace of the two fawns'). The last phrase is an allusion to Song of Songs 4:5 – 'Your two breasts are like two fawns, twin fawns of a gazelle.' The whole of this book, with all its passionate, almost erotic, poetry, was regarded by our Rabbis as an allegory on the relationship between God and Israel. Thus, 'your two breasts' is explained by the Midrash as a metaphoric allusion to Moses and Aaron, 'for just as the breasts are the beauty and glory of woman, so Moses and Aaron are the pride of Israel; and just as the breasts nourish the babe with milk, so Moses and Aaron nourished Israel with Torah'.[5] The Midrash continues to explain the metaphor of 'twins', as applied to Moses and Aaron, in the sense of their having been identical in piety, even though Moses was superior in prophetic attainment.

The poem follows a double alphabetical acrostic pattern, with the last syllable of each alphabetical line rhyming with its partner in the couplet. The two refrains which preface the poem – *selach legoy qadosh* and *chata'nu tzureynu* – were intended to be used, alternately, after each stanza. As frequently occurs with lengthy poems, the refrains are omitted in order to avoid impairing the effect of the poem itself.

בָּרוּךְ שֵׁם כְּבוֹד מַלְכוּתוֹ

Blessed be the name of the one whose glorious kingdom. . . .

מַלְכוּתוֹ בִּקְהַל עֲדָתִי

His kingdom is within my assembled people
(Ro. 39, Bi. 595, De S. 139)

These verses, which serve to introduce the composition *Qadosh 'addiyr ba'aliyyatho*, were intended to serve as refrains throughout the composition; the former after every line, the latter after every couplet. This poem belongs to the genre of *Piyyut* known as *'Ophan*, which was composed for insertion into the first blessing before the *Shema'*, immediately prior to the section commencing *veha'ophanim vechayyoth ha-qodesh*. (In the Polish rite this is actually replaced, on the High Holydays, by the formula *vehachayyoth yeshoreyru*.)

The first refrain anticipates the rallying cry which was inserted by the early Synagogue into the *Shema' Yisrael* – after the first verse – notwithstanding the fact that it constituted an interruption of a biblical passage. Throughout the year, the formula *barukh sheym kevod malkhutho le'olam va'ed* is recited in an undertone, but on *Yom Kippur* the congregation recites it loudly and confidently.

In early talmudic times the word *malkhuth* (kingdom) had a polemical significance, as it was the official term used by Jews to denote the rule of the Roman conquerors. When Jews recited the formula 'blessed be the name of the one whose glorious *kingdom* (*malkhutho*) is forever and ever' they were implying that only God's *malkhuth* would be enduring, but Rome's would be short-lived. Roman inspectors were aware of the implication of this verse, and, for that reason, Jews had to recite it in an undertone for fear of retribution. On *Yom Kippur*, however, the requirement of emphasising God's sole sovereignty gave them the courage to recite it aloud.

The second refrain takes up this theme of God's *malkhuth* (kingdom), and asserts that, although the promised national restoration – as a prelude to the establishment of God's kingdom on earth – has not yet occurred, yet the seeds of the latter are nevertheless germinating within the national spirit of the Jewish people.

The alphabetical acrostic composition, *Qadosh 'addiyr ba'aliyyatho* – each line beginning with the word *qadosh* – was written as an amplification of the sanctification formula – *qadosh qadosh qadosh* – which precedes it.

וְהַחַיּוֹת יְשׁוֹרֵרוּ

The chayyoth sing
(Ro. 40, Bi. 597, De S. 141) – see p. 16

THE REPETITION OF THE *'AMIDAH* BY THE *CHAZAN*
(Ro. 53, Bi. 623, De S. 158) (see pp. 18–20)

אֵמֶיךָ נָשָׂאתִי

I suffer thy terrors

The author of this meditation is Meshullam ben Kalonymos, a tenth–eleventh-century scholar and founding father
of one of the most distinguished families of medieval
Germany for a period of some four hundred years. The
Kalonymos family – which hailed originally from Italy –
produced numerous rabbis, theologians, poets and communal leaders for the communities of the Rhineland. They
had a penchant for poetry, and at least twelve members of
that family contributed towards producing a vast number
of elegies chronicling the sufferings of German Jewry during the tragic period of the Crusades. Meshullam himself
was held in high regard by Rashi as a distinguished talmudical scholar and author of responsa, and he helped to
lay the groundwork for the development of rabbinic learning, as well as a poetic tradition, in Franco-Germany.

This meditation is another example of the *Reshuth*[6] genre,
wherein the Reader makes an urgent plea for divine guidance and indulgence as he assumes the role of intercessor
for his congregation. The opening words sum up his feelings of inadequacy at the awesome responsibility that he
must assume.

The composition is constructed according to an alphabetical acrostic pattern of four-lined stanzas, with four
words to each line. In order to preserve the metric uniformity of only four stresses to each line, the poet was
constrained to employ contracted forms of nouns. Hence,
za'aq ('a cry') for the regular biblical noun *ze'aqah*;[7] *'erekh*
('healing') for *'arukhah*;[8] *chesher* ('rain') for *chashrah*;[9] *keshel*

('stumbling') for *kishalon*;[10] *cheyshel* ('weariness') for *chul-shah*;[11] *peletz* ('quaking') for *pallatzuth*.[12]

אִמַּצְתָּ עָשׂוֹר

You adopted the tenth day
(Ro. 54, Bi. 625, De S. 159)

This alphabetical poem is also by Meshullam ben Kalony-mos. It was composed to follow on from the preceding *Reshuth*, and opens with the concluding word of that com-position. Not surprisingly, we find the same employment of contracted forms of nouns. Hence such forms as *lithechiy* ('for life') for *lithechiyah*; *miteyqa'* ('from the Shofar blast')[13] for *miteqiyyah*, and *'ath* ('the One who came') for *'athah*.[14]

Having focussed, in the *Reshuth*, upon his own difficult situation as Reader and intercessor, he now turns his at-tention to the subject of the congregation he represents. He attempts to wrest divine compassion by alluding to their humble and dejected state and the burden of the fast: 'Their young and old are fasting today; they are hungry and tired. Look at them all standing barefoot, robed in white. . . .'

זָכְרֵנוּ לַחַיִּים

Remember us unto life
(Ro. 55, Bi. 625, De S. 160) (see pp. 21–2)

תַּאֲוַת נֶפֶשׁ

The longing of our soul

This poem follows the reverse acrostic – *tashraq* – pattern, together with the popular metric form of four-lined stanzas, with four words to a line. Again we have the appearance of contracted nouns, so favoured of Meshullam ben Kalony-mos. Thus, *'ahav*[15] ('love') for *'ahavah*; *'eyqed* ('binding') for *'akeydah*, and *'eneq* ('cry') for *'anaqah*.[16]

The poet reminds God of the abiding love which his people have for him, a love as deep and trusting as that of a tender infant for its father. God cannot avoid the consequences of this relationship and cast off his errant children, for he has entered into an irreversible covenant with them when he established the bond of circumcision with their father Abraham. The phrase *beriythekha choq bishe'eyram* ('your covenant is sealed in their flesh') is derived from the blessing recited at the circumcision ceremony.

In the penultimate stanza the poet asks that Abraham, 'the righteous intercessor (on behalf of the Sodomites)', should teach us how to make an effective intercession on our own behalf, so that 'we would gain the protection of a thousand shields'. This is an allusion to the verse, 'your neck is like the tower of David . . . whereon hang a thousand shields' (Song of Songs 4:4). The Midrash on this verse depicts Abraham as complaining to God that, whereas God had promised him 'I shall be a shield *to you*' (Gen. 15:1), this promise did not appear to contain any such commitment to his offspring. The verse in the Song of Songs is represented as God's answer to this; namely, that while God served as one shield to Abraham, his protection of Abraham's offspring would be a thousand-fold.[17]

עַד יוֹם מוֹתוֹ

Until the day of man's death
(Ro. 56, Bi. 629, De S. 161)

As usual, the refrain appears as the heading of the poem. This is borrowed from the almost identical verse which occurs towards the end of the *Unethaneh Toqef* composition. The idea that God waits patiently, until man's last moment of life, in the hope that the evil decision may be reversed, is based upon the verse, 'Say to them, As I live, says the Lord God, I have no pleasure in the death of the wicked, but that the wicked turn from his way and live' (Ez. 33:11).

This composition, also from the pen of Meshullam ben Kalonymos, follows an alphabetical acrostic pattern, though it is unrhymed. It belongs to the genre of *tokheychah* (literally 'reproof'), didactic poems which offer guidance as to right conduct and the development of an appropriate moral philosophy of life. They are written in the spirit of the Wisdom literature, and have a particular affinity with many passages in the books of Job and Proverbs.

The poem opens with a quotation based upon Job 15:14, 'What is man that he can be clean, or he that is born of a woman that he can be righteous?' The second line offers a moralistic maxim to reinforce this assertion of the total vanity of the human estate: 'If the fire can consume fresh trees, how much more easily will it devour dry grass?' The 'fresh trees' stand, metaphorically, for the righteous; the 'dry grass' for the wicked.

In the lines commencing with the letters *zayin* and *cheth*, Meshullam skilfully employs the natural alliteration offered by the flexibility of Hebrew roots, which, by a slight change of vowel, convey a variety of related ideas. Thus: 'Let every creature (*yetziyr*) consider this, and no impulse (*yeytzer*) will lead him astray to sin against the Creator (*yotzeyr*). The womb (*be'eyro*) is his origin, the grave (*boro*) his destiny, and his Maker (*bor'o*) will examine man's account.'

This is continued in the following line: 'Impurity (*tamey'*) flows from his flesh; he defiles himself (*mittammey'*) after his death.'

Having asserted that man is of little consequence, and in no position to think that he can delude his Maker, the poet reminds us that only by accumulating good deeds, acquiring knowledge and leaving behind a good name can we defy death, by bequeathing to posterity a heritage of inspiration and constructive endeavour. If we succeed in achieving that, then indeed, 'the day of death is better than the day of birth'. For on that day we can look forward, with eager anticipation, to having God, at our side, pointing out for us exactly where we succeeded in making our finest and most enduring contribution to life.

אֲחַדְתָּ יוֹם זֶה בַּשָּׁנָה

You have chosen this one day in the year
(Ro. 57, Bi. 631, De S. 163)

In this poem Meshullam employs a complex double pattern
of alphabetical acrostics. The first line of each couplet
follows the ordinary alphabetical acrostic sequence,
whereas the second lines follow a reverse alphabetic acrostic (*Tashraq*, etc.).

The opening line reminds God that he has established
this day as 'a healing balm for the lily (*shoshanah*)'. This is
a popular metaphor for Israel, as first used in the Song of
Songs (2:2): 'As a lily among brambles, so is my beloved
among the maidens.'

In the second stanza attention is drawn to the therapeu-
tic value of prayer and songs of praise, which, after the
destruction of the Temple, provided emotional and spiritual solace to the dispersed nations, while vicariously com-
pensating for the inability to offer sacrifices.

The poet invokes the merit of the patriarch Jacob, described in the Torah as 'the perfect man who dwelt in the
tent'[18] (*yosheyv 'ohaliym*), and he refers to the tradition that
the image of that patriarch is engraved upon the divine
throne.[19]

This tradition is based upon a midrashic rendering of
the tribute given to Jacob by his angelic adversary when
he changed Jacob's name to 'Israel': 'For you strove with
God (*sariytha 'im 'elohiym*) and prevailed.'[20] The Midrash
explains this as 'you became a heavenly authority (*sar*),
residing with God'.

The union of God and Israel is symbolised, according to
the poet, by the fact that 'God has joined his name to
theirs', a reference to the name 'Isra*el*', whose final syllable
represents the name of God. This merging of identity suggests a marriage relationship, which leads the poet to
refer to the beautiful imagery of Jeremiah: 'I remember the
devotion of your youth, your love as a bride (*'ahavath kel-
ulothayikh*).' For the sake of the rhyme, Meshullam inverts
the latter phrase to *kelulath 'ahaviym*.

אַתָּה הוּא אֱלֹהֵינוּ

You are our God

(Ro. 57, Bi. 633, De S. 164) (see p. 24)

מוֹרֶה חַטָּאִים

You teach sinners

(Ro. 58, Bi. 635, De S. 165)

In this poem we have the double name acrostic, *Meshulam biyribiy Qaloniymos chazaqq* (Meshullam son of Kalonymos, be strong!), formed by the initial letters of the first lines of each stanza, and, again, by the initial letters of the second lines. The third lines of the stanzas are taken from the first half of each succeeding line of *Ashrey* (Psalm 145), and with consummate skill the poet manages to fit all of this complex structure into a fine rhythmic and rhyming mould.

The poet emphasises the efficacy of regular worship, and he hails the fervour and love with which Israel addresses its praise to God. He highlights the four services of the Day of Atonement (excluding the *Kol Nidrey* service of the previous evening) and the seven 'praises'. This is an allusion to the verse 'Seven times a day I praise thee' (Ps. 119:164), which the Talmud[21] understands as referring to the blessings before and after the *Shema'*. In the morning we recite two blessings before the *Shema'* and one after; in the evening, two before and two after, making a total of seven 'praises'.

In the ninth stanza God is described as *Kopher 'eshkol* ('a cluster of henna blossoms'), imagery derived from the allegorical interpretation of Song of Songs 1:14. It is employed by our poet in the sense in which the Talmud explains the phrase *'eshkol ha-kopher* (which our poet has transposed), namely, 'the one to whom everything belongs (*sheha-kol shelo*) will grant me atonement (*mekhapper*)'.[22]

The poet looks forward to the restoration of Zion and the Temple service, but asks that, in the meantime, the prayers and confessions of his people should be as acceptable as the offerings of the ancient sanctuary.

אֶדֶר יְקָר אֵלִי

I will declare the glorious majesty of my God
(Ro. 60, Bi. 639, De S. 167)

This poem is introduced by two verses, intended by the
poet to serve, alternately, as refrains to each couplet of
rhyming lines. As we have observed, these are invariably
omitted in our editions from the body of the poem in order
to avoid monotony. In this instance, the poet uses the
refrains in order to construct a name acrostic. Thus, *melekh
shokheyn . . . levadekha melokh*, in the first line, and *ma'aziyn
shav'ah . . . le'ammo meychiysh* in the second, convey the
name *Meshullam*.

The first and second lines of each stanza are both constructed according to an alphabetical acrostic pattern, and
there are but three words to a line. Unlike Meshullam's
previous compositions, which are written from the stand-
point of the human petitioner and his efforts to secure
atonement at this time, this poem is theocentric, focussing,
almost exclusively, upon the general attributes of God. It
contains no specific allusion to *Yom Kippur* – other than
the reference to 'them that afflict themselves' – and the
references to God's indulgent and forgiving nature appear
almost *en passant*.

This description of God's attributes leans towards the
mystical, even though most of the references are drawn
from biblical phraseology. Meshullam introduces the
themes of the celestial court, God's 'tent', the *Seraphim* who
surround him, and, most significantly, *Chashmal*, a category
of angel whose name is derived from the famous vision of
Ezekiel[23] and which is referred to by the Talmud as having
figured in the early system of 'Merkavah mysticism' which
was based upon Ezekiel's vision. What is of particular
interest here is that the Kalonymos family, to which our
poet belonged, was the principal vehicle for transmitting
mysticism – and particularly *Merkavah* literature – to Germany; and it was this family which provided the leading
lights of the pietistic movement of *Chasidey Ashkenaz* which
produced a whole literature of esoteric material.[24] Thus we

may detect in this composition some early indications of the mystical propensities of a founding father of that distinguished tradition.

The Talmud[25] explains the term *Chashmal* as a contraction of three words: *ḥayyoth 'eysh memaleloth*, 'creatures who speak words of fire'. A second etymological interpretation is also offered by the Talmud: *chash*, 'they are silent (only when God speaks; otherwise)', *mal*, 'they speak incessantly.'[26]

אָנָּא אֱלֹהִים חַיִּים

Living God, inscribe for life
(Ro. 61, Bi. 641, De S. 168)

This poem is constructed according to a complicated alphabetical acrostic scheme, which is known as *at-bash*, wherein the first lines of each three-lined stanza follow the ordinary, forward alphabetical acrostic pattern, but the initial letters of the second lines follow a reverse acrostic. According to this scheme only eleven stanzas are required to provide acrostically for every letter of the alphabet.

It is believed that one of the primary reasons for building an alphabetical acrostic into a poem was to facilitate the learning of the poem by heart, as well as to prevent additions or deletions. Where the alphabetical arrangement is as prominent as in the *at-bash* scheme, all of these objectives would stand the best chance of being realised.

The poem is a simple and direct plea to God to have compassion on Israel, to accept her fervent prayers as if they had been sacrifices offered on the Temple altar, and to cleanse us of all our iniquity.

The poet describes Israel as *deveyqekha*, 'those who cleave to you', an image borrowed from Deut. 4:4 – 'And you who cleave (*ha-deveyqiym*) to the Lord your God are alive (*chayyim*) this day'. Because the Torah promises life (*chayyim*) as the reward for 'cleaving' to God, the poet climaxes each line of the opening stanza with the word *chayyim*.

In the second stanza the poet asks that the reward of life

be granted 'at a time of grace' (*'eyth ratzon*), by which he means immediately, while we are engaged in our *Yom Kippur* prayers. He is clearly thinking of the verse from Psalm 69:14, 'O God, let my prayer unto you be a moment of grace (*'eyth ratzon*)'.

Having already petitioned for our prayers to be regarded as if we had offered sacrifices in the Temple of old, the poet makes a further oblique allusion to this in the fifth stanza, simply by employing the word *ha-tzephuphiym*, 'we who are *crowded together* to worship you'. This verb is borrowed from the well-known passage in the *Mishna* which lists, as one of the miraculous occurrences in the ancient Temple, the fact that, although the people stood crushed together (*tzephuphiym*), they were yet able to prostrate themselves fully on the ground.[27] Thus, by applying this verb – charged with Temple association – to his own community, the poet reinforces his earlier plea.

In the ninth stanza God is described as *miqveh yisrael*, 'the hope of Israel', an image drawn from Jeremiah 17:13. The Rabbis gave a homiletical slant to this phrase, based upon the other sense of the word *miqveh*, namely, 'a ritual bath': 'Just as the *miqveh* purifies those who are unclean, so the Holy One, blessed be he, purifies Israel.'[28]

הַיּוֹם יִכָּתֵב

This day it shall be inscribed

(Ro. 61, Bi. 643, De S. 169)

Although this composition appears as an introduction, and is repeated as a conclusion, to the following composition, *'ayummah bachar*, it does not, in fact, have any poetic or thematic association with it. It is simply an exhortation uttered by the Reader in order to rouse his congregation to pray with greater devotion and concentration, and to consider fully the implications of this awesome day when 'life and death are recorded in the book of memorial'.

It is tempting to suggest that in some communities the Readers would proclaim this formula aloud to their congregants whenever the attention of the latter seemed to be on the wane, or decorum impaired, during the lengthy services of this day. Its recitation would certainly have been more decorous than the usual call for silence. Our theory gains support from the fact that the exhortation calls upon the congregation three times to be upstanding while no such instruction is, in fact, observed while reciting the following composition!

אֵימָה בָּחַר

His chosen sons of might
(Ro. 62, De S. 169)

This composition, inexplicably omitted from the Birnbaum edition, is attributed by Zunz[29] to Joseph ben Isaac ibn Abitur, one of the earliest Spanish poets and scholars (900–970 CE), who laid the foundation for the Golden Age of Spanish scholarship, particularly in the field of talmudic learning.[30] A tradition has it that he translated the whole Talmud into Arabic for the benefit of the Caliph al-Ḥakam II.

Joseph found himself at the centre of a bitter controversy over his candidature for the post of Rabbi of Cordova. This position became vacant on the death of the famous Rabbi Moses ben Chanokh (d. 965), whose leadership and erudition had enabled Spain to establish its own rabbinic authority independent of that of the Babylonian Geonim. The Community was split over the appointment into those supporting Joseph and those in favour of Chanokh, son of the previous incumbent. The Caliph supported the latter, and Joseph was constrained to leave Spain after having been excommunicated by the opposing faction, emboldened by the Caliph's support. The ban followed him wherever he wandered, and he suffered miseries. He was eventually befriended by a wealthy silk merchant called Jacob Ibn Jau who was a friend of the Caliph and who persuaded the latter to bring Joseph back to assume a specially created post of Patriarch of Spanish Jewry.[31]

Joseph devoted himself particularly to the creation of *Piyyutim*. He composed many poems for Sabbath and fes-

tivals, and he was the first Spanish poet to describe the
order of the ancient Temple service (*'Avodah*) in poetry.

The present poem follows the alphabetical acrostic pattern, ending with the poet's first name, *Yoseph*. Until the
letter *yod* the alphabetical pattern is easily discernible as
the initial letter of the first lines of each three-lined stanza.
From the letter *kaf* the acrostic appears more frequently,
at the beginning of the first and second lines of each stanza;
and from the letter *samekh* to the end of the poem it is
represented in the first *two* letters of these lines.

This poem was clearly composed to be inserted into the
morning *'Amidah*. Every third line highlights the fact that
it is at this particular service that mercy is sought; and the
plea is intensified by the repetition, throughout the poem,
of the three final lines – *bithephillath ha-shachar* ('in the
morning prayer'), *be'eyth temiyd ha-boqer* ('at the time of the
morning sacrifice') and *bezo'th tephillath yotzeyr* ('during this
early service').

אַךְ אָתִים בְּחִין לְפָנֶיךָ

They come pleading before thee
(Ro. 63, Bi. 643, De S. 170)

Another poem from the pen of Rabbi Meshullam ben Kalonymos. After the introductory word to each line – *'akh*
('truly') – the poet constructs his alphabetical acrostic.
Although in previous poems early editors have omitted the
refrain where its frequent occurrence tended to mar the
rhythm or to inject monotony, for some reason it was
retained here.

The poet describes Israel's total confidence in God's
mercy, and he begs that this will be speedily displayed so
that there will be an end to the nation's unbearable persecution ('Deliver them from the dire destruction').

In his account of the nation at prayer on this sacred day
he describes them as 'washed in purity' (*tevuliym*), a reference to the practice of attending the *miqveh* ('ritual bath')
on the eve of *Yom Kippur*.

וּבְכֵן אָמְרוּ לֵאלֹהִים

So, say to God
(Ro. 64, Bi. 645, De S. 172)

This alphabetical poem by Meshullam ben Kalonymos is a passionate outpouring of reverence and love for God. It calls upon Israel to praise the wonders of the Creator – 'So say to God, how wondrous are your works' (Ps. 66:3) – and it provides a catalogue of those wonders and attributes which are to be praised.

Most of the descriptions are taken directly from biblical phrases whose meaning is quite clear. Having already noted Meshullam's inclination towards mysticism,[32] it is not surprising, therefore, that he should have borrowed mystical references from the visions of Daniel and Ezekiel.

In the seventh stanza he describes God's throne as 'a blaze of flames', his servants as fiery beings, and a river of fire as encompassing them all. This description is derived from Daniel 7:9–10 – 'As I looked thrones were placed, and one that was ancient of days took his seat ... his throne was fiery flames, its wheels were burning fire. A stream of fire issued and came forth from before him.'

The image of God as 'a consuming fire' appears in the Pentateuch itself, though various attempts were made by ancient and medieval exegetes to soften the concept. Thus, the *Targum* on the verse 'For the Lord your God is a consuming fire'[33] renders, 'for the *Memra*' (manifested will) of the Lord your God is a consuming fire', and Nachmanides (thirteenth century)[34] explains it as merely a metaphor for the divine anger and retribution that is visited upon idolators.

One cannot escape the fact, however, that fire plays a part in many biblical accounts of the manifestation of the deity to man, such as in the episodes of the divine appearance to Abraham at the 'Covenant between the pieces',[35] to Moses at the burning bush,[36] in the pillar of fire that went before the Israelites by night[37] and at the Revelation on Mount Sinai.[38]

The ninth stanza continues the mystical theme in its

reference to 'those who bear his chariot' as being 'full of
eyes all around'. This is taken from the well-known description of the celestial court given in Ezekiel 1:18.

In the thirteenth stanza Meshullam includes a reference
to the doctrine of divine predetermination. The phrase
ha-kol tzaphuy, 'All is foreseen', is taken from the maxim of
Rabbi Akivah, 'All (man's fate) is foreseen, yet permission
(to act freely) is granted.'[39]

וּבְכֵן גְּדוֹלִים מַעֲשֵׂי אֱלֹהֵינוּ

And thus, great are the works of our God
(Ro. 67, Bi. 651, De S. 176)

This is also an alphabetical acrostic, though much tighter
in plan, with each phrase, rather than each stanza, commencing with a succeeding letter. It will be appreciated how
much more difficult it is to carry through such a literary
device.

The poem sings of the unique power of God, who, notwithstanding his transcendence ('he has made his habitation in heaven so high'), is, at the same time, capable of
manifesting himself immanently and personally ('He hastens to heed the humble prayers of his people').

There is one stanza, however, which appears, at first
glance, to have been misplaced, since it stands in stark
contrast to the rest of the poem, by castigating man and
his worthlessness, rather than praising God and his greatness. This is the penultimate stanza, commencing *ma'asey
'enosh* ('The works of man'). It will be immediately apparent that this stanza actually interrupts the alphabetical
progression of the poem, intruding between the stanzas
commencing with the letters *reysh* (*rachum limratzav*) and
shiyn (*shomey'a sheva'oth*). Furthermore, its structure differs
from that of the rest of the poem, in that it conforms to a
reverse alphabetical acrostic pattern, following the *Tashraq*
sequence.

However, although this stanza does give the appearance
of having been misplaced, it is, in fact, in the position
originally assigned to it by its author; and it is only as a

result of subsequent, and incomplete, editorial surgery that it has been left in its place with no fellow stanzas of the same ilk to indicate its original force and purpose.

In fact, in the original version of this poem, each stanza describing God's greatness was followed by a contrasting stanza dealing with man's guile, worthlessness and mortality. The first of the two stanzas was introduced by the words *ma'asey 'eloheynu* ('The works of our God'), and the contrasting stanzas were all introduced by *ma'asey 'enosh* ('The works of man'). The change of alphabetical structure was also significant. When describing God's works the acrostic worked forwards, to convey the idea of constructiveness and creativity; when describing man, however, a reverse acrostic was employed to denote his backsliding and contrariness.

At a later time some authorities secured the removal of all the *ma'asey 'enosh* stanzas from their position, presumably because they felt that to make a comparison of God with man was a highly unsatisfactory and irreverent method of highlighting God's attributes, which are absolute and infinite. They therefore placed all those stanzas together *at the end of the poem*, and for some time the *ma'asey 'enosh* collection of stanzas was recited as a separate poem.

Once the reputation of the *ma'asey 'enosh* stanzas had been impugned, it was not long before other weaknesses were discovered. It was realised that making it into a separate poem created more problems than it solved, since it now expressed a most forceful and uncompromising denunciation of man's estate, and thus played into the hand of the accuser on this very day when man's fate hung by a thread.

The difficulty was provisionally overcome by reciting those stanzas in an undertone. This, in effect, doomed their survival in the context of a repetition of the *'Amidah* which was prescribed to be recited aloud.

A later copyist, having deleted the *ma'asey 'enosh* poem because no one was bothering to recite it silently, decided to allow just the first stanza to remain, at the end of the *ma'asey 'eloheynu* poem, as a relic of its original presence.

Later editors, ignorant of all this editorial development, and assuming that the *ma'asey 'enosh* stanza stood as a single independent piece, removed it to its present position as the penultimate stanza. They did this for stylistic reasons, because, contextually, it fitted in best there, qualifying the preceding phrase which made reference to God's human creatures (*kol ma'asav*).[40] The inserted stanza constituted, therefore, an apt definition of the true nature of those creatures.

However, all the difficulties were still not resolved, for it was then realised that the introductory key phrase, *ma'asey 'eloheynu* ('The work of our Lord') could hardly follow on immediately after that chronicle of man's shortcomings, as it might be construed as a criticism of God for creating a weak humanity! A later editor wisely solved this problem by adding the word *'aval* ('but') at the beginning of the phrase. The sense is now clarified: man's actions are, indeed, base and unworthy, 'but the work of our Lord' – in sublime and total contrast – is unique and exalted.

Our recitation of the *ma'asey 'enosh* stanza in an undertone thus goes back to one of the early stages of this editorial saga, when the whole collection of the original *ma'asey 'enosh* stanzas were all recited silently.

הָאַדֶּרֶת וְהָאֱמוּנָה

Majesty and faithfulness are his
(Ro. 70, Bi. 657, De S. 181)

This alphabetical litany originated in a genre of early esoteric literature – the *Heykhaloth* – which has been attributed to the talmudic schools of Rabbis Akivah and Ishma'el (first–second century CE). They were composed in order to induce a state of ecstasy on the part of members of the select mystical fraternity as they embarked upon their spiritual exercises in order to receive revelations of the heavenly *merkavah* ('chariot'). This particular hymn is taken from the work *Heykhaloth Rabbathiy* which contains some of the earliest extant *Piyyutim*.

Tradition has it that Rabbi Akivah heard the angels

singing these songs as he approached the divine chariot, and that he was taught there the full import of its mystical connotation. Rabbi Ishma'el asserted that God is more enthralled when these hymns are sung by Israel than by the angels; and it was on the strength of these assertions that a selection of these hymns has been included in our liturgy. Rudolph Otto[41] has designated these as 'numinous hymns', that is hymns which seek to express in words the atmosphere of mysterious awe – the *mysterium tremendum* – which God's presence generates.

Gershom G. Scholem, in his celebrated book *Major Trends in Jewish Mysticism*, observes that

almost all the hymns . . . reveal a mechanism comparable to the motion of an enormous fly-wheel . . . and within them the adjurations of God follow in a crescendo of glittering and majestic attributes, each stressing and reinforcing the sonorous power of the world. The monotony of their rhythm – almost all consist of verses of four words – and the progressively sonorous incantations induce in those who are praying a state of mind bordering on ecstasy.[42]

This last point is of particular importance; for a mere reading of the translation of this hymn, with no sense for the rhythm to which these lines conform in the original, or knowledge of the mystical exercises to which they originally provided a stimulus, will leave one mystified as to the strange poetic judgment which accorded this repetitive composition a place in our liturgy.

וּבְכֵן ••• וּבְכֵן

And thus . . . And thus . . .
(Ro. 71–7, Bi. 659–63, De S. 182–9)

The succeeding collection of seven hymns, six of which commence with the word *uvekheyn*, all belong to the same genre of 'numinous poems' as *Ha'addereth veha'emunah*. Their insertion at this stage of the *'Amidah* – leading up to the recitation of the *Qedushah* ('Sanctification') – is on account of the fact that the dominant characteristic of this genre is its preoccupation with the concept of God's holiness (*qedushah*) which these hymns attempt to represent and capture in words. Indeed, the kernel of the *Qedushah* – the triple affirmation of God's holiness (*qadosh qadosh qadosh* . . .)[43] – may be considered the climax of the mystic's ecstatic experience.

These hymns, and the mystical spirit they generated, even left their imprint upon the Sephardi version of the *Qedushah* composition itself:

A crown will your myriad angels on high present to you, O Lord our God, together with your people Israel in their earthly assemblies. Together they will recite your triple sanctification.

The scene of the *Qedushah*[44] is set in the heavenly court where the angels are addressing their praises. These 'numinous poems' set the mood for the *Qedushah* by offering a mystical description of the nature of those various categories of angels and their particular modes of praise, as well as by utilising the phraseology of the *Qedushah* for their key words. Thus the hymn *Uvekheyn to'oratz vethuqdash*[45] – 'And thus you are revered and sanctified' – is constructed out of the opening words of the *Qedushah*: *Na'ariytzkha venaqdiyshkha* ('we will revere you and sanctify you'). The following hymn, *leyosheyv tehilloth*[46] – 'Unto the One who is enthroned amid praises' – is similarly inspired by the statement in the opening verse of the *Qedushah* that Israel employs 'the very same mystic utterance as the holy *seraphim*' (*sod siyach sarphey qodesh*). That hymn attempts, therefore, to give expression to that unity of direction and activity which exists between the heavenly and earthly choristers. They truly share the praise of God: The Angels 'say *qadosh*' and Israel responds with *barukh*.

The succeeding hymn, *Uvekheyn seraphiym 'omdym lo* ('And thus *seraphim* stood by him'), opens with a phrase – *zeh 'el zeh sho'aliym* – borrowed directly from the *Qedushah*: *mesh-*

orthav sho'aliym zeh lazeh. It also takes up another of the
Qedushah themes, that of the angels themselves being unable
to determine the precise locus of God's glory: *'ayyey 'eyl
'eyliym* ('Where is the supreme God?'). The reason for this
is their failure to comprehend the panentheistic concept,
that 'the Universe is not where God is located, but he is
the location of the Universe'.[47]

The refrains of this hymn: *seraphiym 'omdiym . . . sheysh
kenaphayim*, etc., from Isaiah 6:2, and *veqara' zeh 'el zeh . . .
qadosh qadosh qadosh*, etc., from 6:3, provide an appropriate
lead-in to the *Qedushah*.

וּבְכֵן לְךָ הַכֹּל יַכְתִּירוּ

(Ro. 77, Bi. 661, De S. 189) (see p. 28)

THE *QEDUSHAH*
(Ro. 78, Bi. 663, De S. 190)

We have referred above to the themes from the *Qedushah*
which have infused the previous collection of hymns. In
order finally to seal this link, the key word of each of those
hymns – *uvekheyn* – is employed again as an introduction to
the *Qedushah* itself: *Uvekheyn ulekha tha'aleh qedushah*.

For fuller treatment of the *Qedushah* prayer, the reader
should consult the standard commentaries on the daily
prayer book.[48] We shall confine ourselves to but two
aspects: one literary, the other historical.

Within the *Qedushah* we have a literary device which has
been defined as 'a *chain technique*, which always links the
last words of the *chazan* with the first words of the congregational responses'.[49] Thus, the last word of the congregational response, *melo' khol ha'aretz KEVODO*, becomes the
first word of the next statement by the reader: *KEVODO
maley' 'olam*. The penultimate word of the same sentence,
barukh, is also taken up as the opening word of the next
phrase. Similarly, the final word of congregational response,
mimmeqomo, becomes the opening word of the next line recited by the Reader; and the same 'chain technique' con-

tinues with the subsequent sentences ending with the words
shema' (*'omriym*), *'echad* and *ledor vador*. Eric Werner, who
describes this chain technique as 'a kind of climactic parallelism', states that it is a most ancient form of semitic
praying.[50]

The insertion into the *Qedushah* of the opening verse of
the first paragraph of the *Shema'*, as well as the last line of
its third paragraph (*'ani adonay 'elokeykhem*), calls for some
explanation. Its origin has been associated with the persecution of the Jews of Babylon by the Persian King, Jezdegaard II (*circa* 455 CE). Among his attempts to curb
even private religious practices was the banning of the
Shema', since its emphasis on God's absolute unity was
construed by the dominant Zoroastrian religion as a denial
of their belief in a dual deity, of good and evil.

The Rabbis of the day were forced to accede to the
removal of the *Shema'* prayer from its usual position in the
liturgy. However, in order to keep alive its recitation, they
smuggled a reference to it into the *Qedushah*, by reciting
just its first and last lines. Presumably these were recited
rapidly and in an undertone so as to be inaudible to the
ear of any Persian inspectors.

During the period of the persecution the *Shema'* would
have been indicated in this way during every *Qedushah*, on
weekdays and Sabbaths. Once the political climate im-
proved, and the decree outlawing its recitation was relaxed,
the custom of including these two verses from the *Shema'*
was abandoned in the case of every *Qedushah*, except that
of *Musaph*. It was retained in this service in order to preserve a record of the deliverance from that particular persecution. The choice of *Musaph* was because the *Shema'* is
not prescribed for that service, and thus no unnecessary
repetition was involved in its recitation.[51]

וּבְכֵן תֵּן פַּחְדְּךָ

And now impose your awe
(Ro. 79, Bi. 665, De S. 193) (see p. 29)

קָדוֹשׁ אַתָּה

You are holy
(Ro. 80, Bi. 665–7, De S. 193–4) (see p. 30)

סְלִיחוֹת

Penitential prayers
(Ro. 81–98, Bi. 669–85, De S. 196–229) (see pp. 125–7, 166–7)

אָבִינוּ מַלְכֵּנוּ

Our father, our King
(Ro. 104, Bi. 695, De S. 236) (see pp. 32–4)

READING OF THE LAW
(Ro. 110–16, Bi. 711–23, De S. 244–54)

The Torah reading (Lev. 16) describes in detail the preparation to be made by Aaron, and all future High Priests, before they entered the Holy of Holies on this sacred day to make atonement for the whole house of Israel.

One cannot atone for others before one's own forgiveness has been secured. Hence a special offering had first to be made on behalf of the High Priest and his own family.

The ritual of the 'goat to 'Aza'zeyl' is described. That goat, symbolically carrying with it the sins of the nation, was cast out into the desert. Two goats were originally selected. The choice of which one was to be used as a sacrifice to God and which was symbolically to be invested with sin depended solely upon the drawing of lots – perhaps indicating how one chance circumstance, experience or association can so easily affect the whole course of our lives, for good or otherwise.

The Torah tells us: 'In the seventh month, on the tenth of the month, you shall afflict your souls. . . .' From the latter phrase our Rabbis inferred five kinds of 'afflictions' which one must experience on *Yom Kippur*. These are abstention from (i) eating, (ii) drinking, (iii) perfuming, (iv) wearing leather shoes and (v) cohabitation.

In the Haphtarah Isaiah expresses the sublime spiritual paradox: that the God who is 'high and lofty' and 'who dwells in the heights' is joined there by – 'the crushed and lowly of spirit!' They are the ones whose companionship God seeks out.

The prophet goes on to castigate mere outward and superficial expressions of piety and fasting. God is impressed only by practical acts of kindness, charity, concern and moral courage, not by how low we can bow down. God is unimpressed by an annual homage; he seeks a more regular dialogue, particularly through the 'delight of Sabbath observance'.

MEMORIAL OF THE DEPARTED

הַזְכָּרַת נְשָׁמוֹת

Memorial of the departed

(Ro. 118–20, Bi. 727–33, De S. 256–9)

At this moment, those who have lost near relatives stand in silent and nostalgic contemplation, entering into the serious spirit of *Yizkor*. *Yizkor* means 'remembering'. But do we ever forget those precious people whose absence has left such a void in our lives? So is this special memorial service really necessary?

The truth is that nature cushions us from morose preoccupation with thoughts about the dead, however precious they were to us. Thus, although visions of our loved ones, and recollections of their actions and words, do periodically flit through our minds, yet, generally, these thoughts have to jostle with competing impressions and experiences while we are being distracted with other activities or conversations. Not so during *Yizkor*. At this moment the departed are given our complete attention – a consecrated attention – as befits their immortal spirit.

Then again, how infinitely more meaningful and symbolic it is to remember the departed in Synagogue, on a *Yom Tov*, in the context of a sacred prayer, making mention of their personal Hebrew names. And all this in an atmosphere of whispered reverence.

We do believe that there is a world beyond the grave, that death is, indeed, a starlit strip between the companionship of yesterday and the reunions of tomorrow, and that, just as we sometimes breathe a sigh of relief when awakening out of a nightmare, so it will be the moment after death.

Colonel David Marcus, who created the Army of modern Israel, had this to say about death:

I am standing upon the seashore. A ship at my side spreads her white sails to the morning breeze and starts for the blue ocean. She is an object of beauty and strength, and I stand and watch her until at length she is only a ribbon of white cloud just where the sea and sky come to mingle with each other.

Then someone at my side says, 'There, she's gone!' Gone where? Gone from my sight – that is all. She is just as large in mast and hull and spar as she was when she left my side, and just as able to bear her load of living freight to the place of destination. Her diminished size is in me, not in her!

And just at the moment when someone at my side says, 'There, she's gone!' there are other voices ready to take up the glad shout, 'Here, she comes!' And that is dying!

'The dead cannot praise God' (Ps. 115:17). However overwhelming is the volume of our grief, especially if our bereavement has been fairly recent, we must still praise God – on behalf of the dead. By so doing, we acknowledge that death is a fact of life, that it is a law, not a punishment, that it is as necessary to the constitution as sleep, and that we shall, assuredly, rise refreshed in the morning.

The memorial prayers are also recited on the last day of Passover, the second day of Pentecost and the eighth day of Tabernacles (*Shemiyniy 'Atzereth*). It might seem inappropriate to detract from the joy of these festivals by reciting a prayer which inevitably promotes sadness and tears. The Rabbis, however, looked more deeply at the psychological effect of their institutions, a fact which explains, for example, the permission to observe a private fast on a Sabbath which they granted to those who had experienced bad dreams. The rationale was that the fast actually restored peace of mind and promoted happiness (*'oneg*) by eradicating the deep-seated fears which were responsible for the bad dreams. It therefore actually aided the troubled person to enjoy the pleasure of the Sabbath.[1] Similarly were our sages aware that to shed a silent tear, and recall one's dear

ones through *Yizkor*, actually had a beneficial and thera-
peutic effect, and that, by releasing the emotions, one's
residual grief was definitely dispelled. For this reason –
totally in consonance with modern views on the psychology
of bereavement – they did not see any conflict between the
recitation of *Yizkor* and the joyous experience of a festival
day.

It was in the context of the liturgical ritual of *Yom Kippur*
that the very practice of reciting a memorial prayer for the
departed[2] first arose. The *Shulchan 'Arukh* merely states that
'it was a custom to contribute charity on *Yom Kippur* on
behalf of the departed'.[3] Moses Isserles, quoting the Mordechai (thirteenth-century German halachic authority),
adds the comment, 'And we make mention of the names
of the departed souls, since they also obtain forgiveness on
the Day of Atonement.' This idea inspired another German
authority, Rabbi Jacob Weil (fifteenth century), to explain
the plural form *Yom Kippurim* (lit. 'Day of Atonements'), in
that it atoned for both the living and the dead.

The *Yizkor* service was clearly popularised in Ashkenazi
circles, who extended its recitation to the three other festivals. The honoured place it subsequently came to occupy
was probably the result of the tragic history of the
Franco-German communities, from the period of the Crusades to the end of the Middle Ages. The endless lists of
martyrs were carefully recorded and preserved in the *memorbuch* or *Yizkor-buch* of the various communities, and read
out at *Yizkor* time. In the course of time the lists were
expanded to include not only the martyred but all departed
members; and this enabled our custom, of reciting *Yizkor*
for individual relatives, to evolve. The *'El maley' rachamiym*
memorial prayer for martyrs of the holocaust and for the
heroes of the State of Israel's defence forces is, therefore,
more in line with the original function of this memorial
service.

THE *MUSAPH* SERVICE

הִנְנִי

The Reader's Meditation
(Ro. – omitted, Bi. 743, De S. Pt II, 1) (see pp. 42–3)

חֲזָרַת הַתְּפִלָּה

The repetition of the *'Amidah* by the *Chazan* (see p. 18)

מִסּוֹד חֲכָמִים וּנְבוֹנִים

From the counsel of the wise and understanding
(Ro. 134, Bi. 765, De S. 15) (see pp. 19–20)

שׁוֹשַׁן עֵמֶק

Lily of the valley
(Ro. 134, Bi. 765, De S. 15)

יוֹם מִימִים הוּחַס

The day pre-eminent above all others
(Ro. 135, Bi. 767, De S. 17)

צְפֵה בְּבַת תְּמוּתָה

Look upon those appointed to death
(Ro. 137, Bi. 771, De S. 19)

אֶשָּׂא דֵעִי לְמֵרָחוֹק

I will fetch my knowledge from afar
(Ro. 138, Bi. 773, De S. 20)

These four compositions, all from the pen of Eleazar Kallir, form one poetic unit, as is clear from their metric and acrostic structure. The first composition forms the acrostic

Shabbat Shabbaton ('Sabbath of Sabbaths'), which is the biblical description of *Yom Kippur* (Lev. 16:31). The second composition is created out of the acrostic *Yom Kippurim*, and the third forms the acrostic *Tzom He'asor* ('Fast of the tenth day'). The employment of this type of 'subject acrostic', drawing attention to aspects of the festival, is a departure from the usual pattern, wherein the poet constructs the acrostic poem either out of his name or out of the letters of the alphabet.

Kallir utilises these three acrostics to form the refrains of the fourth, and final, composition of this group, *'Essa' de'iy lemeyrachok*. The three acrostics are first set out together as an introduction to this composition, each introduced by the word *venaqdishakh* (Ro. 138, Bi. 771–3, De S. 20), before being employed, individually, as a refrain at the end of every third line.

Since *'Essa' de'iy* constitutes the climax of this cluster of four compositions, the poet signs off, as it were, by employing the name-acrostic, *Ele'azar biribbi Kallir*. Purely in order to facilitate the employment of his refrains at least twice in the course of the poem, and not having enough letters in his name to cover the number of lines he required, he was constrained to repeat some of the letters of his name. For the sake of uniformity, he chose to repeat those letters which formed the first line of each of his three-lined stanzas. Thus, the first and second lines of each stanza commence with the same letter.

Although our Ashkenazi rite has these compositions for recitation during *Musaph*, the old Italian and Balkans traditions – as reflected in their respective *Machzorim* – prescribed their recitation during the *Shachrith 'Amidah*. The metric link between these four compositions is also apparent from the uniform length of each line-phrase, comprising a mere three words.

אֱנוֹשׁ אֵיךְ יִצְדַּק

Can man be proved righteous?
(Ro. 136, Bi. 769, De S. 18)

The above four-poem cluster is interrupted in the Polish rite by the insertion of another composition, *'Enosh 'Eykh Yitzdaq*, constructed from an alphabetical acrostic, with five words to each line. This is a *Tokheychah*, a moral exhortation, drawing attention to man's worthlessness as he stands before the supreme judge. The opening sentiment, 'How can mortal man be proved innocent in the presence of his Maker?', derived from Job 9:2, is in line with the existentialist outlook of, say, Kierkegaard (1813–55), who viewed the human situation as one of homelessness and estrangement, and his prevailing mood one of despair and angst, as, facing the yawning abyss of the world, he contemplated his own worthlessness and insignificance, his limited intellect combined with his moral lethargy, all of which inhibit his grasp of true reality.

The poet parts company from Kierkegaard – as does the whole spirit of Judaism – in one major respect: whereas that distinguished Danish theologian and philosopher believed that man's only hope is to take a gamble, in fear and trembling and by a leap of faith, that on the other side of that leap he will find God,[1] the poet here assures the Jew that reality, peace and salvation is to be found on earth, by submitting to the Torah's way of life, 'in love, fear and purity'. The Torah alone can bridge that yawning abyss; it alone can 'resolve the dissonance of this troubled earth'.[2]

אִמְרוּ לֵאלֹהִים

Thus say unto God
(Ro. 144, Bi. 781, De S. 27)

This popular composition calls upon Israel to praise the wonders of the Creator: 'So say to God, how wondrous are your works', a verse taken from Psalm 66:3. It is infused with happy confidence, affirming God as the one who 'hastens the redemption of his people . . . speeds forgiveness to his community and fulfils for us all his promises'.

Nearly all the phrases and allusions are borrowed from the Bible – principally from the Psalms and Isaiah – and their meaning is clear. One phrase, however, has occasioned difficulty: *soleyach l'am zu bazo* (4th stanza), lit. 'forgiving this people with this'. The phrase *'am zu* occurs in the Song of the Red Sea (*'am zu ga'alta* – 'This people whom you have redeemed', Ex. 15:16) and in Isaiah 43:21 (*'am zu yatzartiy liy* – 'This people whom you have created'). But what sense can be made of *bazo* ('with this')? Various suggestions have been offered. Some interpret it as referring to the Torah; namely, God forgives Israel ('with this'), i.e. on account of Israel's merit gained through observing the Torah. The Torah is frequently referred to as *zo*, 'this', as in the liturgical affirmation *Vezo'th ha-torah*, 'And *this* is the law'.

Others explain it as referring to the merit of circumcision which was also accompanied by the demonstrative *zo* ('this') at the time it was promulgated to Abraham: *zoth berithiy* ('*This* is my covenant', Gen. 16:10).

The phrase could be explained far more simply, however, in the sense of 'forgiving this people *at this hour*'. The word *bazo* would then be elliptical for *bazo ha-sha'ah* ('at this time'). Finally, it could also mean 'through this'; namely, through this day of prayer God forgives Israel.

The passage is an alphabetical acrostic, each stanza commencing with a succeeding letter of the *'Aleph Bet*. The composition does, in fact, proceed all the way through the alphabet in this way, though the Polish rite, which we follow, has omitted all the eleven stanzas commencing with the letters between *Kaf* and *Shin*. The stanza commencing with the letter *Tav* (*Taqqiph*) is inserted to constitute a logical conclusion.

וּבְכֵן גְּדוֹלִים מַעֲשֵׂי אֱלֹהֵינוּ

And thus, great is the work of our God

(Ro. 146, Bi. 785, De S. 28) (see pp. 144–6)

וּבְכֵן לְנוֹרָא עֲלֵיהֶם בְּאֵימָה יַעֲרִיצוּ

Therefore in fear they reverence the Revered One

(Ro. 147, Bi. 788, De S. 30)

The authorship of this double acrostic poem has not been ascertained with certainty, though it is attributed to Yannai,[3] one of our earliest liturgical poets (seventh century CE) and principal representative of the old Palestinian school of writers of sacred poetry.[4]

The poet's theme, of the supreme and omnipotent God enthroned upon the adoration of the angels yet still desiring the praise of worthless man, was taken up by later *Payetanim* to become a recurring theme in their High Holyday compositions. In this poem the refrains themselves are intended to provide a justification for the greater pleasure God takes in the praise of humans than in that of the angels. Man has been granted freedom of choice. When he exercises this in favour of his Maker's will, that constitutes true praise – *vehiy' tehillathekha* ('In truth this is your praise'). The praise uttered by the angels is, on the other hand, simply a concomitant of the fact that – *umora'akha 'aleyhem* – 'your awe is imposed upon them'.

This poem belongs to the genre of 'numinous hymns' which we have described above,[5] wherein there is no development or progression of idea and no expression of religious doctrine. It nevertheless pulsates with a mesmeric rhythm, created by the unbroken regularity of the two stresses in each short line as well as in the alternating opening and closing refrains. When chanted against a background of drums and to the accompaniment of ritual dancing, this was the type of song which would have been employed in biblical times by members of the prophetic guilds in order to engender a trance to aid their emotional climb towards a mystical experience.[6] It is not dissimilar to genres of songs sung by primitive tribes as an accompaniment to their rhythmic dances, which were all impelled by a desire to communicate with the supernatural forces. The 'numinous poems' were transfused with adoration of God and were chanted by *merkavah* mystics as a stimulant to their esoteric exercises.

The greater the poet the more confidently he experimented with the classical biblical vocabulary, moulding and adjusting it to his poetic structure. In this poem a number of new Hebrew forms make their appearance. Thus, in the opening stanza we are offered a noun *qedach*, in the sense of 'light' or 'flame'. It was employed in order to rhyme with *qerach* ('ice'), and is derived from the verb *qadach*, 'to kindle a fire'.[7]

In the third stanza, the poet stretches the normal meaning of the biblical root *yakhach* ('to decide', 'prove', 'argue'), in order to create a noun *vekhach* in the sense of 'assembly',[8] parallel to *va'ad* ('council').

In the sixth stanza we also have the phrase *mill'uney mar*, 'from (man) steeped in bitterness'. This less impressive coinage (*l'uney*) was derived from the biblical word *la'anah*, 'wormwood'.[9]

The economy of words which the metre forced upon the poet meant that he was constrained to select phraseology that was pithy and pregnant with meaning. He certainly succeeded most impressively in this poem, and demonstrated thereby his total mastery of biblical usage, and his ability to cull the most apposite imagery from the most obscure and least-known passages of the Holy Scriptures, particularly in the books of Job and Isaiah.

וּנְתַנֶּה תֹּקֶף

We will celebrate the mighty holiness
(Ro. 149, Bi. 789, De S. 32) (see pp. 49–52)

קְדוּשָׁה

Qedushah
(Ro. 151, Bi. 793, De S. 36) (see pp. 27–3, 149–50)

וְכֹל מַאֲמִינִים

And all believe
(Ro. 152, Bi. 797, De S. 39) (see pp. 52–4)

וּבְכֵן תֵּן פַּחְדְּךָ

Now therefore, impose your awe
(Ro. 154, Bi. 801, De S. 42) (see pp. 29–30)

וְיֶאֱתָיוּ כֹל לְעָבְדֶךָ

All shall come to serve you
(Ro. 154, Bi. 801, De S. 43) (see pp. 54–5)

אַתָּה בְחַרְתָּנוּ

You have chosen us
(Ro. 155, Bi. 803, De S. 44) (see pp. 30–1)

וּמִפְּנֵי חֲטָאֵינוּ

But because of our sins
(Ro. 156, Bi. 805, De S. 45) (see pp. 55–7)

עָלֵינוּ

It is our duty
(Ro. 157, Bi. 807, De S. 48) (see pp. 57–9)

אֱ"אֱ הֱיֵה עִם פִּיפִיּוֹת

Our God . . . inspire the lips
(Ro. 158, Bi. 807–8, De S. 49–50) (see pp. 60–1)

אוֹחִילָה לָאֵל

I will hope in God
(*ibid.*)

THE *'AVODAH* – ORDER OF THE SERVICE OF THE HIGH PRIEST IN TEMPLE TIMES
(Ro. 159–68, Bi. 811–36, De S. 52–72)

אַמִּיץ כֹּחַ

You are great in strength

In most editions of the *Machzor* it is not easily recognisable that this *'Avodah* section – describing the *Yom Kippur* ritual in Temple times – is, in fact, one extremely long alphabetical poem, interrupted three times for prostrations and confession. The Birnbaum edition does, at least, commence each succeeding letter of the *'Aleph Bet* with a separate paragraph.

The author varies his alphabetical structure. Until the letter *Samekh* he utilises quatrains – four-lined stanzas – each line commencing with the same letter of the *'Aleph Bet*. For the letters *Samekh* and *'Ayyin* he provides stanzas of eight lines; from *Pay* to *Shin* he increases this to twelve-line stanzas and for *Tav* he provides no less than twenty-four lines.

The number of words per line is also varied, commencing with lines of five words, and, in a most unexpected place, near the very end of the poem and in the middle of his concluding name-acrostic, he changes to lines of four words. The author is the tenth–eleventh-century poet Meshullam ben Kalonymos, generally regarded as having been an Italian scholar, though his tombstone was discovered in Mainz, Germany. His name is interwoven to form the acrostic of the final twenty lines of the poem, which reads *Meshullam Biribbi Kalonymos Chazak*.

His poem commences with a survey of biblical history, beginning with the order of creation, the sin of Adam and Eve and their punishment, the slaying of Abel, the spread of Idolatry, the flood and the Tower of Babel. He refers to Abraham 'the friend of God, who made known His name in the world', and who was the founding father of 'a worthy and beautiful race'. From this people God chose Levi to perform his service, separating one particular branch of that tribe 'to minister in the Holy of Holies' as High Priest and to function as representative of Israel on the holiest day of the year.

This leads the poet into a description of the detailed sacrificial ritual, the immersions, order of robing and the formulae of confession, all as described in the talmudic tractate *Yoma'*.

אָנָּה הַשֵּׁם

O God
(Ro. 161, Bi. 815, De S. 54)

The High Priest, when invoking the name of God for his confession, employed the *Sheym Ha-mephorash*, the secret personal name of God, which was only expressed by the High Priest on this one occasion in the year and by the ordinary priests of the Temple when conferring the daily Priestly Blessing. At ten stages during the *'Avodah* the High Priest expressed the divine name. On hearing the name, all the priests prostrated themselves and responded *Baruch Sheym Kevod Malkhutho Le'olam Va'ed* – the response which was the Temple equivalent of our 'Amen'.

The personal name of God, containing the four letters (*Tetragrammaton*) *yod, hey, vav, hey*, is the one regularly employed in the Torah. The actual vowels that accompany those four letters, to give the name its authentic pronunciation, were never disclosed to anyone outside the High Priestly fraternity. This was not only on account of the sanctity which invested that proper name, but also for fear of it being invoked – and its mystical powers released – for unworthy purposes. The vowels accompanying the *Tetragrammaton* in our Hebrew Bibles are merely arbitrary, being borrowed from the word *'Adonay* ('Lord').

The Talmud[10] tells us that while the High Priest was enunciating the divine name, he took pains to ensure that the chanting of his fellow priests muffled the sound of his voice, so that no one could hear the divine name being distinctly expressed. It is conceivable that as soon as he had said the word *'anna'*, and was preparing to utter the divine name, the priests immediately began to prostrate themselves and to recite their response, so that it was not difficult for the High Priest to draw out the recitation of the name and ensure that it became muffled by the sound of the priests' response. The ordinary priests, themselves, could not even distinguish the name as it was uttered by their senior colleague. The great Rabbi Tarphon, a priest, tells us that he inclined his ear to try and catch the pronunciation of the High Priest, but to no avail.[11]

After the first confessional the *Piyyut* continues with a description of the ritual of selecting the two goats, one slaughtered as a communal sin-offering, the other let loose 'to *'Aza'zeyl*', symbolically carrying away Israel's sin into the waste desert, never to return.

וְיוֹם טוֹב הָיָה עוֹשֶׂה

The High Priest declared a holiday
(Ro. 166, Bi. 825, De S. 61)

The entry of the High Priest into the Holy of Holies was considered an act fraught with considerable personal danger; and it was, therefore, a moment of great relief – not only to himself but also to the Temple worshippers who regarded it as an auspicious sign – when he emerged safely after having made the great national confession.

Summoning courage from his successful mission, he would offer a prayer for national prosperity, security and blessing.

The version of High Priest's prayer found in our *Machzorim* is a poetic expansion of the versions found in the Palestinian and Babylonian Talmud.[12] Here it is cast into an alphabetical acrostic; and it may be more than coincidental that the word *Shanah* ('Year') occurs twenty-four times – a multiple of the number of months in the year. The number twenty-four may reflect the fact that the High Priest was praying for twelve months of happiness both for his own family and, in addition, for the whole community.

The special prayer for the safety of people inhabiting the Sharon Plain – 'that their house may not become their graves' – was necessitated by the fact that the heavy rains made the ground in that area unsuitable for building.

Houses were frequently washed away, and generally had
to be rebuilt twice every seven years![13]

סְלִיחוֹת – PENITENTIAL PRAYERS
(Ro. 169–84, Bi. 837–51, De S. 73–93)

Although, as early as the ninth century, the distinguished
leader of Babylonian Jewry, and pioneering authority on
our liturgy, Rav 'Amram Gaon, declared the *Selichoth* to be
an obligatory part of the Day of Atonement Service, they
have somehow failed to retain their status in the popular
imagination, and, during the past century, have even suffered omission in a number of Ashkenazi communities.
This has been blamed either upon *Chazanim* drawing out
the service in such a way as to leave no time for recitation
of *Selichoth* or on printers who, because of varying customs
governing their recitation, omitted them from their editions, apart from a reference to the fact that 'Selichoth are
recited here according to the custom of the particular
community'.[14]

Selichoth are prayers for forgiveness recited in the *'Amidah*
as a prelude to the *Vidduy* (confession). They are woven
around the 'Thirteen Attributes'[15] of divine mercy, on the
basis of a Talmudic tradition that 'there is a divine promise
that no prayer in which these Thirteen Attributes are invoked will fall on deaf ears.'[16]

Originally the *Selichoth* comprised only biblical verses on
the theme of forgiveness, which were said by the *Chazan*
before the congregational recitation of the 'Thirteen Attributes'. From the tenth century a special genre of *Piyyut*
grew up, with compositions especially made for insertion
into this section of the service. Three distinct types of
Selichoth were established: *Tokheychah* ('Rebuke') – drawing
attention to our guilt, worthlessness, sorry plight and desperate need for mercy and redemption; *'Aqeydah* ('Binding')
– describing the binding of Isaac, and imploring God to
grant forgiveness on the merit of that unique act of faith,
love and obedience; *Gezeyrah* ('Decree') – recalling the
tragic historical circumstances accompanying the various
decrees of persecution inflicted upon our distinguished
sages and communities.

Of the hundreds of *Selichoth* written under these three
categories, it was inevitable that different communities developed a preference for particular compositions. Some
communities were even known to vary their choice each
year, until, in the course of time, certain compositions
became favourites and won a permanent place. Our Polish,
Ashkenazi selection comprises two *Tokheychoth*,* one *'Aqeydah*** and one *Gezeyrah*.***

The second *Tokheychah* serves also as a personal devotional plea for the *Chazan* – a common introductory feature
for separate major components within a service.[17] This
should logically have been placed first, however, in the\
order of *Selichoth*. The *'Aqeydah* is alphabetically constructed
according to four-lined rhyming stanzas, with five words
in each line. The alphabetic arrangement is interesting: the
first phrases follow the normal alphabetical progression
from *'Aleph*, whereas the second phrases, which complete
each couplet, commence with *Lammed* and progress alphabetically from that letter. To mark the concluding stanza,
the letters *Kaf* and *Tav* are employed twice, after which the
author weaves his name – *Meir bar Yitzchak Meir* – into the
acrostic.

אֵלֶּה אֶזְכְּרָה

These things I do remember
(Ro. 178, Bi. 837, De S. 85)

This is one of the most poignant *Selichoth* of the *Gezeyrah*
type, describing the frightful persecution inflicted upon the
Jewish community of Palestine and its rabbinic luminaries
by the Roman Emperor, Hadrian. Having crushed the Bar
Kochba revolt (132–5 CE), Hadrian imposed unacceptable
edicts outlawing the study of Torah, the practice of circumcision and other basic observances, on pain of death. Many
great Rabbis and teachers suffered martyrdom as a result
of their heroic defiance of the edicts, though no talmudic

---

* *'Eyn Peh Lehashiyv* and *'Aniy Hu' Hasho'eyl* (omitted in Birnbaum).

** *'Eth Ha-brith ve-'eth Ha-Chesed* (omitted in Birnbaum).

*** *Eyleh Ezkerah*.

source records the fact of these particular leaders being tried and executed at *one and the same time.*

Bearing in mind other conflicting traditions regarding the names of the martyrs and circumstances of some of their deaths, scholars are of the opinion that legend is responsible for having created this particular dramatic situation which cannot have been strict historical fact.

This period of heroic resistance to the Roman conquerors inspired the creation of several midrashic legends and liturgical poems. The well-known lament *'Arzey Halevanon,* recited on the Fast of Av, is based upon the same theme, and our *'Eyleh 'Ezkerah* is actually prescribed in the Sephardic liturgy for recitation on that fast day!

Ever since the first great rebellion, which culminated in the siege of Jerusalem and the destruction of the Temple (70 CE), the Jews made several desperate attempts to throw off the Roman yoke. With each successive failure the Romans reserved their most intense vengeance for the great leaders of Jewry.

Our author, in order to heighten the dramatic effect, has merely condensed martyrological traditions associated with the great rebellion, the uprising against Trajan (117 CE), and those surrounding the Hadrianic persecutions, into one climactic event concerning the ten martyrs.

It has been suggested that the inspiration for the idea of the number ten came from a circle of mystics of the talmudic period who, in their attempt to link cause and effect, sin and its expiation, depicted the martyrdom of the ten great sages as an effect of the sin of Jacob's ten sons in selling their brother Joseph into slavery, which episode is referred to in the opening section of the composition.

The poet depicts the Roman tyrant as adducing an incontrovertible argument against the sages of his day to support his contention that they should stand trial for the crime of Joseph's brothers in selling him 'for the price of a pair of shoes'.[18] The irony underlying this charge is self-evident: in the absence of any valid and contemporary justification for oppression of the Jew, the antisemite has no compunction in fabricating a charge, even if it requires him to go back more than a thousand years for some evidence of guilt! The implications of this polemical 'midrash' on Jewish guilt for the crucifixion would not have been lost on medieval Jewry.*

THE AFTERNOON SERVICE

It is customary on Sabbaths and festivals to commence the *Minchah* service with *'Ashrey* and *Uva' letziyyon go'eyl*. On *Yom Kippur* these prayers are moved from their usual position to serve as an introduction to the *Ne'iylah* service. The purpose of this is in order that the two *'Amidahs* of *Minchah* and *Ne'iylah* should be separated from each other, so as to emphasise the fact that the latter is an independent service.

READING OF THE LAW
(Ro. 199–204, Bi. 885–95, De S. 116–25)

Amid the abundance of ritual which characterises *Yom Kippur* one can easily lose sight of the fact that it can often be far more difficult to arrive at an appropriate relationship with our fellow-men – particularly with members of the opposite sex – than with God. In our relationship with God one ought to be totally uninhibited; in our pursuit of appropriate moral conduct, however, self-control is necessary.

Hence, even on the holiest day of the year man is not allowed to ignore the area where his weak nature is generally most vulnerable, and for this reason the list of forbidden incestuous and adulterous relationships (Lev. Ch. 18) is read from the Torah.

Another, historical, reason has been offered for the choice of this subject for reading on *Yom Kippur*. In the early period of the second commonwealth *Yom Kippur* was a day when a romantic match-making ritual was enacted. The girls of marriageable age would dress up in white and dance in the vineyards, inviting the young men to select their life's partner.[1] A portion of the law which draws attention to the prohibited categories of marriage partners (*'arayoth*) was therefore most appropriate.

The Book of Jonah is read as the *Minchah Haphtarah*. It

expresses God's concern for all his creatures and his delight in their repentance. The pathetic attempt of Jonah to flee from his spiritual mission is but a reflection of what most of us do before the memory of *Yom Kippur* has had time to fade from our minds. Like Jonah, most of us are more interested in our own comfort than in what is happening to our less fortunate fellow human beings. Like Jonah, in times of crisis – as when he was swallowed by the great fish – we plead, pray and make firm resolve. When deliverance comes, however, we conveniently forget God – at least until the next *Yom Kippur*! In this respect, however, Jonah has indeed something to teach us, for when deliverance came to him, he did not forget God, but proceeded immediately to fulfil his mission.*

אֵיתָן הִכִּיר אֱמוּנָתֶךָ

The steadfast patriarch discerned your truth
(Ro. 215, Bi. 917, De S. 138)

This is an alphabetic composition in praise of the patriarchs Abraham and Isaac, the former who discovered God and disseminated faith, and the latter who demonstrated, by the *'Aqedah*, the extent to which faith must be exhibited.

The poem is divided into two parts: the first half – until the letter *lammed* – is employed as a poetic accompaniment to the first (*'Avoth*) blessing of the *'Amidah*; the second half of the poem is assigned to the second (*Gevuroth*) blessing. As the second section of the poem deals with the theme of life and death, which, at the *'Aqedah*, hung in the balance, it is most appropriately related to the subject matter of the second blessing of the *'Amidah*.

The line commencing with the letter *teth* states: 'He sustained the wayfarers (*'ovriym*) with your own food; he made known to passers-by (*shaviym*) that there is none like you.' This is an allusion to the midrashic tradition that Abraham would invite passers-by into his home, and, after having fed them, he would call upon them to thank the one

---

* On Jonah, see p. 93.

who provided the food. After their initial surprise that a host should presume to ask his guests for thanks, Abraham would explain that there was a God in heaven who was the true provider. He then proceeded to teach his guests how to recite Grace After Meals.[2]

The phrase *'ovriym ve-shaviym* actually means 'a wayfarer', 'traveller' (lit. 'those who pass one way, and who return home'), and it is indisputably in this sense that our poet is applying it. However, when used independently, the words may also mean 'transgressors' and 'penitents' respectively. The Routledge and Birnbaum translations have mixed the two meanings to give an incorrect rendering of the second phrase.

מֵאֹהֵב וְיָחִיד לְאִמּוֹ

The only child, beloved of his mother
(Ro. 216, Bi. 919, De S. 140)

This section of the above poem attributes the deliverance of Isaac from the *'Aqedah* to the merciful initiative of the angels rather than to the original divine plan. This idea was inspired by the actual biblical account which speaks of 'an angel of God from the heavens' calling out to Abraham to stay his hand.[3]

This poetic idea might easily be refuted by reference to the Ethics of the Fathers, which enumerates 'the ram selected by Abraham (in place of his son)' as one of ten things which were created on the eve of the very first Sabbath of Creation.[4] According to this tradition the deliverance of Isaac was uppermost in God's mind at the very dawn of creation.

Such a conflict of ideas will not perplex those familiar with the rich and variegated tapestry of midrashic folklore. Midrash is more a patchwork quilt than an integrated and uniform mosaic. It reflects the highly personal and vivid imagination of the talmudic sages as they dreamed their way back into biblical time to supplement whatever domestic, romantic, social and spiritual details the biblical chronicle had left to the imagination.

The literal meaning of the line *richapho rachum limromo* is 'the Merciful One spirited him (Isaac) away to his heavenly place', an allusion to the midrashic view of Rabbi Judah that Isaac actually died of fright as his father's sword approached his neck. However, when his soul heard the angel's command to Abraham not to touch his son, the soul re-entered Isaac's body, and he revived.[5]

The motive underlying this fantastic piece of folklore is in order to establish the personality of Isaac as an expiatory symbol, an idea reflected in the final line of this poem: 'Regard him as if offered in the Temple this day.'

אֶרְאֶלִּים בְּשֵׁם תָּם מַמְלִיכִים

Heavenly beings acclaim God in the name of the perfect man

(*ibid.*)

Having sung the praises of Abraham and Isaac in the previous composition, this poem completes the picture by highlighting the merit of the third patriarch, Jacob, described in the Torah as 'a perfect man (*Tam*) who stayed in the tent'.[6]

According to the Midrash, the image of Jacob is engraved on the divine throne.[7] The second line of the poem alludes to this idea, and depicts the angels as flocking to the throne solely in order to view the beauty of that patriarch's countenance.

'His children are standing like angels this day'. According to our Rabbis, on the Day of Atonement Israel stands like angels: free of sin, divorced from any preoccupation with their physical needs and totally absorbed in the praise of God. The practice of wearing white garments on *Yom Kippur* is also in order to present ourselves in the guise of angels, in order to win divine mercy.

The poem embodies an acrostic on the author's name: *'Eliyyah biribiy mordechay*, Elijah bar Rabbi Mordechai.

אֱמוּנַת אוֹם נוֹטֶרֶת

A people that preserves its faith

יְכַפֵּר וְיִסְלַח

He will atone and forgive

תְּפִלָּתֵנוּ מִמְּעוֹנוֹת

From your habitation accept our prayer
(Ro. 217, Bi. 921, De S. 140)

These three lines, as printed in our *Machzor* editions,
appear as brief, independent petitions, with no relation to
any poetic compositions. In fact, they each represent the
refrain lines of compositions that have been omitted from
our editions. A glance at the first line will actually reveal
the name acrostic *El'azar* (Kallir): *'Emunath . . . lema'ankha
'azor . . . ża'aqah ŕetzey.*

מִיכָאֵל מִימִין מְהַלֵּל וְגַבְרִיאֵל

Michael praises on the right hand and Gabriel
(*ibid.*)

This line constitutes the refrain verse of the following composition: *'Er'elley hod potzchiym*, which Routledge and De
Sola include, but which Birnbaum has omitted. The refrain
was intended to be recited after every fourth line (taken
from the angelic vision of Isaiah 6:2–3) which constitutes
the end of each stanza. To avoid monotony these were
omitted, apart from in the opening and closing stanzas.

Because the Isaiah passage refers to 'One angel calling
to another' (*veqara' zeh 'el zeh*), the poet mentions only two
representatives of the angelic hierarchy, Michael and Gabriel. In rabbinic lore there are actually four main categories of angels singing God's praises, the other two being
Uriel and Raphael. In the prayers prescribed for recitation
before retiring to sleep at night all these categories are
petitioned to keep watch over the individual: 'In the name
of the Lord, the God of Israel, may Michael be at my right

hand; Gabriel at my left; before me, Uriel; behind me, Raphael; and above my head the divine presence of God.'[8]

כִּי רְכוּבוֹ בָּעֲרָבוֹת

For his throne is in the heavens
(Ro. 218, Bi. 921, De S. 142)

This poem is by one of our earliest Palestinian poets, Yannai,[9] and was written as a prelude to the *Qedushah* prayer which is based upon Isaiah's vision of the heavenly throne. This poem sets out to enlarge Isaiah's rather narrow conception of a heavenly court wherein God's praise is confined. It achieves this through its references to the many celestial realms – all of which are referred to in the Bible – where God's attributes are equally manifested: *'aravoth* (heavens), *shechaqiym* (skies), *me'onah* (dwelling), *zevul* (habitation), *'araphel* (dark regions), *Shemey Shamayim* (highest regions), *Shamayim* (firmament).

In the second part of the *Qedushah* there is a shift of direction from the angelic arena to the earthly domain, wherein man praises and God responds mercifully. To correspond with this in our composition, the poet moves to describe the adoration of God that is expressed here on earth not only by man, but by every element of nature: the waters, soil, trees, mountains and hills.*

---

* For commentary on the remainder of the *'Amidah*, see p. 149 (*Qedushah*); 29–31 (*Uvekheyn teyn pachdekha*), 125–7, 166–7 (*Selichoth*); 118 (*Zekhor rachamekha*); 123–4 (*'Al cheyt*).

THE *NE'IYLAH* SERVICE

On Sabbaths and festivals we recite four services: *Ma'ariv*, *Shachrith*, *Musaph* and *Minchah*. *Yom Kippur* is the only festival when a fifth service, *Ne'iylah*, is added. In Temple times, however, *Ne'iylah* was recited on certain other occasions, notably on the special fast days instituted by the authorities, during periods of drought, in order to pray for rain. It also formed part of the order of service recited by the *Ma'amadoth*, the lay fraternities which corresponded to the priestly duty-rotas in the Temple. While the latter were officiating, twice a year for a week, in Jerusalem, the *Ma'amadoth* assembled to conduct a prayer vigil, which included four fast days, on which *Ne'iylah* was added.[1] The Muslim practice of reciting five daily services was almost certainly borrowed from that old Jewish tradition.

Ne'iylah is an abbreviated name. The full name of this service, as mentioned in the *Mishna*,[2] is *Ne'iylath She'arim*, 'closing of the gates', though the precise sense of this term was a matter of dispute in talmudic times. Rav understood it temporally, namely, 'the service recited (at sundown) at the time of the closing of the *heavenly* gates. R. Yochanan applied it, in its literal sense, to the service recited at the time of the closing of the gates of the *Temple*'.[3] Maimonides favoured Rav's explanation of the term.[4]

REPETITION OF THE *'AMIDAH* BY THE *CHAZAN*

The Ark is opened for the repetition of the *'Amidah*, and it remains open for the duration of the whole service. The open Ark ensures that the congregation remains standing – an appropriate posture for that most solemn moment when the divine judge is passing his final sentence upon us, and our spiritual exertions are to reach their climax.

The honour of performing this *mitzvah* of opening the

Ark (*Petiychath Ne'iylah*) is one of the most prized of the whole year. In many communities it used to be put up for auction, and the highest bidder would frequently present the honour to a worthy elder.

מִסּוֹד חֲכָמִים וּנְבוֹנִים

From the counsel of the wise and understanding
(see pp. 19–20)

אָב יְדָעֲךָ מִנֹּעַר

The patriarch who knew you from childhood
(Ro. 253, Bi. 977, De S. 192)

This alphabetical acrostic poem, by Eleazar Kallir, is employed here in a rather piece-meal manner, and only as far as the letter *lammed*. In certain Ashkenazi communities of Germany, however, the whole poem was recited. Our tradition has divided up (the first half of) the poem so that its first four lines (until the letter *daleth* in the phrase *degalav lavo'*) are employed in the first blessing of the *'Amidah*, its second group of four lines (until the letter *cheth* in the phrase *chusan berakhah*) supplement the second blessing, and its subsequent four lines (*teva' ziyv* . . . until *le'eyth qatz chaz vayyiyra'*) are included in the third blessing.

The poem is a tribute to the faith of the patriarchs, by whose merit Israel now petitions for mercy. According to the poet, Abraham's discovery of God's existence came in his early childhood, a statement derived from the talmudic view[5] that he was then a mere three-year-old. This is based upon the verse 'Because (*'eyqev*) Abraham listened to my voice and kept my commandments' (Gen. 26:5). The numerical value of *'eyqev* is one hundred and seventy-two; and the verse may therefore be understood as implying that for that period out of the one hundred and seventy-five years of his life[6] he kept God's commandments. Thus, at the age of three he must have already known God; and even at such a tender age he entreated God 'to let his descendants enter through this gate (of mercy)'.

In the insertion into the second *'Amidah* blessing, Isaac is described as 'the one called seed of his father' (*haniqra' la'av zera'*), a reference to Genesis 21:12 where God consoles Abraham, at his having to banish his son Ishmael, by informing him that 'through Isaac shall your posterity be proclaimed'. The continuation of the line (*veniphneh lasur mimmoqshey ra'*), 'And he turned aside from every evil snare', has been variously explained as referring either to the evil influence of Ishmael[7] or that of the daughters of the Canaanites[8] or to the episode of King Abimelech who was planning to abduct his wife, Rebecca.[9] The final line of that quatrain (*chusan berachah ba'asher zara'*), 'he was enriched by the blessing on his crops', would seem to support the last interpretation, as, immediately after the restoration of his wife by Abimelech, the Torah states, 'And Isaac sowed (*vayizra'*) in that land, and found in the same year a hundredfold; and the Lord blessed him' (Gen. 26:12).

שַׁעֲרֵי אַרְמוֹן

Gates of the Temple
(Ro. 255, Bi. 981, De S. 194)

This alphabetical poem calls upon God to open the gates speedily to Israel, though it is unclear which particular gates he has in mind: those of heaven, those of the Temple, or both. Again, we recite only the first half of this poem, until the letter *lammed* (*lelo' 'alman*).

קְדוּשָׁה
(see pp. 149–50)

וּבְכֵן תֵּן פַּחְדְּךָ ···· אַתָּה בְחַרְתָּנוּ
(see pp. 29–31)

אוֹ"אֱ וּמִי יַעֲמוֹד חֵטְא ···· מְרוּבִּים צָרְכֵי עַמָּךְ

Who could stand if you recorded sin – Your people's needs are many
(Ro. 260, Bi. 989, De S. 200)

A glance at the initial letters of each line will reveal that we have represented here only the concluding section of a

poem which is constructed out of a reverse alphabetical
acrostic pattern. Our composition commences with the letter *vav* and works backwards to the letter *'aleph* (*'Az ya'alu
veyir'u beruach nediyvah*), employing each letter twice for con-
secutive lines. Following on from the letter *'aleph*, the poet
weaves an acrostic on his name, *Shelomoh Ha-qatan*, that is
Rabbi Solomon ben Judah Ha-Bavli (tenth century). Solomon hailed from Babylon and appears to have lived for
a time in northern Italy before moving to Germany where
he fostered poetic activity and founded the great Ashkenazi
payetanic tradition.

His poem is a tender plea for acquittal to a God who –
in the words of Ezekiel, to which the poet alludes – 'does
not desire the death of a person but that he returns from
his evil ways and lives'.[10] It pleads also for an end to the
sufferings of Israel and calls for the bestowal of the divine
gift of intellectual enlightenment in order to understand
the Torah better, and, consequently, to appreciate more
fully the ways of God and the mystery of Jewish existence.

The stanzas commencing with the letter *mem* (*merubiym
tzorkhey 'amkha*), until the end of the poem, appear to run
on as an essential part of the main composition. In fact
they are the second half of a separate poem by Joseph
(Bekhor Shor) ben Isaac of Orleans, a twelfth-century
northern French Bible commentator, Tosaphist and poet.
These stanzas have been tacked on to the previous poem
upon which they seem to have been modelled. The differing
acrostic pattern of this section is clearly apparent. It is a
forward alphabetical acrostic, beginning with two *mem* lines
followed by one *nun* line, and maintaining this pattern for
alternate letters throughout the poem.

The beginning of this section – *merubiym tzorkhey 'amkha*
– is a quotation from the Talmud,[11] where it appears as
the formula of a plea to be recited when in danger of one's
life, at the approach of either wild beasts or bandits:

Master of the Universe,[12] the needs of your people, Israel,
are many and their knowledge slender. May it be your
will to provide for each and every one sufficient for his

livelihood . . . and to every individual whatever he is in
need of.

It is difficult to understand the precise relevance of this
formula to the emergency in question, for it appears more
suited to be recited as a prayer for livelihood when in
financial straits. Perhaps it was on account of its wider
applicability that our poet employed it here as a petition
for sustenance in the coming year.

The poet proceeds to lament the fact that the age of the
great composers of prayer has long since passed, and, lacking inspiring and eloquent *Chazanim* to lead the congregation, we have no means of achieving salvation from our
troubles through the medium of fervent prayer.

From the stanza commencing *Qadosh re'ey*, to the end of
the poem, the author speaks in the first person, clearly
adopting the role of a *Chazan* offering prayers on behalf of
his congregation. It is written in the style of the usual
Reader's *Reshuth*,[13] recited at the beginning of the repetition
of an '*Amidah*. As *Ne'iylah* does not have such a *Reshuth*, it
is conceivable that this section was originally intended to
serve that particular purpose.

It will be observed that the Birnbaum edition inter-
sperses the stanzas of this long composite poem with references to the Thirteen Attributes ('*Eyl melekh*).[14]

This seems to have been the original practice, which was
probably curtailed whenever time was short, since *Ne'iylah*
had to be concluded before nightfall. There are still a
number of varying traditions regarding the frequency of
the recitation of the Thirteen Attributes in this service.

אֶנְקַת מְסַלְּדֶיךָ

Let the cry of those who praise you
(Ro. 262, Bi. 997, De S. 204)

This single stanza, of four short phrases, is, in fact, merely
the opening verse of a poem, the rest of which was omitted
probably in order not to prolong the service. The rest of
the poem, which was included in the book of *Selichoth* used

in Lithuanian communities, bears the author's name-acrostic: *Siylano*. Siylano was the religious leader of the community of Venosa in southern Italy during the ninth century. He was also one of that country's first liturgical poets, disseminating there the traditions of the school of poetry in Palestine, and particularly that of Kallir whose style he clearly emulates.

There is an interesting, though tragic, episode in Siylano's life which is recorded in the famous Chronicle of Achima'atz (1034), a fellow countryman and poet. A visiting emissary, from the Jerusalem talmudic academy, gave a sermon in Siylano's synagogue in Venosa. As the visitor could not speak Italian, he supplied Siylano with a copy of his address for him to translate. The emissary later discovered that Siylano had doctored his translation in order to incorporate a vitriolic condemnation of his community. When the former returned to Jerusalem and reported the matter, it was decided to excommunicate Siylano for bringing the Palestinian representatives into disrepute, a situation which could affect the financial support upon which Palestine depended from the diaspora communities. The ban was later lifted as a mark of gratitude to Siylano for his vigorous support of the rabbinic authorities, through the medium of his poetry, in their struggle against the Karaite heresy.

יִשְׂרָאֵל נוֹשַׁע בַּיָי

Israel has been saved by the Lord
(*ibid.*)

Once again our *Machzor* quotes here only the opening stanza of a poem written by Shephatyah ben 'Amittai, ninth-century spiritual leader of Oria in southern Italy.

The penultimate stanza of the poem contains a plea for the destruction of Christian Rome (*Kalley Sey'iyr*). This may be related to the anti-Jewish decrees imposed by the Byzantine emperor, Basil I (867–86). Shephatyah was sent to the royal court at Constantinople in order to plead for the decrees to be rescinded. While there, he successfully exorcised an evil spirit from one of the princesses, in appreciation of which a reprieve was granted to his own and four other Italian communities. It is conceivable that this poem, with its opening sentiments 'Israel has been saved by the Lord' (Is. 45:17), might have been composed to mark this particular deliverance.

יַחְבִּיאֵנוּ צֵל יָדוֹ

He will shelter us in the shadow of his hand
(*ibid.*)

Once again our *Machzor* represents here only the opening stanza of a fairly lengthy poem written by Isaac ben Samuel of Dampierre in France, a prominent Tosaphist and one of the leading rabbinic authorities in the second half of the twelfth century. He is popularly referred to as *Riy Ha-Zaqeyn* (Rabbi Yitzchaq the Elder), and was a disciple of the renowned Rabbi Jacob (*Rabbeynu*) Tam.

The Lithuanian tradition included the whole of his poem in the repetition of the *Musaph 'Amidah*, whereas our Polish rite borrowed only the opening stanza. This stanza contains an acrostic on his first name *Yitzchaq* (*Ȳachbiy'eynu īẕeyl . . . C̄hon . . . Q̄umah*).

יַשְׁמִיעֵנוּ סָלַחְתִּי

Let us hear 'I have forgiven'
(*ibid.*)

This stanza is, again, merely the opening verse of a poem bearing the name acrostic of its author, Solomon ben Samuel. In the late thirteenth century he taught in a *yeshivah* in Acre, which in that period had become a distinguished centre of scholarship in Palestine, helped by the arrival of hundreds of Rabbis who made their way there after their expulsion from England and France.

Solomon was involved in a bitter controversy with the grandson of Maimonides, David ben Abraham, who held the office of *Nagid*,[15] and who sought to have Solomon excommunicated because of his widely publicised opposition to the teachings of Maimonides.

Solomon probably shared the tragic fate of the Acre community which suffered massacre in 1291 at the hands of the conquering Mamluks.

יְיָ יְיָ אֵל רַחוּם ....

The Lord, the Lord, a God full of compassion . . .

אֶזְכְּרָה אֱלֹהִים וְאֶהֱמָיָה

Lord I remember, and am greatly amazed
(Ro. 263, Bi. 997–9, De S. 204–5)

The Thirteen Attributes ('Adonay 'Adonay . . .), which introduce the poem *'Ezkerah 'Elohim ve'ehemayah* are intended to serve as a refrain, to be repeated after every four-lined stanza. To avoid monotony, as well as to save time, the refrains were omitted other than at the beginning and end.

The initial letters of each stanza are arranged to form the name acrostic *'Amitai*, a reference to the Italian poet 'Amittai ben Shephatyah (late ninth century). The Routledge edition has adopted a revised version of the second stanza, reading, instead of *Middath ha-rachamiym 'aleynu hithgalgeliy*, the phrase *rachamekha 'aleynu galgeyl*. Other reasons apart for preferring the original text, the revised version impairs the name acrostic by supplanting the letter *mem*.

'Amittai was the son of Shephatyah ben 'Amittai, author of the poem *Yisra'el Nosha' ba'adonay*.[16] Like his father, whom he succeeded as spiritual leader of Oria in Southern Italy, he wrote poetry to express his reaction to the persecution of his day, and, in particular, that imposed by the Byzantine emperor, Basil I.[17] In this particular poem these feelings reach their apogee, as he laments the fact that 'each town stands solid on its site, whereas God's own city is razed as low as the grave'.

The final stanza expresses a prayer that God, who responds to the anguish of his people, 'should place our tears in a flask that they may be preserved', to ensure that mercy is never withheld, particularly during periods of 'cruel decrees'.

רַחֵם נָא קְהַל עֲדַת יְשֻׁרוּן

Have mercy upon the whole community of Yeshurun

שַׁעֲרֵי שָׁמַיִם פְּתַח

Open the gates of heaven

We have already demonstrated the interrelationship of the *Selichoth* and the *Hosha'noth* recited on the festival of Tabernacles.[18] The presence of these two lines among the *Selichoth* of the *Ne'iylah* service is a further testimony to this; for these represent the opening and closing lines of a *Hosha'na'* composition (*'Az ke'eyney 'avadiym 'el yad 'adoniym*) recited on *Hosha'na' Rabba'*, the seventh day of Tabernacles. That entire *Hosha'na'* composition was certainly at one time recited during *Ne'iylah*.

אֱלֹהֵינוּ ⋯ כִּי אָנוּ עַמֶּךָ

For we are your people

אָשַׁמְנוּ

We have transgressed
(Ro. 264, Bi. 1001–2, De S. 206) (see pp. 119–122)

אַתָּה נוֹתֵן יָד לְפוֹשְׁעִים

You give the hand to transgressors
(Ro. 265, Bi. 1003, De S. 207)

Already in Geonic times it was regarded as inappropriate to recite the detailed confessional of *'Al Cheyt'* in the *Ne'iylah* service. The day has all but passed by now and it can safely be assumed that we have abased ourselves and acknowledged our misdeeds as fully as possible. In its place, therefore, the two compositions *'Attah notheyn yad* and *'Attah hivdalta 'enosh* were introduced, the first of which

makes a specific reference to the act of confession: 'You
have taught us, O Lord our God, to make confession before
you of all our iniquities.' That *'Attah notheyn yad* stands in
place of the detailed confessional *'Al Cheyt'* may also be
seen from the verse which precedes the former: *halo' kol
ha-nistaroth vehannigloth 'attah yodey'a* ('Do you not know all
that is secret or revealed?'). An examination of all the other
services wherein *'Al Cheyt'* is recited will confirm that that
confessional is always introduced by such a statement
affirming God's knowledge of man's secret thoughts as well
as his revealed actions.[19] Furthermore, the paragraph
which introduces *'Al Cheyt'* always commences with the
phrase *'Attah yodey'a* ('You know'); and it is precisely this
phrase which precedes our *'Attah notheyn yad* composition.

From the talmudic description of the *Ne'iylah 'Amidah*[20]
we learn that, at that period, immediately after *'attah vechartanu*,[21] the Reader continued with the passage *mah 'anu
meh chayyeynu*, which is the second half of the composition
'attah notheyn yad. We may therefore regard the latter as
having been composed as an introduction to the section
mah 'anu.

The phrase *'attah notheyn yad* is rendered in all our translations as 'You reach out your hand', to convey the idea
that God attempts to provide opportunity, help and incen-
tive for transgressors to repent. However, a medieval commentary[22] draws attention to the fact that *yad* may also
mean 'ability', 'freedom of action',[23] thus conveying the very
opposite idea, that God actually enables transgressors to
defect from the righteous path by not restricting their freedom of choice. This interpretation calls to mind the famous
talmudic maxim: 'Whosoever seeks to purify himself finds
that heaven assists him; whoever seeks to defile himself
finds that heaven opens the door for him to enter (the
impure regions).'[24]

There is one statement in this composition – and repeated in the next paragraph – which appears problematic:
'You have taught us ... to make confession before you
... so that we may cease to perpetrate robbery (*'osheq*).'
Why was just robbery singled out from all other sins? The

answer is that the author was clearly influenced by the talmudic view that desire for money (*chemdath mamon*) is the most potent of all seductions. 'The majority sin through theft (i.e. dishonest dealings)', say the Rabbis, 'and the rest through sex.'[25] The Rabbis further assert that, of all the sins perpetrated by the generation of the flood, 'their final fate was only sealed because of the sin of theft'.[26]

Since *Yom Kippur* only atones for sins committed against God, not for those against our fellowman,[27] this reference to theft or dishonesty is an implied call for us to determine to make restitution, or pay compensation, to those of whom we may have taken wrongful financial advantage.

אַתָּה הִבְדַּלְתָּ אֱנוֹשׁ מֵרֹאשׁ

You set man apart from the beginning
(Ro. 265, Bi. 1005, De S. 207)

The previous composition ends with a rather deprecatory assessment of human worth: 'for man is in no wise superior to the beast, for all is vanity.' In order to ensure that that teaching is not distorted into a philosophy of nihilism, our composition hastens to point out that, for all man's short-comings (as implied in the word *'enosh*),[28] yet, 'God set him apart' from the beasts, and endowed him with an intellectual and moral spirit. This is the import of the word *vata-kiyreyhu*, 'you gave him perception'.[29]

The second verse – 'For who can say to you: "What are you doing?" Even though man be righteous, what can he give you?' – is difficult to relate to its context, being, in any case, a combination of two totally independent biblical verses.[30] It is probable that, having acknowledged man's uniquely independent intellectual capacity, the author was seeking to ensure that this did not lead to a doctrine of human infallibility. Although God 'set man apart (intellectually) from the beginning', yet man must realise the limitations of his intellect, and must not seek to ask critically of God, 'What are you doing?' And just as man must not demand justification of God's actions, so must he realise that 'even though man be righteous, what can he give you?'

Human righteousness is not a reciprocated gift which man condescends to bestow upon God for his kindnesses to us. Righteousness, in addition to being a Divine and moral imperative, is also a gift to ourselves; it is an augmentation of the quality of living.

Having quoted the verse 'What can he (man) give you' (Job 35:7), the author is moved to draw attention to all the gifts bestowed upon us by God. Hence the continuation, *vatiteyn lanu* ('And you have given to us . . .'), which refers specifically to the gift of *Yom Kippur*, and, with it, the incomparable benefit of atonement and salvation.

שְׁמַע יִשְׂרָאֵל

Hear, O Israel

בָּרוּךְ שֵׁם כְּבוֹד מַלְכוּתוֹ

Blessed be the name of his glorious Kingdom

יי הוּא הָאֱלֹהִים

The Lord is God!
(Ro. 271, Bi. 1017, De S. 215)

For all that we have spent a whole day reciting some very inspiring and interesting poetic compositions, we rightly climax our prayers with two of the most familiar and beloved lines known to the Jew: the first two lines of the *Shema'*. Following the recitation of this affirmation of faith in God the Jew sets off each morning to pursue his daily tasks with a commitment to the dignity and sanctity of labour. It gives him a sense of God's presence in every human situation, with the ethical and moral responsibilities which this imposes. These *Shema'* verses, when recited each night, also express the Jewish conviction that sleep is not oblivion, but rather the time when the soul experiences its spiritual refreshment: 'To him I entrust my spirit, when I sleep and when I awake.'[31] Thus, as *Yom Kippur* reaches its climax this jubilant public proclamation of the *Shema'* gives expression to our feelings of spiritual elation and our confidence that, our prayers having been accepted, God will watch over us by day and by night, and will bless all our activities with success throughout the coming year.

The *Shema'* verse is recited but once. Our authorities were sensitive to any repetition of this affirmation of faith in the one God in case it was misconstrued as recognition of the heretical concepts of duality or trinity. The second verse of the *Shema'*, which affirms the eternity of God's Kingdom, is repeated three times, corresponding to his sole sovereignty in the past, in the present and in the future.

The final verse – 'The Lord is God' – was uttered by the Israelites gathered on Mount Carmel to witness Elijah's vindication of the power of God over the prophets of Ba'al.[32] The two names of God in this, our shortest, affirmation, represent his two-fold manifestations: the first name signifying God's attribute of mercy, the second that of strict justice. We affirm, hereby, that whatever lies in store for us in the coming year – whether blessing or suffering – proceeds from a righteous God who has decided our fate through the most delicate equipoise of those two attributes.

The repetition of this verse seven times was viewed as a mystical farewell to the *Shekhiynah* (divine presence) which had descended from the seventh, and highest, heaven in order to be most accessible to Israel. Just as the seven-fold repetition of Psalm 47 on *Rosh Hashanah* escorted the *Shekhiynah* down to the throne of mercy,[33] so, in the same way, we now escort her on her return. In this spirit we sound the Shofar to accompany the ascending divine presence, in fulfilment of the verse, 'God ascends with trumpet sound, the Lord amid the sound of the shofar' (Ps. 47:6).

There are also other explanations of the blowing of the Shofar at this point. The most popular explanation, rejected however by Maimonides, was that it is to recall the ancient biblical institution of the Jubilee (fiftieth) year, which was inaugurated by a trumpet fanfare at the conclusion of the *Yom Kippur* of the forty-ninth year of the fifty-year agricultural cycle. In the course of time, the calculation of the Jubilee fell into desuetude, and because of the doubt as to which year was, in fact, the Jubilee, it became customary to sound the Shofar every year.

This interpretation, which links the Shofar blowing to an institution associated with our ancient homeland, has the benefit of providing, at the same time, an explanation of the final joyful shout, 'Next year in Jerusalem' – *Leshanah haba'ah biyrushalayim.*

NOTES

THE MORNING SERVICE – FIRST DAY

1 R. Shimon b. Zemach, Responsum no. 160; *Hagahoth May-muni*, Laws of the Sabbath, ch. 30.

2 Dan. 10:5–6; Enoch 87:2; Testament of Levi 8:1.

3 See section commencing *'illu phiynu maley' shirah* ('Though our mouths were full of song as the sea . . .'), Ro. 79, Bi. 167, De S. 96.

4 Its philosophical ideas seem to have been influenced by Saadya Gaon's famous treatise, *'Emunoth Ve-de'oth*.

5 Midrash *Shochar Tov*, *ad loc.*; Tal. *Ber.* 7ᵃ.

6 The Spanish and Portuguese (*Sephardic*) Jews pronounced this word as *Qerovotz*, as a result of which a popular interpretation was suggested, explaining it as an acrostic of the initial letters of the verse *Qol Rinah Viyeshu'ah Be-'oholey Tzaddiqim*, 'The sound of joyful singing and salvation in the tents of the righteous' (Ps. 118:15).

7 The *Piyyutim* evolved in Palestine under the influence of the great literary works of Midrash (third–seventh century CE), though it is impossible to determine exactly when the first composition of this genre made its appearance.

8 Composers of *Piyyut*.

9 On Yannai, see pp. 12–13, 52–3.

10 The term *Yotzer* is derived from the concluding formula of the first *Shema'* blessing: *Yotzer Hame'oroth*.

11 See his comment on Ecclesiastes 5:1.

12 Maimonides is bitterly critical of the *Chazanim* who 'are extravagant in praise, fluent and long-winded in the hymns they compose'. See *Guide for the Perplexed* (Friedlander, ed.), p. 86.

13 See Julius Guttmann, *Philosophies of Judaism*, pp. 172 ff., 351.

14 Tal. *R.H.* 10ᵇ.

15 Jer. *Ta'anith* 2:13 (66ᵃ).

16 Cf. *Shul. Ar., O.H.* 581:2.

17 Ex. 32:13.

18 *Ber. Rabb.* 56:5.

19 Gen. 27:1.

20 See Rashi *ad loc.*

21 Ezek. 1:5–7.

22 I Sam. 4:4, II Sam. 6:2, Is. 37:16, Ps. 80:2 *et al.*

23 Isaiah 6:2.

24 Tal. *Ket.* 104ᵃ.

25 See G. G. Scholem, *Major Trends in Jewish Mysticism*, pp. 57 ff.

26 Rudolph Otto, *The Idea of the Holy* (tr. of *Das Heilige*), ch. VI.

27 See Mishna *Berachoth* 5:4; Maimonides, *Hil. Teph.* 9:1.

28 Moses Maimonides, Joseph Karo, Jacob Emden and the Vilna Gaon were all vehemently opposed to the intrusion of *Piyyutim.*

29 Gen. 18:25.

30 Mid. *Vay. Rabb.* 10:1.

31 Mid. *Ber. Rabb.* 14:6.

32 Tal. *R.H.* 10ᵇ. Some commentators explain the final phrase of the poem – '*Tesher* on which she was visited' – as an allusion to the month *Tishri*. Others explain the word as 'a gift', the equivalent of *teshurah* (I Sam. 9:7).

33 Tal. *R.H.* 16ᵃ.

34 F. Heiler, *Prayer – History and Psychology*, tr. S. McComb (Galaxy Books, 1958), p. 355.

35 Austrian Jewish novelist (1833–1924), *Paradise, Parables*, 25.

36 This is precisely how Rashi (Tal. *Sotah* 40ᵃ) interprets the obscure phrase *'al She'anachnu modiym lakh*, found near the end of the *Modiym Derabbanan* prayer; namely, 'We give thanks unto you . . . *for having implanted within us the urge to give thanks.*'

37 Tal. *Ber.* 29ᵃ.

38 It occurs as the conclusion of the blessing *Borey' nephashoth*, recited after eating various foods and drinks. See *The Authorised Daily Prayer Book* (Singer), 387.

39 D. Goldschmidt, *Machzor Leyamim Nora'im*, (Jer. 1970), I. 72 n.8.

40 Is. 42:13.

41 Mid. *Ber. Rabb.* 58.1.

42 Tal. *R.H.* 10ᵇ.

43 Gen. 21:1.

44 Mid. *Ber. Rabb.* 53:5.

45 Cf. Jud. 13:18.

46 Tal. *R.H.* 8ᵇ.

47 Gen. 12:3.

48 Tal. *Avod. Zar.* 4[b].

49 Mishna *R.H.* 4:5.

50 Est. 4:16.

51 Ro. 155–91, Bi. 806–63, De S. 44–103.

52 I. Elbogen, *Monatsschrift*, 55, 437.

53 This phrase occurs in the *Ha-yom harath 'olam* prayer, recited three times during *Musaph* after the Shofar blowings which accompany each of the three main sections of *malkhuyoth*, *zikhronoth* and *shopharoth*.

54 Tal. *Ta'anith* 25[b].

55 See his *Siddur 'Avodath Yisrael* (1937) p. 109, and commentary.

56 This issue, of whether or not to recite *'Aviynu Malkeynu* on a Sabbath, is dealt with in a modern volume of responsa by Chief Rabbi Ovadia Yoseph (*Yechaveh Da'ath* (1977), I, no. 54, 155–61). He quotes the *Orchoth Chayyim*, who offers a historic-halachic reason for prohibiting its recitation on a Sabbath, which takes into consideration the fact that this prayer was originally introduced by Rabbi Akivah for recitation on public fast days, 'and no public fasting is permitted on the Sabbath'. Leaving aside the question of the close textual association of *'Aviynu Malkeynu* with the weekday *'Amidah*, Rabbi Yoseph views the matter in relation to the halachic consideration that 'we may not petition for personal needs on the Sabbath'. The *'Aviynu Malkeynu* certainly does petition for personal needs, and it was for that reason that other authorities prohibited its recitation both when *Rosh Hashanah* occurred on the Sabbath and on the intermediate Sabbath of the Ten Days of Penitence. They permitted its recitation, however, on Sabbath *Yom Kippur* because of the urgency of making a final desperate plea ('If not now, when?') before judgment was finally sealed (*Sepher Ha'Ittim*).

A consensus of the most distinguished codifiers of the halachah draws a distinction, however, between purely 'personal petition' for our private wishes and petition such as that expressed throughout the *'Aviynu Malkeynu*, which is rather a 'communal petition' wherein the needs of the individual are indistinguishable from those of the community. They categorise *'Aviynu Malkeynu* as a 'communal petition', which is permitted to be made on the Sabbath.

57 I Sam. ch. 1.

58 Tal. *R.H.* 10[b]–11[a].

59 Gen. 21:1.

60 I Sam. 2:21.
61 Ju. 7:19.
62 Ex. 18:19.
63 Zeph. 1:14–16.
64 Is. 27:13.
65 Nu. ch. 16.
66 Singer, *The Authorised Daily Prayer Book*, p. 371.
67 Tal. *R.H.* 16[b].
68 *Ibid.*

THE *MUSAPH* SERVICE

1 The translation of this stirring plea is given here in the light
   of Routledge's total omission of the prayer and De Sola's
   omission of a translation.
2 This rendering follows the talmudic interpretation (*Ta'anith*
   16[a–b]).
3 Zec. 8:19.
4 See also *Magen Avraham* on *Shulchan 'Aruch*, 582:4.
5 The version in the *Machzor* of D. Goldschmidt (Jer. 1970)
   actually has the identical word *na'alah* for our *na'aleh* (see vol.
   I, p. 158).
6 This seems to be the import of the difficult opening phrase
   which we understand, literally, as 'turn from your (highest)
   habitation to sit upon the (*kes*) throne (of mercy)'.
7 Tal. *Sukk.* 51[a–b].
8 Mish. *R.H.* 1:2.
9 Tal. *Ta'an.* 24[b].
10 Day of Atonement *Machzor*, Ro. 166, Bi. 825, De S. 61.
11 Tal. Jer. *Ta'an.* 2, 13(66[a]). See above, p. 15.
12 Tal. *R.H.* 11[b].
13 De Sola ed. includes, before this, the poem *'ometz 'addiyrey kol
   chephetz*. It is omitted in the other editions.
14 Mish. *R.H.* 1:2.
15 *Jahrbücher für jüdische Geschichte und Literatur*, 1 (1974), 187.
16 Jer. *R.H.* 1:3.
17 On the background of the Amnon legend, see *Jewish Encycl.*
   I, 526.
18 Mid. *Shemoth Rabbah* 30:1.
19 M. Zulay, *Yediy'oth ha-makhon lecheyqer ha-miqra'*, VI, 199–201.
20 See on Ps. 91:1 – 'He that made his presence (*Shekhinah*) to
   dwell in the secret celestial realms, will reside in the shadow

of the Almighty's clouds of glory.'

21 E. Urbach, *Chazal – Pirqey 'Emunoth Vedey'oth* (Jer. 1969), p. 39.

22 This approach concurs with the view of R. Joshua that 'in the final redemption, even if Israel does not repent her redemption is guaranteed' (San. 97[b]). This view is contested in the Talmud by R. Eliezer.

23 *Ramban*, commentary to Gen. 1:1.

24 See comment of Rashi on Tal. *Sukk.* 41[a], *R.H.* 30[a].

25 Rashi maintains that this verse refers to the future Temple although the verb is couched in the past tense. The prophets, when they describe something they see vividly as taking place in the future, regularly use the past tense, for it is as if they have already witnessed it. This device is called by grammarians 'the prophetic perfect'.

26 *The Authorised Daily Prayer Book* (Singer), p. 105.

27 Maim, *Yad, Hilkhoth Melakhim*, 11:4.

28 Tal. *Meg.* 16[b]. The blessings of the weekday *'Amidah – veliyrushalayim* and *'eth tzemach*, followed by *shema' 'qoleynu* and *retzey*, will be seen to conform to the talmudic sequence.

29 See, however, Z. H. Kalisher, *Derishath Tziyyon* (1862), a tract devoted to proving that animal sacrifices may – and should – be reinstituted independently of the Temple, the merit of which would hasten the advent of the Messiah.

30 See, however, note 33 below.

31 Support for the view that *'Aleynu* was composed in the Persian period is based on the reference to God as 'King of the King of Kings'. 'King of Kings' was an honorific title of Persian monarchs – hence the necessity, at that time, of such a cumbersome reference to God.

32 N. Wieder, *'Be-'etyah shel Gematria 'anti-Notzrith ve-'anti Isla'-mith'*, *Sinai*, 76 (Tishri, 1975), pp. 1–14.

33 He is referred to throughout the Talmud as, simply, *Rav*, the Master. In addition to his unique contribution to talmudic law, he also had a formative influence on Jewish liturgy. Its ascription to him is based on the talmudic (Tal. Jer. *R.H.* 57a) term for *'Aleynu: teqi'atha' debey Rav* ('Shofar composition of the school of Rav'), though it is unlikely that he, personally, composed this prayer.

J. Heinemann, in his monumental work, *Ha-tephilah bitquphath ha-tanna'im veha'amora'im* (ch. 10), suggests that the first paragraph (only) of *'Aleynu* actually dates back to Temple

times, to the recitations of the duty-rotas of Priests and laymen (*'Anshey Ma'amad*) who ministered at the Temple twice
a year for a week at a time. The latter used to read from the
Torah chapters of the Creation three times daily, probably
to emphasize that, although God is worshipped, primarily, in
the Temple, we should not lose sight of his cosmic role. The
'Aleynu, which acclaims God as the 'Lord of all things . . .
who formed the world in the beginning', was composed as an
appropriate closing prayer to those readings from the Torah
on the subject of creation.

34 Wieder, *loc. cit.*

35 This is another factor which is noted by the proponents of
the theory that this prayer was composed at an early period
while the Temple was still standing.

36 For comment on the second paragraph of *'Aleynu*, see below,
p. 62.

37 On the *Reshuth*, see above, pp. 19–20, 60.

38 See *Yom Kippur Machzor*, Ro. 159, Bi. 807–9, De S. 49–51.

39 For this usage, see Is. 13:14 where *She'on* and *Hamon* are
synonymous.

40 Commentary to the Siddur *'Otzar Ha-tephilloth* (Hebraica
Press, New York, 1966), p. 450.

41 See *The Scientific Study of Jewish Liturgy* (Ktav, New York,
1970), pp. 106–8.

42 For further remarks on the practical distinction between the
concepts of 'son' and 'servant', see pp. 32–3, 64.

43 Tal. *R.H.* 32a.

44 *Tosaphoth, ad loc.*

45 This is the considered view of A. Buchler in his oft-quoted
article 'The Reading of the Law and Prophets in a Triennial
Cycle', *Jewish Quarterly Review* (OS), 5(1873), reprinted in *The
Scientific Study of Jewish Liturgy*, pp. 181–302. For his comment
on the dating of the *Haphtaroth* as a statutory part of the
Synagogue service, see pp. 230–1.

46 See above, p. 63.

47 This also explains why the concluding formula of the blessing
of the *'Amidah* is *'Oseh Ha-Shalom* (the old Palestinian version).
instead of our usual formula: *ha-mevarekh 'eth 'ammo yisra'el
bashalom*.

48 Lev. 9:22; Tal. *Sotah* 38b.

49 See E. Werner, 'The doxology in Synagogue and Church',
HUCA, XIX (1945/46), 275–351.

TASHLIKH

1 *Sepher Maharil, Hilchoth Rosh Hashanah*, p. 38. Cf. Isserles on Tur *O.H.* ch. 583.
2 Jacob Z. Lauterbach, 'Tashlik, a study in Jewish ceremonies', *HUCA*, 11 (1936), pp. 207–340.
3 See I Kings 1:33–4.
4 Tal. *Horayoth* 12ª; *Kerithoth* 5ᵇ.
5 See Lauterbach, *op. cit.*, 313 ff.
6 Only the Birnbaum edition includes these Psalms.

THE MORNING SERVICE – SECOND DAY

1 See pp. 62–7.
2 *Avoth* 5:1.
3 The classical commentator, Abraham Ibn Ezra, points to this expression as a proof that Isaiah already knew that the earth was round, and that the term 'four corners of the earth' was merely a metaphor of distance. See his comment on this verse.
4 Cf. Ps. 115:16.
5 Tal. *Kid.* 36a.
6 For the promise of *Chesed le-Avraham*, see Micah 7:20.
7 For an explanation of this reference and for supplementary comments on this composition, see pp. 15–16.
8 On Simeon bar Isaac, see above pp. 75–6.
9 On the *Reshuth*, see p. 195 n.37.
10 *Mid. Vay. Rabb.* 34(10).
11 Maimonides, *Yad, Hilchoth Yesodei Ha-Torah*, ch. 2.
12 Jeffrey M. Cohen, 'Pearls of Prayer', *Jewish Chronicle*, 4 June 1982, p. 39.
13 Ro. 30, Bi. 67, De S. 35.
14 See p. 15.
15 Ex. 34:6.
16 Tal. *R.H.* 17a.
17 Tal. *B.B.* 15a; see also Targum on Ps. 89:1.
18 pp. 78–80.
19 Mid. *Ber. Rabb.* 56:3.
20 The judicial terms *qatteygor* and *sanneygor*, employed in this line, are commonly found in the Talmud, being direct borrowings from the Greek legal offices of *Kategoros*, 'public prosecutor' and *sunegoros*, 'defence attorney'.
21 Tal. *R.H.* 16b.

22 These are known as *teqiy'oth dimeyushav*, 'notes blown while permitted to sit'.
23 These are known as *teqiy'oth dime'umad*, 'notes blown while standing (for the *'Amidah*)'.
24 See *Tosaphoth* to Tal. *R.H.* 16[b]. He quotes this interpretation in the name of the *'Arukh*.
25 Isaiah 25:8.
26 See Ro. 99, Bi. 219, De S. 123. For commentary on *ta'iyr vethari'a* see p. 24.
27 See Ro. 197 (middle), Bi. 244 (bott.), De S. 263.
28 See pp. 76, 81.
29 Is. 27:13.
30 Nu. ch. 16.

THE JEWISH DOCTRINE OF REPENTANCE

1 Jonah 3:7–8.
2 Deut. 6:5.
3 Lev. 26:40.
4 II Samuel 12:13.
5 Tal. *Mo'ed Katan* 25a; *Hagigah* 22b; *Sanhedrin* 100a; *Baba Metzi'a'* 33a.
6 Tal. *Yoma'* 86b.
7 Tal. *Sanhedrin* 99a; *Berakhoth* 34b.
8 Mishna *Yoma'* 8:9. The limitation of *Yom Kippur*'s efficacy to religious transgressions was derived from the verse, 'From all your sins *before the Lord* shall you be cleansed' (Lev. 16:30).
9 *Tosephta'*, *Baba Metzi'a'* 8:26.
10 *Yoma'* 87a; Maimonides, *Hilkhoth Teshuvah* 2:9.
11 Maimonides, *ibid.* 2:11.
12 For a more detailed statement of their outlook see Gershom G. Scholem, *Major Trends in Jewish Mysticism* (London, 1955), pp. 80–118; also A. Rubin, 'The concept of repentance among the Hasidei Ashkenaz', *Journal of Jewish Studies*, vol. XVI, nos 3–4, p. 161.
13 Isaiah 6:6–7.
14 Ezekiel 18:23.
15 Mid. *Canticles Rabba* 5(3).
16 *Yoma'* 85b.
17 *Ibid.* 86a.
18 *Ibid.* See Rashi's comment *ad loc.*
19 See p. 195 n.42.

20 Cf. Mishna *'Avoth* 4:11, 4:17, Tal. *Shabbat* 32a; *Yoma'* 87a; *Nedarim* 32b; *Sanhedrin* 87b, etc.
21 *Yoma'* 87a; Maimon. *Hilkhoth Teshuvah* 1:4.
22 *Yoma'* 86a.

THE EVENING SERVICE

1 Lev. 23:27.
2 Mishna, *Yoma'* 8:1.
3 The same abstention applies to the Fast of the Ninth of Av.
4 Ps. 60:10.
5 Tal. *B.B.* 53ᵇ.
6 Song of Songs 7:2.
7 This is based upon the scriptural reference 'And you shall see it (sc. the fringe) and remember all the commandments of the Lord your God.' The Rabbis inferred from this that the law applies only as long as you can 'see' the *tzitzith*, i.e. in natural daylight.
8 See pp. 14, 117.
9 *Sepher Raviah* (ed. Aptowitzer), II pp. 187–8.
10 Tal. *Kerithoth* 6ᵇ.
11 J. S. Bloch, *Israel and the Nations* (Berlin, 1927), p. 278.
12 Bathja Bayes, *Encyclopaedia Judaica*, 10, p. 1168.
13 See *'Otzar kol minhagey Yeshurun* (Lemberg, 1920), p. 71. It is of interest that Yemenite tradition does not attribute any particular significance to *Kol Nidrey*. In their *Machzor* it is relegated to a minor position towards the end of the service, and is recited without any accompanying melody.
14 Nu. ch. 30.
15 Mishna *Hagigah* 1:8.
16 See L. Zunz, *Die Ritus*, p. 106; N. Wieder, *The Judaean Scrolls and Karaism*, ch. 5 and Appendix.
17 Pl. of *Gaon*, 'Excellency'. This was the title given to the heads of the great Babylonian academies of rabbinic learning, seventh–eleventh centuries CE.
18 A. B. Ehrlich, *Miqra' Kipheshuto* (Ktav, 1969), p. 298.
19 Mishna *Nedarim* 1:2.
20 *Loc. cit.* 1:1.
21 Maimonides, *Peyrush Ha-Mishnayoth*, *Ned.* 1:2.
22 Nu. 30:3.
23 *Siddur Rav Sa'adya Ga'on*, ed. I. Davidson, S. Assaf and B. Joel (1941), p. 261.

24 Lev. 23:32.
25 D. Goldschmidt, *op. cit.*, p. 11.
26 See S. Baron, *A Social and Religious History of the Jews* (New York, 1958), VII, 90–3.
27 Y. Kaufmann, *The Religion of Israel* (London, 1961), p. 11.
28 Kaufmann, *op. cit.*, pp. 62–3.
29 Gen. 3:1, Amos 9:3.
30 Gen. 1:21.
31 Is. 51:9.
32 See pp. 108, 111.
33 Ex. 34:6.
34 Tal. *'Eruvin* 22ª.
35 Mid. *Vay. Rabb.* 29(24).
36 II Sam. 22:26.
37 Levi ben Gershom, 1288–1344. French Bible commentator and philosopher.
38 II Sam. chs 11–12.
39 I Sam. 13:14.
40 Tal. *R.H.* 17ª.
41 *Loc. cit.* 17ᵇ.
42 Ex. 34:6–7.
43 *Ibid.*
44 Tal. *Meg.* 22ª.
45 Magen Avraham on *Orach Chayyim* Sec. 282.
46 Daniel Goldschmidt, *op. cit.*, vol. II, p. 28.
47 See Ju. 14:5, Amos 3:4, 8, Ps. 104:21, Is. 5:29 *et al.*
48 Job 9:2.
49 Job 4:17. For our view, that Job was here replying to this specific point, we follow N. H. Tur-Sinai, *The Book of Job* (Jerusalem, 1967), p. 154.
50 Cf. Gen. 8:21.
51 Josh. 2:1.
52 See Ps. 89:1. The Rabbis explain the heading *'Eythan ha-'ezrachi* as referring to Abraham (Tal. *B.B.* 15ª).
53 M. Adler, *Jews of Medieval England* (1939), p. 127.
54 Tal. *R.H.* 17ᵇ.
55 Gen. 8:21.
56 See A. Rosenfeld, *The Authorised Selichot for the Whole Year* (London, 1979), p. 14 and *passim*.
57 Mid. *Cant.* 2:16.
58 Tal. *Yoma'* 87ᵇ.

59 *Ibid.*

60 Ro. 48, Bi. 551, De S. 54.

61 Tal. *Yoma'* 87[b].

62 For *Kol Nidrey*, see Ro. 47, Bi. 549, De S. 52.

63 See *Authorised Daily Prayer Book* (ed. Singer), p. 9. The opening words, *Ribbon ha-'olamim* are there expanded into *Ribbon kol ha-'olamim.*

64 For *Kol Nidrey*, see Ro. 29, Bi. 517, De S. 29.

65 Tal. *Yoma'* 87[b].

66 Arthur Marmorstein, 'The confession of sins for the Day of Atonement', in *Essays Presented to J. H. Hertz, Chief Rabbi* (London, 1942), p. 298.

67 See Ro. 164, Bi. 821, De S. 58.

68 On this prayer book, see David Kaufmann, 'The prayer book according to the ritual of England before 1290', *Jewish Quarterly Review*, Old Series, vol. 4 (1892), and the edition of Chief Rabbi I. Brodie (3 vols, 1962–7).

69 This confessional is introduced there by the phrase *modeh 'aniy lephanekha*, which actually accounts for the presence of this phrase in our prayer book even though it is clearly a formula of confession, meaning 'I *admit* before thee'. Our rite has actually omitted the succeeding confession, and the translators were, therefore, constrained to overcome the hiatus by rendering it 'I *give thanks* before thee'. See. D. Kaufmann, *op. cit.*

70 For the well-known rabbinic parable on the joint responsibility of body and soul, see Mid. *Lev. R. (vayyiqra')* 4:5.

71 E. Munk, *The World of Prayer*, vol. II, p. 248. For an explanation of the distinction between all the categories of sacrifice enumerated in this composition, see Munk (*ibid.*).

72 Many of the texts of these and other *Selichoth* and *Hosha'noth* are identical, except that the former occur with the response *'aneynu*, the latter with *hosha'na'*.

73 J. Heinemann, *op. cit.*, ch. 6.

74 *Ibid.*, see English preface, p. vii.

75 Mishna, *Ta'anith* 2:4.

76 See II Sam. 21:1.

77 See I Kings 8:35–7.

78 'May he who answered . . ., he will answer *you*' (instead of 'he will answer *us*').

THE MORNING SERVICE

1 Tal. *Yev.* 49[b].
2 On *Yotzeroth*, see pp. 12–13, 128.
3 The great Saadia Gaon actually objected to the presence of the *'or chadash* verse on that account, and the Sephardi rites consequently omit it.
4 Mid. *Cant. Rabb.*, 5:2.
5 *Ibid.* 4:12.
6 On the *Reshuth*, see p. 195 n.37.
7 Jer. 18:22.
8 Jer. 30:17, II Chr. 24:13.
9 II Sam. 22:12.
10 See Prov. 16:18.
11 *Chulshah* is post-biblical. The form *cheyshel* is coined from the single occurrence of the verb *chashal* in Deut. 25:18.
12 Is. 21:4, Job 21:6.
13 This form does occur once in the Bible, in Ps. 150:3.
14 For the regular form of the 3rd pers. masc. perf. of the verb *'athah*, 'to come', see Deut. 32:2.
15 The form *'ahav* does not occur in the Bible, other than in the plural *'ahavim*, Ho. 8:9; Prov. 5:19.
16 Mal. 2:13.
17 *Cant. Rabb.*, 4:4.
18 Gen. 25:27.
19 Mid. *Ber. Rabb.* 78:6.
20 Gen. 32:29.
21 Jer. Tal. *Ber.* 1, 8.
22 Tal. *Shabb.* 88[b].
23 Ezekiel 1:27.
24 See *Encyclopaedia Judaica*, 7, 1377 ff.
25 Tal. *Hagigah* 13[b].
26 The word *mal* is from the root *mll* 'to speak', from which comes the word *millah*, 'a word'.
27 Mishna *'Avoth* 5:5.
28 Mishna *Yoma'* 8:9.
29 L. Zunz, *Ritus*, p. 107.
30 A. H. Weiss, *Dor Dor Vedorshav*, IV, p. 277.
31 See *Encycl. Otzar Israel*, I, p. 47.
32 See pp. 138–9.
33 Deut. 4:24.
34 *Ramban, Commentary on Pentateuch, ibid.*
35 Gen. 15:17.

36 Ex. 3:2.
37 Ex. 13:21.
38 Ex. 19:18. For the significance and use of fire in Samaritan tradition, see Jeffrey M. Cohen, *A Samaritan Chronicle* (E. J. Brill, 1981), pp. 205–11.
39 Mishna *'Avoth* 3:15.
40 In the *Musaph* version this is also the case. There it follows on from the phrase *ma'asey 'adonay*, 'God's deeds', which refer specifically to his dealings with men, and in particular the men who oppress Israel.
41 Rudoph Otto, *The Idea of the Holy* (1923), ch. 6.
42 Gershom G. Scholem, *Major Trends in Jewish Mysticism* (London, 1955), pp. 59–60.
43 Is. 6:3.
44 Ro. 78, Bi. 663, De S. 190.
45 Ro. 73, Bi. omitted, De S. 184.
46 Ro. 73, Bi. omitted, De S. 185.
47 *Pesiqta' Rabbathiy* 21:10.
48 See, for example, J. M. Cohen, *Understanding the Synagogue Service* (1974); E. Munk, *The World of Prayer*, 2 vols (1961); B. S. Jacobson, *Meditations on the Siddur* (1966); A. Kohn, *Prayer* (1971); J. H. Hertz, *The Authorised Daily Prayer Book With Commentary* (1947).
49 See Eric Werner, 'The doxology in Synagogue and Church', *Hebrew Union College Annual*, vol. XIX (1945/46), pp. 275–351.
51 Jeffrey M. Cohen, *op. cit.* 92–3.

MEMORIAL OF THE DEPARTED

1 See *Tur, O.H.*, 220.
2 The Sephardim refer to their memorial prayers by the name *'Ashkavah*, 'laying to rest', with the implied suggestion that their recitation brings reward of tranquil repose to the departed. These are recited also on the eve of *Yom Kippur*, before the *Ma'ariv* service.
3 *Shulchan 'Arukh, O.H.*, 621.

THE *MUSAPH* SERVICE

1 Nathan A. Scott, Jr, *Mirrors of Man in Existentialism* (1978), ch. 1.

2 *Ibid.*, p. 14.
3 See M. Zulay, *Piyyutey Yannai*, (1938), p. 332.
4 We only have knowledge of the name of one poet – Yose ben Yose – before the period of Yannai. On Yannai, see p. 190 n.46.
5 See pp. 17–18, 147.
6 See I Sam. 10:5, 19:20–24 *et al.*
7 See Dt. 32:22, Jer. 15:14, 17:4 *et al.*
8 This coinage suggests that the poet understood the verb *ven-ivvakhechah* (Is. 1:18) as 'let us *assemble* for judgement'. It is clearly that particular biblical occurrence which inspired his creation.
9 See Dt. 29:17, Amos 5:7, 6:12 *et al.* The passive participle *l'uney mar*, as coined by the poet, would mean, literally, 'poisoned' or 'infected'.
10 Tal. *Kidd.* 71ᵃ.
11 Tal. Jer. *Yoma'* 3:7.
12 *Yoma'* 53ᵇ *Ta'anith* 24ᵇ; Jer. Tal. *Yoma'* 5:3.
13 Tal. *Sotah* 44ᵃ.
14 D. Goldschmidt, *op. cit.* (Jerusalem, 1970), vol. II, Intro. p. 13.
15 Exodus 34:5–7.
16 See p. 117.
17 See above pp. 9, 42–43, 60–61, 201.
18 This is a reference to Amos 2:6, 'For they sold the righteous for the price of a pair of shoes.'

THE AFTERNOON SERVICE

1 Mishna *Ta'anith*, 4:8.
2 Mid. *Ber Rabb.* 56:6.
3 Gen. 22:4, 15–18.
4 Mishna *Pirqey 'Avoth* 5:5.
5 Mid. *Pirqey d'Rabbi Eliezer*, ch. 31.
6 Gen. 25:27.
7 See p. 201 n.19.
8 *The Authorised Daily Prayer Book* (Singer), p. 395.
9 See M. Zulay, *op. cit.* p. 334.

THE *NE'IYLAH* SERVICE

1 Mishna *Ta'anith* 4:1, 3; Tal. *Ta'anith* 26ᵇ.
2 *Ibid.*

3 The idea seems to have been that the sun is enclosed within the heavens at night time. See comment of *Mar'eh Ha-panim* on Tal. Jer. *Ber.* 4:1. Rav may also have understood it in a theological sense, namely, 'the service recited at the time of the closing of the *gates of mercy*'.

4 Maim. *Yad, Hilchoth Tephillah*, 1:7.

5 Tal. *Ned.* 32ª.

6 Gen. 25:7.

7 See Gen. 21:9.

8 The evil of the Canaanites prompted Abraham to seek out a wife for Isaac from among his own kinsmen in Mesopotamia (see Gen. 24:4). Isaac's later assessment of the Canaanites was the same, prompting him, likewise, to advise his son Jacob not to intermarry with them (Gen. 28:1,8).

9 Gen. 26:7–11.

10 Ez. 18:32.

11 Tal. *Ber.* 29ᵇ.

12 While the Talmud – and the quotation from it in our poem – does not include an introductory formula invoking God by name, the *Divry Chamudoth*, a commentary on the *Rosh* (*ibid.*), insists that it must have been included in the authorised version of this prayer, as it is inconceivable to address a plea to God without calling upon him with the conventional mode of address.

13 On the *Reshuth*, see p. 195 n.37.

14 See pp. 117, 166.

15 *Nagid* was the title of the leader of the Jewish community in Moslem countries.

16 See p. 181.

17 *Ibid.*

18 See pp. 125–7.

19 This may well have been inspired by the biblical juxtaposition of these two themes. See Dt. 29:28 and Dt. 30:1–3.

20 Tal. *Yoma'* 87ᵇ.

21 Ro. 257–8, Bi. 985–6, De S. 197–8.

22 This unpublished commentary, written by a contemporary of Rashi (tenth–eleventh century), is referred to in *'Otzar Ha-tephilloth*, ed. S. Goldman (New York, 1966), p. 582.

23 For this nuance of the combination of the verb *natan* with the noun *yad*, cf. Dt. 16:17, Ez. 46:5, 11, *et al.*

24 Tal. *Yoma'* 38ᵇ.

25 Tal. *B.B.* 165ª.

26 Tal. *San* 108ª.
27 Mishna *Yoma'* 8:9.
28 The word *'enosh*, from the verb meaning 'to be weak', is used
   in the Bible, instead of the usual noun *'ish*, to emphasise
   man's transience and frailty. It is from the same root, *'anash*,
   that the noun *'ishah*, 'woman', is derived, suggesting something more 'delicate' and physically weaker than her male
   counterpart.
29 Cf. the noun *hakarah*, 'perception', 'recognition'.
30 Cf. Job 35:7 and Eccl. 8:4.
31 Quotation from the familiar *'Adon 'Olam* poem.
32 I Kings 18:39.
33 See p. 40.

BIBLIOGRAPHY

This bibliography lists all the works cited in the text and the notes to the text. An asterisk after the title of the book denotes works of a more popular nature, suitable for the general reader.

Adler, H. (ed.), *Service of the Synagogue**, 6 vols, London, Routledge & Kegan Paul, 1906.

Adler, M., *The Jews of Medieval England**, London, Jewish Historical Society, 1939.

Aptowitzer, V. (ed.), *Sepher Ravyah*, 2 vols, Berlin, Mekitzei Nirdamim, 1913–35.

Baer, S. (ed.), *Seder 'Avodath Yisra'el*, Roedelheim, Israel Lehrberger, 1868.

Baron, S., *A Social and Religious History of the Jews**, New York, Columbia University Press, 1958.

Bayer, B., 'Kol Nidrey (Musical Rendition)', in *Encyclopaedia Judaica*, vol. 10, pp. 1167–9, Jerusalem, Keter, 1971.

Birnbaum, P. (ed.), *High Holyday Prayer Book**, New York, Hebrew Publishing, 1951.

Birnbaum, P., *Tephiloth Yisra'el U-musar Ha-yahaduth*, New York, Shulsinger, 1971.

Bloch, J. S., *Israel and the Nations**, Berlin, Harz, 1927.

Brodie, I. (ed.), *'Etz Chayyim*, 3 vols, Jerusalem, Mosad Ha-rav Kuk, 1962–67.

Buchler, A., 'The reading of the Law and the Prophets in a triennial cycle', *Jewish Quarterly Review* (Old Series), vol. 5, 1873; reprinted in *The Scientific Study of Jewish Liturgy*, New York, Ktav, 1970.

Chavell, C. (ed.), *Peyrush Ha-Ramban 'al Ha-Torah*, Jerusalem, Mosad Ha-rav Kuk, 1959.

Cohen, J. M., *Understanding the Synagogue Service**, Glasgow, Private Publication, 1974.

Cohen, J. M., *A Samaritan Chronicle*, Leiden, Brill, 1981.

Cohen, J. M., 'Pearls of Prayer', *Jewish Chronicle*, 4 June 1982, p. 39.

Davidson, I., *Machzor Yannai*, New York, Jewish Theological Seminary of America, 1919.

Davidson, I., Assaf, S. and Joel, B., *Siddur Rav Sa'adya Gaon*, Jerusalem, Reuben Mass, 1963.

Ehrlich, A. B., *Miqra' Kipheshuto*, New York, Ktav, 1969.

Elbogen, I., *Toledoth Ha-tephilah Veha-'avodah Beyisra'el*, Jerusalem, Dvir, 1924. (Hebrew transl. of *Der Juedische Gottesdienst*, Frankfurt am Main, J. Kauffmann, 1924.)

Encyclopaedia Judaica*, Keter Publishing House, Jerusalem, 1972.

Friedlander, M. (ed.), *The Guide for the Perplexed*, London, Routledge & Kegan Paul, 1904.

Goldman, S. (ed.), *'Otzar Ha-tephiloth*, New York, Hebraica Press, 1966.

Goldschmidt, D. (ed.), *Machzor Leyamim Nora'im*, 3 vols, Jerusalem, Koren, 1970.

Guttmann, J., *Philosophies of Judaism*, New York, Schocken Books, 1964.

Heiler, F., *Prayer – History and Psychology**, New York, Galaxy Books, 1958.

Heinemann, J., *Ha-tephilah Bitequphath Ha-tanna'im Veha-'amora'-im*, Jerusalem, Magnes Press, 1964.

Hertz, J. H. (ed.), *The Authorised Daily Prayer Book With Commentary**, London, Shapiro Vallentine, 1947.

Idelsohn, A. Z., *Jewish Liturgy and its Development**, New York, Schocken Books, 1932.

Jacobs, L., *Hasidic Prayer**, London, Routledge & Kegan Paul, 1972.

Jacobson, B. S., *Meditations on the Siddur**, Tel Aviv, Sinai, 1966.

Jacobson, B. S., *Nethiv Binah*, 5 vols, Tel Aviv, Sinai, 1976–78.

Kalischer, Z. H., *Drishath Tziyyon*, K. Dombrowski, 1866.

Kaufmann, D., 'The prayer book according to the ritual of England before 1290', *Jewish Quarterly Review* (Old Series), vol. 4 (1892), pp. 20–63.

Kaufmann, Y., *The Religion of Israel*, London, George Allen & Unwin, 1961.

Kohn, A., *Prayer**, London, Soncino, 1971.

Lauterbach, J. Z., 'Tashlikh, a study in Jewish ceremonies', *Hebrew Union College Annual*, vol. 11 (1936), pp. 207–340.

Levy, E., *Yesodoth Ha-tephilah*, Tel Aviv, Tzioni, 1963.

Marmorstein, A., 'The confession of sins for the Day of Atonement', in *Essays Presented to J. H. Hertz, Chief Rabbi*, London, Edward Goldston, 1942, pp. 293–305.

Munk, E., *The World of Prayer**, 2 vols, New York, Feldheim, 1961.

Otto, R., *The Idea of the Holy* (Translation of *Das Heilige*), Oxford University Press, 1928.

Petuchowski, J. J. (ed.), *Contributions to the Scientific Study of Jewish Liturgy*, New York, Ktav, 1970.

Petuchowski, J. J. (ed.), *Understanding Jewish Prayer**, New York, Ktav 1972.

Rosenfeld, A. (ed.), *The Authorised Selichot for the Whole Year**, New York, Judaica Press, 1979.

Rosenthal, E. I. J. (ed.), *Saadya Studies*, London, Oxford University Press, 1943.

Rubin, A., 'The concept of repentance among the Hasidei Ashkenaz', *Journal of Jewish Studies*, vol. XVI (nos 3–42), pp. 161–73.

Scholem, G., *Major Trends in Jewish Mysticism*, London, Thames & Hudson, 1955.

Scott, N. A. Jr., *Mirrors of Man in Existentialism*, Cleveland, Ohio, Collins, 1978.

Singer, S., *The Authorised Daily Prayer Book**, London, Singer's Prayer Book, 1962.

Sola, De, D. A. (ed.), *The Complete Festival Prayers**, 5 vols, London, Shapiro Vallentine, 1948.

Tur-Sinai, N. H., *The Book of Job*, Jerusalem, Kiryath Sepher, 1967.

Urbach, E., *Chazal – Pirqey 'Emunoth Vedey'oth*, Jerusalem, Magnes Press, 1969.

Weiss, I. H., *Dor Dor Vedorshav*, 5 vols, Jerusalem/Tel Aviv, Ziv, undated (reprint of original edition, New York and Berlin, Platt & Minkus, 1924).

Werner, E., 'The doxology in Synagogue and Church', *Hebrew Union College Annual*, vol. XIX (1945–6), pp. 275–351.

Wieder, N., *The Judaean Scrolls and Karaism*, London, East & West Library, 1962.

Wieder, N., 'Be-'etyah shel gematria 'anti-notzrith ve-'anti-Isla'mith', Sinai, 76 (Tishri, 1975), pp. 1–14.

Yoseph, O., *Sepher Yechavveh Da'ath*, 3 vols, Jerusalem, Yeshivat Porath Yoseph *et al.*, 1977.

Zulay, M., *Piyyutey Yannai*, Berlin, M. Zulay, 1938.

Zunz, L., *Die Synagogale Poesie des Mittelalters*, Berlin, Julius Springer, 1855.

Zunz, L., *Die Ritus des Synagogalen Gottesdienstes*, Berlin, Julius Springer, 1859.

PRIMARY RABBINIC SOURCES

Gersonides (R. Levi b. Gershom), *Commentary on the Torah*, var. edns.

Jacob ben Asher, *Tur*, Warsaw, 1882.

Karo, Joseph, *Beth Yoseph*, commentary on the *Tur*.

Magen Avraham (R. Abraham Abeli Gombiner), commentary on the *Shulchan 'Arukh*, var. edns.

Maharil, Sepher (R. Jacob Ha-Levi Moellin), 1st edn, Sabionetta, 1556.

Maimonides, Moses, *Commentary on the Mishnah*, var. edns.

Maimonides, Moses, *Yad Ha-Chazakah*, var. edns.

Maimonides, Moses, *Guide to the Perplexed*, trans. M. Friedlander, London, 1904.

Maimuni, Abraham, *Hagahoth Maimuni*, ed. A. H. Freimann, Jerusalem, 1937.

Midrash, Pirqey de Rabbi Eliezer, Warsaw, 1852; trans. G. Friedlander, N.Y., 1965.

Midrash, Rabbah, Romm, Vilna, Jerusalem, var. edns.

Midrash, Shochar Tov, ed. S. Buber, Romm, 1891; Jer. 1966.

Mishnah, var. eds.; trans. H. Danby, Oxford, 1933; Commentaries: P. Blackman, Oxford, 1951–56 (7 vols); P. Kehati, Jerusalem, 1963, 12 vols.

Rashi (R. Solomon ben Isaac), comm. on Bible and Talmud, var. edns.

Sepher Ha-'Ittim (Judah ben Barzillai), ed. R. J. Schorr, 1902.

Shulchan 'Arukh, see Karo, Joseph.

Siddur Rav Sa'adya Gaon, see Davidson, I.

Talmud, Babylonian, Romm, Vilna, Vienna, Jerusalem, var. edns.; English trans. ed. I. Epstein, London, 1948–52.

Talmud, Palestinian, Krotoschin, 1886; *Talmud Yerushalmi Ha-Gadol*, 6 vols, Vilna, 1922.

Tashbatz (*Teshuvoth Shimon b. Tzemach Duran*), Amsterdam, 1738–41.

Tosephta', ed. M. S. Zuckermandel, Jerusalem, 1963.

Tur, see Jacob ben Asher.

INDEX

Note: main entries are given in bold type.

Aaron, 20, 68, 130, 151
Abba Arikha, 59; *see also* Rav
Abel, 163
Abimelech, 178
Abraham, **20–1,** 39, 73, 81, 82, 86, 116, 127, 134, 143, 159, 163, **171–2, 177–8**
absolution, *see* vows
abstentions, five, 99
Achima'atz, Chronicle of, 181
Acre, 182
Acrostics, alphabetical, 7, 15, 24, 28, 44, 52, 54, 77, 78, 80, 114, 118, 126, 134, 136, 139, 142, 144, 158, 159, 165, 171, 177; double, 47, 123, 137, 160; name, 20, 76, 83, 138, 157, 163, 183; reverse, 23, 46, 107, 133, 144–5, 179; subject, 157
Adam, 21, 45, 56, 77, 163
adulterous relationship, 170
affliction, *see* suffering
Ahazuerus, 50
Akivah, Rabbi, 33, 144, 146
'Al cheyt, 123–5
'Aleynu, 29, 57–9, 195
alliteration, 135
al Qumisi, Daniel, 103
altar, 68
Amalek, 65
'Amen, 164
'Amidah, **11, 18,** 19, 22, 29, 30, **34,** 43, 47, 55, 56, 60, 66, 67, 78, 83, 84, 145, 166, 171, 176, 177, 182, 185
Amittai ben Shephatyah, 183

'Amram Gaon, 166; *Seder Rav 'Amram,* 104
Amnon, Rabbi, 52
angelic choir, 16, 26, 148
angels, clothed in white, 4; guardian angels of heathen nations, 5; intercede for Isaac, 172; Israel compared to, 173; of peace, *see* 'Arelim; sent to Abraham, 78; shedding tears, 16; *see also* Gabriel, Michael, Raphael, Uriel
anthropomorphisms, 14
antiphonal chant, 110
antisemitism, 168
'Aqdamuth, 6
'Aqedah, *see* Isaac, binding of
Arabic metre, *see* metre
Aramaic, 51, 54, 104
'arayoth, 170
'Arelim, 17
Ark curtain, 3; opening of, 19, 83, 176–7
'Ashkavah, 202
Ashkenazi communities, 8, 44, 75, 100, 101, 177; formula, 106; poetic tradition, 179; prayer rite, 33, 108, 155, 157
at-bash, 47, 139
atonement, 20, 93, 137, 138, 187
attributes of God, 112, 138, 145, 188
auto da fé, 58
Av, Fast of, 56, 99, 114, 168
'avaryanim, 102
Avignon, *see* Machzor Avignon
'Aviynu malkeynu, 32–4, 192
'Avodah, 30, 60, 68, 108, 142, 162–5
'Avoth, 171

Avudarham, D., 67
'Aza'zeyl, 151, 165

Ba'al, Prophets of, 188
Ba'al Toqe'a, 39
Babel, Tower of, 10, 56, 163
Babylonia, 103, 179
Babylonian, *see* Geonim; prayer
  rite, 30, 67; Talmud, 165
Baer, Seligman Isaac, 33
Balkans Prayer rite, 157
bandits, prayer against, 179
baptism, forced, 75
Bar Kochba, 167
Bar Mitzvah, 69
Basil I, 181, 183
Bathsheba, 89, 112
bereavement, 155
Bimah, 18
Birkath ha-zeman, 107
Birnbaum, P., 61, 69
Bloch, Joseph S., 102
Blois martyrs, *see* martyrs
Brüll, N., 51
burial, 101

Cairo Genizah, 49, 52
Caliph al-Hakam II, 141
Canaanite religion, 58, 110
Canaanites, daughters of, 178
cantor, *see* Chazan
Carmel, *see* Mount Carmel
celestial court, 138, 144, 148;
  realms, 175
censorship, 59
Chanokh ben Moses, 141
Charamey, 105
charity, 155
chashmal, 138
Chasid, 112
Chasidey Ashkenaz, 7, 91, 138
Chasidic Synagogues, *see*
  Synagogues
Chasiduth, 112
chatta'th, 88
Chayyoth, 16, 26

Chazan, **9**, **11**, 18, **19**, 20, 33,
  42–3, 78, 166, 167, 180, 190
Cherubim, 16
Chosen People, 53
Christianity, 58, 59, 86, 102, 173,
  181
circumcision, 101, 134, 159, 167
Clifford's Tower, 115
collectors' tax, 89; customs, 89
confession, 120, 121–4, 163, 164,
  166
Constantinople, 181
conversion, 102
converts, 103
Cordova, 141
coronation, 39
creation, 15, 77, 109; myth, 110;
  first Sabbath of, 172
crucifixion, 169

dancing, ritual, 160, 170
Daniel, 143
David, *see* King David
David, House of, 57; Tower of,
  134
David ben Avraham, 182
Day of Atonement, 89, 94, 95,
  106
Day of Judgment, 39, 50, 72, 83
dayyan, 106
death, day of, 135
demons, 72
dew, prayer for, 3
divine garments, 13–14, 113;
  spirit, 69
doxology, 70
dreams, 154
dukhaning, 68

earth, round, 196 n.3
ecstacy, 147
Elchanan (bar Simeon), 75–6
Eleazar of Worms, 59
Eliezer b. Yoel HaLevi *(Raviah)*,
  101
Elihu, 26
Elijah, 127, 188

Elijah bar Mordechai, 173
Eliphaz, 116
Ellul, 16
Emden, Rabbi Jacob, 8
England, 182
English Jewry, 122
enlightenment, 129
'esarey, 104
Essenes, 17
Ethics of the Fathers, 172
Ethiopians, 105
'Etz Chayyim, 122
Eve, 163
evil spirits, 73
excommunication, 37, 101, 141, 181, 182
exile, 55–6, 87
existentialism, 158
Ezekiel, 16, 92, 138, 143, 144, 179

fast days, 34, 38, 125, 126, 176
fasting, 99, 133; on day before Rosh Hashanah, 48
fire, 143
fish, 73
flood, 46, 163
flood, generation of the, 10, 46, 186
forgiveness, 95–6, 114–15, 124–5
France, 182
Franco-Germany, 19, 30, 132, 155
Frankfort, 44
French, 105; prayer rite, 127

Gabirol, Ibn, 13
Gabriel, angel, 174–5
Gaon, 198 n. 17
Garden of Eden, 56
gematria, 5
Genizah, Cairo, see Cairo Genizah
Geonim, Babylonian, 103, 121, 141, 184
Germany, 19, 52, 132, 138, 177,

179; pietists of, see Chasidey Ashkenaz
Gersonides, 112
Gevuroth, 171
Gezeyrah, 166–7
Gideon, 37
Glory, Hymn of, 4
God: as consuming fire, 143; assists the penitents, 94; enthronement of, 39, 148; enwraps himself in tallith, 100, 113; fatherhood of, 32–3; fear of, 79; Israel's relationship with, 64, 78, 97, 94, 114, 119, 129, 133–4, 136, 139, 170; judicial qualities of, 28, 188; kingdom of, 62, 131; kingship of, 8–9, 30, 33, 39, 57, 59, 112; love of, 94, 133–4, 143; memory of, 64–5; mercy of, 15–16, 53, 81, 87, 92–3, 111, 118, 138, 142, 188; names of, 15, 120; panentheistic concept of, 149; probes the righteous, 80; profanation of name of, 95, 122; the hope of, 140; thrones of, 8, 45, 64, 78, 112, 136, 143, 173, 188; Unity of, 13
God's anger, 143; chariot, 146; existence discovered, 177; gifts to man, 187; holiness, 109, 148; immanence, 144; omnipotence, 109, 143, 160; omniscience, 109, 185; praise of, 137, 148; reconciliation with Israel, 129; Secret name, 164; Shekhinah, see Shekhiynah; shield for Abraham, 134; surveillance of world, 64; tent, 138; Thirteen Attributes, 100, 112–13, 117, 120, 166, 180, 183; transcendence, 144; Unity, 6, 150; word, 77, 93
Golden Calf, 16
Goldschmidt, D., 109, 115
Grace after Meals, 172

Hadrian, 167
Hagar, 35
HaLevi, Judah, 13
Ha-melekh, 8, 30
Hamnuna, Rav, 121
Hannah, barrenness of, 23, 35; Prayer of, 23
Haphtaroth, 35–6, 66, 87, 152, 170
heaven, highest, 188
hegeh, 118
Heinemann, J., 126
hereafter, 10, 39
Heykhaloth, 146; *Rabbathiy*, 146
High Priest, confessions of, 164
entry into Holy of Holies, 165; Prayer of, 47, 165
holocaust, 155
Holy Land *see* Israel
holy nation, 128
Holy of Holies, 131, 163, 165
Hosea, 82, 116
Hosha'na Rabbah, 3, 6, 184; as the day of judgment, 6
Hasha'noth, 126, 184
human destiny, 64

Iberians, 102
Ibn Ezra, Abraham, 13, 54
Ibn Ezra, Moses, 13
Imitatio Dei, 65
immersion, 164
incestuous relationships, 170
ingathering of the exiles, 39
Isaac, ashes of, 21; binding of, 39, 82, 85–6, 167, 171, 172; birth of, 25, 35, 177–8; impaired sight of, 16; returns from the dead, 173; surrenders his life, 45
Isaac ben Samuel, 182
Isaiah, 17, 24, 77–8, 91, 109, 128, 149, 152, 159, 161, 175
Ishmael, 35, 178
Ishma'el, Rabbi, 146
Islam, 58
Israel, people of, 117–18; State of, 14, 155
Isserles, M., 155
Italian communities reprieved, 182; prayer rite, 104, 127, 157
Italy, 132, 179, 181, 183
'Iyyun Tephilah, Sepher, 62

Jacob, 136, 168, 173
Jacob ben Judah, 122; *see also 'Etz Chayyim*
Jacob Ibn Jau, 141
Jacob *(Rabbeynu)* Tam, 182
Jaffe, Rabbi Mordechai, 8
Jeremiah, 87, 109, 136, 140; his parable, 117
Jericho, 37
Jerusalem, 55, 56, 67, 168, 176, 189
Jesus, 58
Jezdegaard II, 150
Job, 26, 109, 116, 135, 161
Jochanan ben Nuri, 29
Jonah, 35, 88, 93, 127, 170–1
Joseph, 48, 168
Joseph ben Isaac Ibn Abitur, 141–2
Joseph ben Isaac of Orleans, 179
Joshua, 37, 58, 116, 127
Jubilee, 37, 64, 188–9
Judah Ha-Nasi, 17
Judgment, precise moment, 28; *see also* Day of Judgment

Kaddish, 43–6
Kafka, Franz, 22–3
Kallir, Eleazar, **12–13**, 15, 23, 24, 25, 27–8, 44–5, **46**, 47–8, 75, 76, 77, 81, 84, 156, 174, 177, 181
Kalonymos ben Meshullam, 52
Kalonymos family, 132, 138
Karaites, 20, 103, 181
Kaufmann, Y., 110
Kavod, 54
Kethuvim, 65–6
Kiddush, 107
Kierkegaard, S., 79, 158

kindness, 129
King David, 57, 66, 79, 88–9, 112, 127
King Manasseh, 95, 128
King Nimrod, 127
King Saul, 112
King Solomon, 127
kittel, 3–4, 100
kiynuyey, 105
Kneseth Yisrael, 80
Knowledge, Tree of, 23
Kol Nidrey, 7, 100
Korach, 40; sons of, 40
Krauss, S., 103

lashes, forty, 91
Lauterbach, Jacob Z., 72
Le-David Ha-Shem 'Oriy, 4–6
Leviathan, 109, 110
Levites, 68
Levy, 163
l'eyla', 43–4
life, 21–2; Book of, 22; Tree of, 23
light, *see* enlightenment
litanies, 126, 146
Lithuanian Prayer rite, 181, 182
Luria, Rabbi Isaac, 73
Luria, Rabbi Solomon, 8

Ma'amadoth, 176
Ma'aseh Bereyshith, 17
Ma'aseh Merkavah, 17
Machzor Avignon, 49
Machzorim, handwritten, 12
Maimonides, Moses, 13, 14, 56, 79, 105, 123, 176, 182, 190
Mainz, 163
Malkhuyoth, 29, 57, 60, 62–3, 66, 76, 85
Mamluks, 183
man, 145, 186–7; man's intellect, 186
Manasseh, King, *see* King Manasseh
maqriy', 39
Marcus, David, 153

mar'iyth ha'ayin, 100
Marmorstein, A., 121
Marranos, 102
martyrdom, 57, 86
martyrs, 57, 155; Ten, 168
match-making, 170
Meir bar Yitzchaq, 167
Meir ben Samuel, 106
Meir of Rothenburg, 100, 101, 114
Memorbuch, 155
memory, 64
Memra', 54, 143
mercy, *see* God, Mercy of; gate of, 177
Merkavah mysticism, 139, 146, 161
meruba', 82
Meshullam ben Kalonymos, **132**, 133, 134, 136, 137, **138**, 142, 143, 163
Messiah, 57, 70
messianic alarm, 41; era, 29, 56, 57; hope, 54
metre, 115
Michael, angel, 174
Midrash, 12, 172; polemical, 169
Minchah service, 93, 170–3
Min ha-meytzar, 40
miqveh, 140, 142
Mishna, 17, 29, 51, 140, 176
mitzvoth, 31
Miy Shebeyrach, 35
Moellin, Jacob, 44, 72, 73
Mohammet, 58
Monarch, crowning of, 73
monarchy, 14, 25, 49, 57
money, 186
Mordechai 50; (German halakhist), 155
Moses, 73, 113, 130, 143
Moses ben Chanokh, 141
Moses ben Nachman, 56, 143
Mount Carmel, 127, 188; Moriah, 21
Musaph, 3
Muslim services, 176

mysterium tremendum, 17, 147
mystical fraternity, 146, 168
mysticism, 143

Nacheym, 56
Nachmanides, *see* Moses ben
  Nachman
Nagid, 182
Nathan, 89
Natronai Gaon, 104
Nedarim (Tractate), 103
neder, 104
Ne'iylah, 170, 176–89
ne'iylath ha-Sandal, *see* shoes
Ne'iylath She'arim, 176
Neviy'iym, 65–6
New Years, four, 47
nicknames, 122
nihilism, 186
Nimrod, King, *see* King Nimrod
Nineveh, 88, 93
Nishmath, 6
Noah, 56
nouns, contracted forms, 132–3
numinous hymns, 17–18, 147,
  160

'Ophan, 15, 16, 131
Oral Law, 104
Oria, 181, 183
Otto, Rudolph, 17, 147

Palestine, 77, 167, 181, 182
Palestinian School of Poetry, 181;
  Prayer rite, 30, 31, 67;
  Talmud, 165
Passover, *see* Pesach
Patriarchs, 16, 22
Payetanim, 12, 94, 160
Peli'im, 26
penance, 88, *see also* repentance;
  of correspondence, 91
Pentecost, *see* Shavu'oth
persecution, 102
Persian Dualists, 10, 13, 58, 150,
  188; inspectors, 150; *see also*
  Zoroastrian religion

Persians, 12
Pesach, 5, 47, 55, 154
Petiychah, 19
Petiychath Ne'iylah, 177
Piyyut, early, 59
Piyyutim, **11–13**, 49, **67**, 70, 141,
  146, **166**
Piyyutim, Propriety of, 19
Polish prayer rite, 16, 33, 157,
  159, 182
poor man, 79
Pope, Jewish, 75
Posen, 44
Prayer, 22, 23, 136; Semitic, 150
predetermination, 144
priestly blessing, 68–9, 164
Priests, 68–9; Kingdom of, 128
primordial light, 10
printers, 166
printing, 83
prostrations, 59, 140, 163, 164
Proverbs, Book of, 135
Psalm *27*, *see* Le-David Ha-Shem
  'Oriy
Psalm: **47**, 40; **74**, 109; **33**, 73;
  69, 140; **89**, 81; **130**, 83; **145**,
  137
Psalms, Book of, 24
psalm verses, 65–6, 158

Qedushah, 18, 26, 27–8, 70, 131,
  149–50, 175; chain technique
  of, 149
Qedushath Ha-shem blessing, 29
Qedushath Ha-Yom blessing, 30
qehillah qedoshah, 128
Qerovoth, 11
Qerovotz, 190, n.6
Qinnoth, 114
qinnusey, 105
qonamey, 105
Qorban, 105
Qarovah, 11
Queen Esther, 29
Qumran, 17

rain, prayer for, 3, 126

Raphael, angel, 175
Rav, 120, 176, 194; see also Abba
    Arikha
Reader, see Chazan
Reader's desk, 9
Reading of the Law, 34–6, 86–7,
    151–2, 170–1; melody for, 34
Rebecca, 178
refrains, 130, 134, 138, 142, 149,
    157, 174
repentance, 47, 53, 87, 88–96,
    128, 172; biblically prescribed,
    91; motives for, 94; of
    opportunity, 91; preventive, 91
Reshuth, 19, 20, 60–1, 78, 80, 83,
    133, 180
retzey, blessing 56
Rhineland, 132
Richard I, 115
righteousness, 187
Rinath Yisrael Prayer Book, 57
Riy Ha-Zaqeyn, 182
robbery, 185
Rome, 24, 84, 131, 168, 181
Rosh Hashanah, 5, 9, 14, 22, 36,
    38, 47; birth of Isaac on, 21,
    25; Joseph released from prison
    on, 48; world created on, 15

Saadia Gaon, 107, 108
Sabbath, see Shabbat
sacrifices, 89, 136, 140, 165;
    restoration of, 55–7
Safed, Mystics of, 40
Samuel, 35, 127
Samuel He-Chasid, 7
sanctification formula, see
    Qedushah
Sarah, 25, 35
Satan, 5–6, 40–1, 50–1, 73, 83–4,
    116
Saul, see King Saul
Scales of justice, 53, 81, 113
Scholem, Gershom G., 147
sectarianism, 20
Seder Rav 'Amram, see 'Amram

Selichah composition, 114, 115,
    125–7
Selichoth, 16, 30, **48, 112–18,
    125–7, 166–7,** 180–1, 184
Sephardi communities, 13, 101;
    formula of Kol Nidrey, 106;
    poets and scholars, 141; prayer
    rite, 33, 148, 168
Sephardim, 18
Sepher Maharil, 44, 72; see also
    Moellin, Jacob
Seraphim, 17, 26, 91, 138
serpent, 110
sex, 186
sex, opposite, 170
sexual passion, 25, 89
Shabbat, 34, 37, 48, 72, 84, 141,
    150, 152, 154, 192; first Shabbat
    of Creation, 172
Shabbat Rosh Chodesh, 31, 55
Shabbat Shabbaton, 157
Sharon Plain, 165
Shavu'oth, 5, 6, 47, 55, 154
Shekhiynah, 54, 188
Shelomoh Ha-qatan, 179
Shema', 12, 18, 131, 150, 187–8;
    Blessings of: 10, 11, 12, 128–9,
    131
Shemiyniy 'Atzereth, 154
Shemuel (talmudist), 120–1
Shephatyah ben Amittai, 181
Shevarim, 38, 63
Shevu'oth, 105
Sheym Ha-mephorash, see
    Tetragrammaton
Shir Ha-Kavod, see Glory, Hymn of
shoes, 68, 99–100, 168
Shofar, 4, 66–7, 83–4, 112, 188;
    historic role of, 36–8, 64; notes
    of, 38, 39, 63; significance of,
    39–41
Shopharoth, 60, 63, 65–7, 76, 85
shrouds, 3
Shulchan 'Arukh, 155
Simeon bar Isaac, 26, 75, 78, 80,
    81, 82, 84
sin (and atonement), 88–96

Sinaitic Revelation, 39, 67, 143
sin-offerings, 82
Siylano, 181
slaughtering knife, 82
slaves, 64, 99
Sodomites, 20, 81, 134
soldiers, 51
Solomon, *see* King Solomon
Solomon ben Judah, *see Shelomoh Ha-qatan*
Solomon ben Samuel, 182–3
Songs of Songs (Canticles), 99, 119, 129, 130, 134, 136, 137
Song of the Sea, 159
soul, 123–4, 187
Spain, 102, 141
stair-like progression, 109
suffering, 62, 94, 95
Sukkah, 6
Sukkoth, 3, 5, 6, 47, 55, 125–7, 154, 184
Synagogues, Chasidic, 9

Tabernacles, *see Sukkoth*
Tablets, Two, 129
tallith, 100; as divine robe, 14, 100, 113; priests, 69
Talmud translated into Arabic, 141
Targum, 54, 112
Tarphon, Rabbi, 165
Tashlikh, 72–4
Tashraq, see acrostic, reverse
Temple, 59, 137, 173; Altar, 68, 139; Ark, 16; destruction of, 99, 136, 168; gates of, 176, 178; miracles, 140; rebuilding of, 56–7, 86; restoration of service, 57, 137; service, 142; Shofar sounded daily, 37
Teqiy'ah, 38, 63; *Gedolah*, 63
Teru'ah, 38
Tetragrammaton, 120, 164
theft, 89–90
Thirteen Attributes, *see* God's Thirteen Attributes
Tokheychah, 134, 158

Torah, 65, 158–9, 179; study outlawed, 167
Tosaphist, 179, 182
Tosaphoth, 65, 83
Trajan, 168
transgressors, 100–2, 172, 184–5
tzitzith, 100

Ugarit, 110
Unethaneh toqeph, 49–52, 134
Unity, Hymn of, 4, 6–8
universalism, 54, 62
Uriel, angel, 175
uvekheyn, 29–30, 147–51

vegetarian ideal, 82
Venosa, 181
Vidduy, see confession
Vidduy Rabba', 121
Vidduy Zuta', 121
Visigoths, 102
vows, absolution of, 103–4; annulment of, 106

washing, ritual, 68
water, 72–3
Weil, Jacob, 155
Werner, E., 150
white colour, 1, 133, 173
Wieder, N., 51, 58
Wiesel, Elli, 58
wild beasts, prayer against, 179
Wisdom Literature, 135

Yaakov ben Mosheh Moellin, *see Sepher Maharil*
Yakhin Lashon commentary, 33–4
Yannai, 12, 13, 52–3, 160, 175
Yehudai Gaon, 103–4, 106
Yekutiel b. Mosheh, 20
Yemenite prayer rite, 127
Yeytzer, 116–18
yishar Kochakha, 39
Yizkor, 153–5
Yizkor-buch, 155
Yoma', 164
Yom Kippur, 4, 9, 14, 22, 35, 44,

48, 59, 60, **89**, **94**, 95, **99**, 107,
111, 120, 123, 125, **129**, 131,
137, 140, 152, **155**, 157, 163,
171, **173**, 176, 186, 187, 188
Yom Kippur services, 93, 101, 120,
137
Yom Tov, 67, 111, 153
Yom Tov ben Isaac, 115
York Massacre, 115
Yose ben Yose, 108, 111

Yotzeroth, 12, 13, 15, 128
Yovel, see Jubilee

zechuth 'avoth, 16
Zichronoth, 36, 60, 63, 64, 65, 66,
67, 76, 85, 86
Zoroastrian religion, 10, 150
Zulay, M., 53
Zunz, L., 101, 141